The Disease of Liberty

Thomas Jefferson, History, & Liberty
A Philosophical Analysis

M. Andrew Holowchak

Series in American History
VERNON PRESS

Copyright © 2025 Vernon Press, an imprint of Vernon Art and Science Inc, on behalf of the author.

All rights reserved. No part of this publication may be reproduced, stored in a retrieval system, or transmitted in any form or by any means, electronic, mechanical, photocopying, recording, or otherwise, without the prior permission of Vernon Art and Science Inc.

www.vernonpress.com

In the Americas:
Vernon Press
1000 N West Street, Suite 1200
Wilmington, Delaware, 19801
United States

In the rest of the world:
Vernon Press
C/Sancti Espiritu 17,
Malaga, 29006
Spain

Series in American History

Library of Congress Control Number: 2023951273

ISBN: 979-8-8819-0172-1

Also available: 978-1-64889-819-8 [Hardback]; 978-1-64889-884-6 [PDF, E-Book]

Product and company names mentioned in this work are the trademarks of their respective owners. While every care has been taken in preparing this work, neither the authors nor Vernon Art and Science Inc. may be held responsible for any loss or damage caused or alleged to be caused directly or indirectly by the information contained in it.

Cover design by Vernon Press. Image: The Battle of Bunker's Hill, June 17, 1775 by John Trumbull (Public domain). https://artgallery.yale.edu/collections/objects/41

Every effort has been made to trace all copyright holders, but if any have been inadvertently overlooked the publisher will be pleased to include any necessary credits in any subsequent reprint or edition.

To my longtime friend David D.

Table of Contents

	Preface	vii
	Part I. The Meaning of History	1
Chapter I	**Prolegomena to the Praxis of History**	3
Chapter II	**Jefferson on the Praxis of History**	19
Chapter III	**The Argument for Interested History**	35
	Part II. The Nature & Civic Possibility of Liberty	49
Chapter IV	**The Advances of Science**	51
Chapter V	**The Nature of Humans**	71
Chapter VI	**The Lexical Ambiguity of "Liberty"**	99
	Part III. Liberty as Pandemic	117
Chapter VII	**Jefferson on the American Revolution**	119
Chapter VIII	**The Revolution of 1800**	145
Chapter IX	**The Spread of Liberty in the Americas**	165
Chapter X	**The Spread of Liberty across the Globe**	185
	Epilog	199
	Index	205

Preface

In a letter to Judge Spencer Roane (6 Sept. 1819), Thomas Jefferson writes of "the true principles of the revolution of 1800": the principles of a second American Revolution. He adds: "That was as real a revolution in the principles of our government as that of 76. was in it's form; not effected indeed by the sword, as that, but by the rational and peaceable instrument of reform, the suffrage of the people." The difference between the first and second American Revolutions is stark. The first was a revolution by sword—a sanguinary, years-long uprising with intent to overthrow and success in overthrowing British yoke. The second was a revolution by reason—a willful and peaceable election by the American people of an executive and legislative aiming to place federal power where it belongs: in the people. "the nation, Jefferson adds, "declared it's will by dismissing functionaries of one principle [Federalists], and electing those of another [Republicans], in the two branches, executive and legislative, submitted to their election."

Over one year later (26 Dec. 1820), Jefferson writes to Marquis de Lafayette of the advance of liberty throughout the globe.

> the light which has been shed on the mind of man thro' the civilised world, has given it a new direction from which no human power can divert it. the sovereigns of Europe who are wise, or have wise councellors, see this, and bend to the breeze which blows. the unwise alone, stiffen and meet it's inevitable crush. the Volcanic rumblings in the bowels of Europe from North to South, seem to threaten a general explosion, and the march of armies into Italy cannot end in a simple march. the disease of liberty is catching: these armies will take it in the South, carry it thence to their own country spread there the infection of revolution & representative government, and raise it's people from the prone condition of brutes to the erect attitude of man.

Jefferson's prose is silver-tongued, perhaps overly so—that is, magniloquent. In a flush of excitement, he throws together metaphors of all sorts: light being shed, a blowing breeze, volcanic rumblings, the march of armies, and liberty as a "disease" that infects through revolution and leads to representative government—a contagion that raises prone brutes to erect men.

It is impossible to attempt a biography of Jefferson without saying much about Jefferson's investment in liberty. No other American figure, perhaps no other figure, has politically invested so fundamentally, so unremorsefully, so completely in the notion.

Yet that political investment, it is seldom recognized, is essentially a philosophical investment.[1] As a student of history and as a natural scientist, inasmuch as his time would allow for study of nature, Jefferson follows the naturalists and philosophers of his day and makes purchase of the view that there is a natural progression from the tribalism of Native Americans and Africans to civilized living in keeping with advances of human knowledge. That progression is an unfolding or maturation of human liberty—a term, like "gravity," denoting something invisible and in Newton's day inexplicable, yet vital and real. Liberty is the movement from the independency of tribal living, a vagarious sort of life without laws and with no efficient use of the land, to the civic liberty guaranteed by communal living in societies or states in which each is equal under the laws, in keeping with humans' nature, and land is used most efficiently for human wellbeing.

The movement of liberty can be abetted by visionary humans or retarded by recalcitrant humans. Liberty, when unchecked, can go too far. Communal living, as Plato and his disciple Aristotle noted over two millennia ago, unchecked by just laws, can readily avalanche toward the bedlam of radical liberalism and radical equalitarianism, where each person perceives himself to be executor of his own laws.[2] On the other hand, liberty, when over-checked, cannot go sufficiently far. Communal living with surfeit of laws will choke the civic liberty for which it is intended to provide succor.

Jefferson's solution to those extremes of unchecked liberty and over-checked liberty is representative government—a concession that not all citizens have the time and talent to legislate, though they do have time and talent to oversee their representatives. Representative government has the added benefit of being workable in a society or state of great expanse of land. In the America of Jefferson's day, he envisages a federative nation over a large span of land with an executive and legislative, checked by the strictures of the Constitution, and a tenured judiciary, without sole power to interpret the Constitution. There then will be the several states, each sovereign concerning all issues not expressly mentioned in the Constitution, and next, the many counties of each state, each with its own government to oversee its parochial affairs, and the numerous wards of each county, each with powers to direct its affairs. In such a manner, liberty for each citizen can be guaranteed if, at each echelon of

---

[1] An exception being Adrienne Koch's *The Philosophy of Thomas Jefferson* (New York: Columbia University Press, 1943).
[2] Plato's and Aristotle's notion of *demokratia*.

government, there are no paternalistic unconstitutional intrusions to its manner of governing by the echelons above it.

What guarantee is there that citizens will take the time to oversee their elected representatives at all echelons of governing?

That, of course, is a hefty problem. John Adams thought that the *hoi polloi* was too uninterested to care, and so his solution was to have checks and balances within the governmental system. The people simply could not be trusted. Jefferson, believing that each person was born with a moral sense that linked him to all others through a proclivity to beneficence, needed no checks and balances, but instead "incentives" to stimulate morally correct action. Those incentives in America included needed political reforms—e.g., riddance of entails and primogeniture, freedom of religion, free presses, and systemic educational reform—to ensure sufficient civic liberty to allow both for self-sufficiency in conduct of, and knowledge to conduct, citizens' personal affairs and for the needed political space for benevolent actions. Jefferson successfully championed such reforms as a parochial ambassador for liberty in Virginia.

Still, Jefferson was not merely a parochial ambassador for liberty, he was also a global ambassador for liberty. There was inevitability to the spread of liberty, hence, Jefferson's employment of "disease," was used harmlessly to connote contagion. The key to contagion was overthrow of authorities like Aristotle and the Catholic Church that shackled people to dogmata, at odds with reality. Once people were shown by experience that their authorities were fallible, because their views were false, it was time to use human reason and the human senses for disclosures about the way nature works. The prize was the republicanizing of the globe—*viz.*, the mating of liberty and reason—and the liquidation of barbarism on it.

For the light of human enlightenment to shine brightest, the partnership of government and sectarian religion needed to be broken—Anglicanism in England and in parts of Colonial America—and in its place, there needed to be partnership of government and science. Hence, educational reforms to advance government of and for the people were essential to accommodate the rapid growth of knowledge at the time. There is today no greater symbol of partnership of knowledge and Jeffersonian republicanism than Jefferson's crown jewel of University of Virginia: the Rotunda. It occupies the most prominent and privileged position between the two rows of pavilions—a spot where one might have expected a church or chapel to occupy—and its chief function was to be the school's library.

In this book, thus, I tell the story of Jefferson's dream of a global community of nations, interacting amicably and peacefully, and held together by their natural feelings toward each other of benevolence, inspired by a naturalized Christianity.

In the first part, "The Meaning of History," I focus on the significance of a study and preservation of history, practiced aright, in preparation for critical discussion of Jefferson's notion of liberty. It has three chapters. Part II's focus is an explication of how liberty, for Jefferson, has come to be the axial concept driving his political philosophy—how liberty has become hypostatized (a thing, or something real, and not merely a notion or a phlizz). It comprises three chapters. In the last part, I cover Jefferson's conception of liberty as the dynamic force behind the American Revolution, his "ascendance" to the presidency in 1800—what he calls in 1819 "the revolution of 1800"—his vision of the spread of liberty across the continent, the hemisphere, and, he hoped, even the globe. In the epilog, I proffer discussion of why the lofty vision failed to enroot, even in the United States.

Before ending, readers who are familiar with my work might wonder why I write another book on what essentially concerns Jefferson's political philosophy, after having written *Thomas Jefferson's Political Philosophy and the Metaphysics of Utopia*. The reason is this. Since publication of that book in 2017, I have become fascinated, if not ensorcelled, by Jefferson's almost pathological obsession with "liberty." Like John Stuart Mill after him, Jefferson recognized the real worth of that meaty concept, and he aimed to tackle the selfsame question with which Mill obsessed in *On Liberty:* How can humans be "free" in any meaningful sense of the word, and yet live as social animals? And so, unlike my 2017 book, the focus of this book concerns Jefferson's obsession with liberty, which here, I claim, was not merely an inspirational notion, but something *real*. Hence, unlike my 2017 book, this book is essentially philosophical, analytically so.

How can liberty be real? Is the question mere rot?

I wax philosophical here. It is impossible to make sense of Jefferson's obsession with liberty unless one presumes that liberty for Jefferson is something, in some sense, real—that it is an actual, realizable state of persons and, derivatively, of states, as well as a driving force in nature. The scenario for Jefferson is like that of Aristotle, for whom humans have both formal and final *aitia* (roughly, "causes"). For Aristotle, an axe is, by its formal nature, a chopping thing and it reaches its final nature when it chops. Likewise, for Jefferson, we might say that a human is, by nature, a free animal and he reaches his final nature when he is free—*viz.*, there are no obstacles to him acting in pursuance of his volitions in a social setting.

Liberty, for Jefferson, is as real as virtue, a state of moral being for virtue-ethics theorists for a person, and the particular virtues: e.g., justice, courage, self-control, generosity, and wisdom. For the ancients and for modern virtue-ethics philosophers, virtue describes a state of an organism that has achieved a sort of moral perfection, or moves asymptotically toward it—a capacity for a human, doing the right thing, at the right time, in the right place, and for the right reason and a disposition that other virtuous persons easily perceive.[3] A person, for Aristotle, is generous if and only if he gives what he can give to those in need of just what they need.[4] In that regard, virtue is comparable to physical health. To say, "Person P possesses physical health," is to say, "Person P is in such-and-such an optimal physical state, given his (unique) physical constitution." One physically healthy is identifiable by robustness, cheeriness, energy, and activity—qualities that other physically healthy people recognize more readily than those physically debilitated. Likewise, to say, "Person P possesses virtue," is to say, "Person P is in such-and-such an optimal psychical state, given his (unique) psychical constitution."

It is the same with liberty—which is, for Jefferson, a state of being, like virtue. There is *personal liberty*, which is the freedom to make and act on choices. To say, "Person P possesses personal liberty," is to say, "Person P is in such-and-such an optimal condition, given his (unique) physical constitution, to lead a self-sufficient life." There is also *civic liberty*. In the civic state, to say, "State S possesses civic liberty" is to say, "State S is in such-and-such optimal condition to afford all its members to have personal liberty, insofar as circumstances allow." For Jefferson, there is more than that to the story. The aim of Jeffersonian republicanism is to provide a schema of government, tailored to circumstances, that allows for each citizen, equal in rights, to have optimal personal freedom for the expression of virtue—that is, to create a political milieu in which all persons have the largest possible personal freedom and are incentivized to act virtuously. Civic liberty occurs when a state or society champions basic human rights—such as freedom of religion, freedom of presses, and access to basic education for all citizens—and when it creates avenues for its citizens to act intelligently, honestly, and beneficently, but otherwise refrains from intervention is citizens' affairs. Civic liberty, like a person's physical health, is an ideal to be approximated, yet that does not make it, like health, any less real.

---

[3] Aristotle, *Nicomachean Ethics*, trans. H. Rackham (Cambridge: Harvard University Press, 1990), 1106b17–22.

[4] For the ancient Stoics, virtue was a matter of seeing things as they are, forming corresponding judgments without the intrusion of the passions, and acting accordingly, though they argued that actions were determined. I leave in abeyancy the prickly notion of whether virtue can be completely actualized, like Plato, Aristotle, and the Greeks and Romans believed.

It is difficult for anyone who has spent his whole life in a country, where he is free to do as he chooses to do, to understand, and appraise correctly, the true worth of liberty—a genuine state of a person's or state's being. Those things cannot be done until liberty is lost. In that regard, liberty is like water. When water is plentiful, it is not valued; when it is scarce, it is valued above all other things.

Proof of the worth of liberty—that liberty might really be something actual—comes through the testimonies of those who first experience civic liberty when they have never before experienced it. The feeling is typically too sublime and too oily for words. I offer two illustrations.

The sublimity of liberty is illustrated by the arrival of Petro Grigorenko—the only Soviet general to have been exiled, though many were killed, by Soviet dictator Joseph Stalin—and his wife to New York City, after being exiled. He sums thus the experience. "America is a sea of light where night is turned into day." He and his wife, he adds, "had traveled not just to another country but to another planet."[5] Grigorenko describes a feeling, not arbitrary and subjective, but generated reflexively, naturally, and without the consent of will. It is the feeling that all persons feel, when living for a time in an oxygen-depleted milieu, who then enter an oxygen-rich milieu.

The oiliness of liberty is illustrated by the testimony of Victor Kravchenko in his autobiography, *I Chose Freedom*. While trying to express his feelings about removal to a free country, the United States, he adds: "The citizens of a free country have nothing in their personal experience to make my feelings and my behavior credible. The utterly tragic must seem to them merely eccentric." The tragedy to which he refers is his life in the unfree USSR. He gives in a subsequent chapter the advice that his father gave to him, while still a boy. "Always remain true to the fight for freedom. There is no life without liberty. … We are either swine or we are men, and if we are men we cannot submit to be slaves."[6]

Before ending, I add two points: one procedural, the other editorial. First, I have adopted the convention here, as in other publications, of labeling Jefferson's epistolary writings by reference only to his correspondent and to the date of the letter, if known, thereby giving readers the opportunity to refer to the edition of Jefferson's writings that is most readily available to them. There are several major compilations of Jefferson's writings, the most widely used are the following: *The Writings of Thomas Jefferson: Being his Autobiography,*

---

[5] Petro G. Grigorenko, *Memoirs* (New York: W.W Norton & Co., 1982), 451.
[6] Victor Kravchenko, *I Chose Freedom* (New York: Charles Scribner's Sons, 1946), 4 and 16.

Correspondence, Reports, Messages, Addresses, and Other Writings, Official and Private: Published by the Order of the Joint Committee of Congress on the Library, from the Original Manuscripts, Deposited in the Department of State, 9 Vols., ed. Henry Augustine Washington (Washington: Taylor & Maury, 1853-4); *The Works of Thomas Jefferson*, ed. Paul Leicester Ford, 12 Vols. (New York: Putnam, 1902); *The Writings of Thomas Jefferson, Definitive Edition*, 20 Vols., ed. Andrew Adgate Lipscomb and Albert Ellery Bergh (Washington. Thomas Jefferson Memorial Association, 1907); and *The Papers of Thomas Jefferson*, 42 Vols. (to date), ed. Julian Boyd et al. (Princeton: Princeton University Press, 1950-). There are also several one-volume compilations of Jefferson's writings—the best of which is Merrill D. Peterson's *Thomas Jefferson: Writings* (New York: The Library of America, 1984). Moreover, many of Jefferson's writings are readily available online—e.g., Hathi Trust Digital Library, The Online Library of Liberty, and Founders Online. Non-epistolary writings, in contrast, are fully referenced throughout this book. Second, I thank the two anonymous reviewers for their aidful comments, leading to the improvement of this work.

Part I
The Meaning of History

Chapter I

Prolegomena to the Praxis of History

History Thomas Jefferson considered to be one of the three categories of human knowledge. Following Francis Bacon, Jefferson broke down learning into disciplines related to memory, reason, and imagination—thus, the corresponding disciplines of history, philosophy, and the fine arts. History he divided, in keeping with personal interests, into ancient, modern, American, British, and ecclesiastical.

History, especially ancient history, was ever dear to Jefferson.

For one, Jefferson was by disposition an obsessive chronicler of events through note-taking. He always kept with him a white marble slab on which he would jot down things worth remembering. "I had always made it a practice whenever an opportunity occurred of obtaining any information of our country, which might be of use to me in any station public or private, to commit it to writing." Those memoranda, adds Jefferson, he would later jot down on "loose papers, bundled up without order, and difficult of recurrence."[1] Knowing what we know of Jefferson, it is impossible to believe that the bundles were without order; one must understand disorder in a Jeffersonian sense.[2]

Yet there is another reason, more significant and not unrelated to the first, for his love of history. Human affairs were not motionless. History was on the move. As a true child of the Enlightenment, Jefferson believed that humans' potential had failed to be actualized for millennia. That was because views of human nature were skewed due to a sort of "philosophical" complacency. The sorts of questions that people asked could be found in religious texts, like the Bible, or in Aristotle's works, which for millennia came to predominate the

---

[1] Thomas Jefferson, *Autobiography*, in *Thomas Jefferson: Writings*, ed. Merrill D. Peterson (New York: Library of America, 1984), 55.

[2] Jefferson seemingly had a system for everything. He kept all letters in his vast correspondence and endorsed each received letter, after he read it. An endorsement consisted of name of sender, place of its origin, date of when it was written and received, and often its main subject (e.g., invention, yellow fever, or madman). By noting the date of composition and date of arrival, Jefferson could glean information about the efficiency of the postal system. He would then file the letters by alphabet and then add his endorsement to his Summary Journal of Letters. He also kept indices of his letters. See Jack McLaughlin, *To His Excellency Thomas Jefferson: Letters to a President* (New York: W.W. Norton & Company, 1991), xxiii–xxv.

biological, physical, and political sciences. There was no need to question such authorities. Aristotle's former teacher, Plato, argues that most humans by nature were cognitively slothful, unfit for intellectual matters, but suitable for production. That view predominated until key concepts such as liberty and equality began to be taken seriously during the Enlightenment.

Like Aristotle, Jefferson believed that humans, in possession of rationality, were special in the cosmos. *Pace* Aristotle, it was not that each human was fully rational—Jefferson always maintained that very few people had large rationality[3] and, he added, possession of large rationality was not a measure of desert of rights[4]—but that each human had rationality sufficient to manage his own affairs, to adjudicate religious nodi, and to involve himself to a sufficient degree in political matters inasmuch as his talent and time would allow. Human rationality allowed for the practice and advances of science by those at least sufficiently rational to be practitioners.

In this chapter, I cover certain preliminary issues concerning Jefferson's views on the praxis of history. Hence, this chapter is a sort of prolegomenon to study of Jefferson's views on history, which are themselves prolegomena to study of his views on liberty. I begin with thoughts by naturalists, philosophers, and doctors on the study of humans by humans, turn to the notion of stages of human development (stadialism and conjectural history), and end with Jefferson's take of stadialism which I call medialist. All such issues have a direct bearing on Jefferson's view of liberty.

"If I would have called man a simian or vice versa..."

The "Races" of Humans

The advances of Enlightenment science were the result of an eruption of knowledge, inconsistent with Aristotle's static, telic cosmos. Discoveries were made in all areas of science—in what are today physics, chemistry, biology, astronomy, paleontology, archeology, and even politics *inter alia*—and thus they led to the relatively quick dismissal of Aristotle's *Weltanschauung* (see chapter 3). Numerous inventions—e.g., the spinning jenny and the cotton gin—led to augmented productivity of farmed and manufactured goods and ease of the burden of human living. Trade with and colonization of new territories—e.g., Australia, Africa, and the Americas—led to observations of humans living in "uncivilized" tribes, without knowledge or concern for the abundant conveniences of civilized living.

---

[3] TJ to John Randolph, 1 Dec. 1803, and TJ to Edward Livingston, 4 Apr. 1824.
[4] TJ to Henri Grégoire, 25 Feb. 1809.

Civilized Europeans had read about the barbarism of peoples in other lands from the time of the early Greek historian Herodotus and, later, the Roman historian Tacitus, so its existence was not shocking, but it was difficult to grasp. How was it possible for humans to have a common origin, as almost all educated persons thought at the time, and yet to vary culturally and even physically so remarkably?

The notion of humans taking to studying humans was not new to Enlightenment naturalists. That had begun in early Greek thinking—in the medical practice with Hippocratic physicians and in the works of Aristotle. The Hippocratic writer of "Airs, Waters, Places" (c. 400 B.C.) notes that seasons of the year, temperature of the winds, and the nature of water and soil in a particular parcel of land affect health and a physician's assessment of it, so a physician must observe the habits of a people. "The constitutions and the habits of a people follow the nature of the land where they live." In general, all people flourish in moderate climates, with rich and moist soil, with water that is cool in winter and warm in summer, and with plants that grow tall and fleshy and animals that mature to a hardy bulk.[5] The implication throughout the work is that the observable differences in the types of men, even the races of men, are explicable over time by their acclimation to environmental circumstances and their habits, beneficial or injurious. The best climates produce the best men; inferior climates, inferior men. Aristotle (384–322 B.C.) notes that laws must be conformable to constitutions (*politeiai*), which are of one, of a few, or of the many. Constitutions, in turn, must be conformable to the occupations, wealth, birth, and merit of a citizenry as well the number of citizens, the climate and land, the nature of the people (conditioned by climate and land), and their customs.[6]

With general acceptance of an empirical perspective in the eighteenth century, much of what thinkers, following Aristotle or the Catholic Church, thought about the world was shown to be wrong. Nicolas Copernicus showed, *pace* Aristotle, Ptolemy, and the Church, that heliocentrism was at least as plausible as geocentrism. Tycho Brahe, in observing the strange behavior of comets and exploding stars outside the sphere of the moon, showed, *pace* Aristotle, that there was superlunary change—change in the region of the planets, the sun, and the "fixed" stars in which all things, Aristotle had stated, ever remained the same. Galileo Galilei showed, *pace* Aristotle, that heavy things did not fall to the center of the cosmos on account of and in proportion

---

[5] Hippocratic Author, "Airs, Waters, Places," in *Hippocratic Writings*, ed. G.E.R. Lloyd (New York: Penguin Classics, 1983) 148–69.
[6] Aristotle, *Politics*, trans. Ernest Barker (Oxford: Oxford University Press, 1995), 1288b10–1289a26, 1289b27–1290a29, and 1325a16–1328b23.

to their weight, shown by Galileo to be irrelevant to rate of a body's fall. Johannes Kepler, *pace* Aristotle, showed that the orbits of planets were elliptical and of variant velocities, not comprising circles and not of uniform motions. Invention of the telescope and the microscope disclosed macroscopic and microscopic wonders and oddities. With the relatively quick explosion of Aristotle's *Weltanschauung*, which had predominated for some two millennia, philosophers like Francis Bacon and Isaac Newton promulgated abandonment of justification by appeal to authority. Authorities were no longer to be trusted. The world needed to be studied anew.

The new post-Aristotelian milieu for thinkers of the day was both frightful and exciting. The world was alien and everything was to be explored and analyzed from scratch. The only discipline that was untouched by the wondrous disclosures that led to the breakdown of the Aristotelian *Weltanschauung* was Euclidean geometry. Naturalists—e.g., Linnaeus, Buffon, Goldsmith, Cuvier—turned to study of biota of all sorts, humans among them, and they too used geometry in analysis. Much of my account below is paraphrased from a prior publication.[7]

Swedish zoologist, botanist, and physician, Carl Linnaeus (1707–1778) taxonomized living organisms into a widely accepted system. In 1758, he publishes the first edition of *Systema Naturae* in which he limns four species of primates: Homo (humans), Simia (e.g., apes and orangutans), Lemur, and Vespertilio (bats). By the tenth edition, Linnaeus taxonomizes "homo" by geographic location and color of skin and splits them under four kinds of Homo Diurnus (day man) and one kind of Homo Nocturnus (night man).

Homo Diurnus

Homo Rusus (Americanus), cholericus, rectus (red man, bilious [angry], straightforward)
Homo Albus (Europeus), sanguineus, torosus (white man; blooded [hopeful], brawny)
Homo Luridus (Asiaticus), melancholicus, rigidus (yellow man; black-biled [depressed] man, inflexible or cruel)
Homo Niger (Afer), phlegmaticus, laxus (black man; phlegmatic [stolid], lazy or relaxed)

Homo Nocturnus

Ourang Outang

---

[7] M. Andrew Holowchak, *Rethinking Thomas Jefferson's Views on Race and Slavery: "God's justice can not sleep forever"* (Newcastle upon Tyne: Cambridge Scholars Press, 2020), chap. 3.

That Linnaeus categorizes orangutans as "homo" implies that the key difference between humans and orangutans is one of habit: Humans are diurnal; orangutans, nocturnal. Yet even that distinction is forced. He writes in a letter to Johann Georg Gmelin (25 Feb 1747): "I seek from you and from the whole world a generic difference between man and simian that follows from the principles of Natural History. I absolutely know of none. If only someone might tell me a single one! If I would have called man a simian or vice versa, I would have brought together all the theologians against me."[8] One sees plainly here the large influence still of the Church in meddling with the hypotheses or disclosures of naturalists.

The nonpareil French naturalist, Georges-Louis Leclerc (1707–1788), Comte de Buffon—a perfect contemporary of Linnaeus insofar they shared their year of birth—also took it on himself to discuss the races of humans in "On the Degeneration of Animals" (1766) and "On the Epochs of Nature" (1778). Buffon notes, consistent with Hippocratic writings, that exposure to certain types of food and land over time leads to "the general and constant characters in which we recognize the different races and even nations which compose the human genus." Exposure to the right sorts of climates and food types lead to human thriving; their absence, to human degeneration. Human thriving also can be enhanced by better nutrition and some degree of humanizing climate.[9]

In *An History of the Earth, and Animated Nature* (1774), Irish novelist, poet, playwright, historian, and naturalist Oliver Goldsmith (1728–1774) lists six "varieties" of humans, determined by climate, alimentation, and culture:

People at the Poles	African Negroes
Tartars	Native Americans
Southern Asiatics	Europeans

Negroes he describes as "this gloomy race of mankind," Asiatics as cowardly and effeminate, and American natives as thoughtless and serious. All were degenerative varieties.[10]

In *Le règne animal* (1817), French zoologist and paleontologist Jean Léopold Nicolas Frédéric, better known as Baron "Georges" Cuvier (1769–1832),

---

[8] From Justin E.H. Smith, "Natural History and the Speculative Sciences of Origins, in *The Routledge Companion to Eighteenth Century Philosophy*, ed. Aaron Garnett (New York: Routledge, 2014), 723.
[9] Georges-Louis Leclerc, "De la dégénération des animaux," in *Histoire naturelle, générale et particulière*, vol. 14 (Paris: Imprimerie Royale, 1766): 313–16, and "Des époques de la nature," in *Histoire naturelle, générale et particulière: supplément*, vol. 5 (Paris: Imprimerie royale, 1778): 1–254.
[10] Oliver Goldsmith, *An History of the Earth, and Animated Nature*, 8 vols. (Philadelphia: Edward Poole, [1774] 1823), 239–250.

attempts to arrange all created beings into a "system of nature" according to "natural methods" and according to "true fundamental relations." There are for Cuvier three "races" of humans, the "first order" of mammals:

Caucasians (Whites)

Mongolians (Yellows)

Ethiopians (Negroes)

Caucasians have beautiful oval heads, varied complexions, and varied color of hair, and comprise the most highly civilized nations. Mongolians have high cheekbones, flat visage, narrow and oblique eyes, straight black hair, scanty beard, and an olive complexion. They have had great empires, but are "stationary." Negroes, "confined to the south of Mount Atlas," are of black complexion, with crisped and wooly hair, compressed cranium, and a flat nose. Their hordes "have always remained in the most complete state of utter barbarism."[11]

It is here worth noting lack of consensus by these early scientists on race. All agree on the categories of white, yellow, and black men. Some add other categories, pursuant to regions of the globe. In the main, lightness of coloration of skin is linked with intelligence and embrace of civilization; darkness, with lack of intelligence and barbarity.

Other preeminent figures had opinions or hypotheses.

Scottish philosopher and historian David Hume (1711–1776), an advocate of abolition writes: "I am apt to suspect the negroes to be naturally inferior to the whites. There scarcely ever was a civilized nation of that complexion, nor even any individual eminent either in action or speculation. No ingenious manufactures amongst them, no arts, no sciences." The savagery of Blacks Hume explains by natural differences.[12]

German philosopher and cosmologist Immanuel Kant (1724–1804) offers an epigenetic explanation of "variety" among humans. He posits an original human stem (*Menschenstamm*) and buds (*Keime*), which allow for adaptation to different milieus. Thus, for Kant, tincture of skin is symptomatic of natural organic differences and abilities—different buds from the original stem. He also differentiates "race" and "species" by viable offspring. Different races (*Racen*) of the same stem can interbreed and produce fertile hybrids or

---

[11] Baron Cuvier, *The Animal Kingdom, Arranged in Conformity with Its Organization*, trans. H. M'Murtrie, vol. 1 (New York: G & C & H Carvill, 1831), 4–6 and 30–32.

[12] David Hume, "Of National Characters," in *Essays: Moral, Political, and Literary*, ed. Eugene F. Miller (Indianapolis: Liberty Fund, 1987), 208n10.

"blended forms" (*Mittelschlage*); different species (*Arten*), always of a different stem, cannot.[13]

Lifelong Philadelphian Dr. Benjamin Rush (1746–1813), intimate friend of Thomas Jefferson and one of the foremost physicians of his day, thought that black skin color was symptomatic of leprosy. He writes to Jefferson (4 Feb. 1797): "I am now preparing a paper for our Society in which I have Attempted to prove, that the black Color (as it is called) of the Negroes is the effect of a disease in the Skin of the Leprous kind. The inferences from it will be in favor of treating them with humanity, and justice, and of keeping up the existing prejudices against matrimonial connexions with them."

Constantin Francois de Chassebœuf, Comte de Volney (1757–1820) writes of Chinese as governed by "insolent despotism," Indians vegetating "in an incurable path" due to filiopiety, Tartars as ignorant and ferocious, Arabs as mired in tribal anarchy and familial jealousies, and Africans as seemingly "irrevocably doomed to servitude."[14]

Except for Kant, whose works were not readily accessible in translations, Jefferson read and in general assimilated the views of all the men of science to whom I have referred in this section. There is nothing to show that he agreed with Rush's view of Blacks being leprous.[15]

"The gradual shades of improving man"

Stadialism

Progress in the sciences and study of the differences between the races of humans led to attempts at explaining those differences within the context of history, which Enlightenment scholars thought, in general, was progressing. One commonly accepted explanation of cultural differences between peoples was stadialism—the hypothesis that all societies pass through well-defined

---

[13] Immanuel Kant, "Von den Verschiedenen Rassen der Menschen," in *Der Philosoph für die Welt*, ed. Johann Jacob Engel, vol. 2, (Leipzig: Dyk, 1777), 125–64, and "Bestimmung des Begriffs einer Menschenrasse," in *Berlinischev Monatsschrift*, vol. 6, 1785: 390–417.
[14] Constantin Francois de Volney, *The Ruins*, trans. Thomas Jefferson (Fairford, England: The Echo Library, 2010), 68.
[15] In *Notes on Virginia*, he writes: "Whether the black of the negro resides in the reticular membrane between the skin and scarfskin, or in the scarfskin itself; whether it proceeds from the colour of the blood, the colour of the bile, or from that of some other secretion, the difference is fixed in nature, and is as real as if its seat and cause were better known to us." Thomas Jefferson, *Notes on the State of Virginia*, ed. William Peden (Chapel Hill: University of North Carolina Press, 1954), 138.

stages. My account in this and in the following section follows closely my account in a prior publication.[16]

Stadialism, which became popular in the late eighteenth century, had roots in antiquity. Plato, in Books VIII and IX of his *Republic*, perhaps the most influential book on political philosophy that has been written, describes the life-cycle of a polis: a kingship degenerates into a timocracy; timocracy, into oligarchy; oligarchy, into democracy; and finally democracy, into a tyranny. He offers this account for decay:

> Everything that comes into being must decay. Not even a constitution such as this will last forever. It, too, must face dissolution. And this is how it will be dissolved. All plants that grow in the earth, and also all animals that grow upon it, have periods of fruitfulness and barrenness of both soul and body as often as the revolutions complete the circumferences, of their circles. These circumferences are short for the short-lived, and the opposite for their opposites.[17]

Plato's account, however, begins with a relatively perfected city-state (*polis*), in which the different classes each do what they have to do for the betterment of the polis. In contrast, stadialists begin with the most primitive social units and describe the upward process of movement toward the most perfect state.

Stadialism was birthed in Scotland and held by Scottish and French thinkers[18]—e.g., Adam Smith, David Hume, Adam Ferguson, John Millar, Lord Kames, William Robertson, Claude-Adrien Helvétius, and Anne-Robert-Jacques Turgot.[19] Given Europeans' exposure to the barbarism of certain other cultures, the aim was to explain sequentially how human progress was possible by recourse to advancing stages from pastoralism to industrialism.

Stadialism was, *faute de mieux*, a methodological heuristic used by historians to offer a link between human barbarity and the enlightened man of the

---

[16] M. Andrew Holowchak, "Differences of Circumstance, Differences of Fact: Jefferson Medialist View of History," in *American Studies in Scandinavia*, Vol. 47, No. 1: 2015, 3–21.

[17] Plato, *Republic*, trans. G.M.A. Grube (Indianapolis: Hackett Publishing Company, 1992), 546a.

[18] "That stadialism arose in Scotland was not coincidental," writes Neil Hargraves, "[as] 18th century Scotland was in many ways a museum of archaic social forms, from the 'barbarous' highlanders to the feudal remnants of the lowlands." Neil Hargraves, "Enterprise, Adventure and Industry: The formation of 'Commercial Character' in William Robertson's *History of America*, in *History of European Ideas*, Vol. 29, 2003, 35.

[19] Karen O'Brien, "Between Enlightenment and Stadial History: William Robertson on the History of Europe," in *Journal of Eighteenth-Century Studies*, Vol. 16, No. 1, 1993: 53–54.

eighteenth century. Following the path of conjectural history, the aim was not to recapitulate the true path from barbarism to civilized living, but the path most conformable to reason. And so, stadialism was not a method that aimed to replace traditional "narrative" approaches to history, but instead one meant to complement them.[20]

Most stadialists posited four stages—hunting, pasturage, agriculture, and commerce[21]—though there were two groups of stadialists: cyclicalists and linearists. Cyclicalists (e.g., David Hume) posited that social systems had a life cycle from nascency, growth, and maturity to senescence, decline, and eventual death. Decline and death were due to social flaccidity from artificial and superfluous luxuries like the "benefits" of commercial society. Linearists (e.g., Adam Smith and Lord Kames) posited that social systems passed through stages—the last of which marked a stage of excellence, toward which social systems were thought to converge. Not all movement for either was smooth. There were glitches and retrogradations through what Adam Smith called humans' "drowsy stupidity,"[22] or in Lord Kames' words, their degeneration "into oysters," through inaction.[23]

Jefferson too made purchase of stadialism, as evidenced by a letter to William Ludlow (6 Sept. 1824). To Ludlow, Jefferson describes "a philosophic observer" on his trip from the Rocky Mountains to the seaport towns:

> These he would observe in the earliest stage of association living under no law but that of nature, subscribing and covering themselves with the flesh and skins of wild beasts. He would next find those on our frontiers in the pastoral state, raising domestic animals to supply the defects of hunting. Then succeed our own semi-barbarous citizens, the pioneers of the advance of civilization, and so in his progress he would meet the gradual shades of improving man until he would reach his, as yet, most improved state in our seaport towns.

Having limned four stages, Jefferson sums, "This, in fact, is equivalent to a survey, in time, of the progress of man from the infancy of creation to the

---

[20] H.M. Höpfl, "From Savage to Scotsman: Conjectural History in the Scottish Enlightenment," in *Journal of British Studies*, Vol. 17, No. 2, 20.
[21] For more, see M. Andrew Holowchak, "Differences of Circumstance, Differences of Fact: Jefferson Medialist View of History," in *American Studies in Scandinavia*, Vol. 47, No. 1: 2015, 3–21. My account here follows closely that given in this essay.
[22] Adam Smith, *Wealth of Nations*, ed. Edwin Cannan (London: Methuen & Co., 1904), 735.
[23] Lord Kames, *Sketches of the History of Man*, vol. 1 (Edinburg, 1774), 152–53.

present day." The wording is suggestive of possibility of something beyond the present day, whether further improvement or decay.

Jefferson's letter to Ludlow, indicative of his uptake of stadialism, shows four stages of advancement that showcases economic improvement through efficient usage of land. Economic efficiency is part and parcel of political advance and stability which allows for moral advance and stability. For Jefferson, political aims are always answerable to moral aims—human thriving or human happiness.

Native Americans are illustrations of stage one. In general, they live off land, yet do not cultivate or improve it. Untied to the land, they freely roam over vast parcels of it to find food and other goods like hides of buffalo to sustain themselves. They need no laws beyond the laws of nature.

American frontiersmen are illustrations of stage two. They settle on a parcel of land and use it, along with the animals they have domesticated, to sustain themselves. Putting to some use the land, they require less of it than do Native Americans, who hunt and forage over large parcels of land, hence frontiersmen's manner of living is more economical than Indians.'

American husbandmen are illustrations of stage three. They make most efficient use of the land by clearing out useless plants, felling trees, and growing climate- and soil-friendly plants for human consumption or human use. Enriching the soil and using tested strategies like crop-rotation and dunging, when dung is available, they required less land than do frontiersmen. Tied to their land and not to the caprices of commerce, they are the most independent and dependable citizens.

Urbanites of the seaport towns, presumably of the eastern United States at the time, are illustrations, for Jefferson, of stage four, which Jefferson calls curiously the "most improved state." Why Jefferson considers such urban living to be an improvement over agrarianism, given his unwavering commitment to agrarianism as the most praiseworthy and prevalent occupation in an ideal Jeffersonian republic,[24] is unclear. The sense of "improved" is perhaps meant to be "developed," and if so, Jefferson is hinting at overdevelopment.[25]

The view Jefferson expresses in his letter to Ludlow is in keeping with eighteenth-century Scottish-Enlightenment thinking, characterized by the push for agricultural improvement, the creation of public spaces for scientific societies and clubs, and in general, the belief in the advance of all sciences, even politics and morality.

---

[24] M. Andrew Holowchak, "Jefferson's Moral Agrarianism: Poetic Fiction or Moral Vision?" in *Agriculture and Human Values*, Vol. 28, 2011: 497–506.

[25] For this, I am indebted to one of the reviewers of this manuscript.

Study of the varieties of human culture and the different races of man gave birth to conjectural history. Conjectural history entailed drawing inferences about the past beyond the safe limits of "reliable historical evidence" in some effort to serve present-day normative needs, which included foremost moral progress and human thriving.[26] In sum, conjectural history was essentially presentist. Thus, history was not merely a descriptive discipline, whose aim was veridical narrative, it was also a normative discipline, whose aim was moral improvement. The normative aim of stadialists trumped the descriptive aim. The theoretical economy that served a moral purpose in the writing of history was preferable to trying to be true to the actual anfractuous and etiologically complex course of nature. In that regard, veridicality was an ancillary concern.

For conjectural historians, explanatory convenience, not etiological correctness, was the chief desideratum because of evidentiary gaps and the presentist aims of historians. Scottish philosopher and mathematician Dugald Stewart (1753–1828) writes that without facts to guide historians through the stages, "we are under the necessity of supplying the place of fact by conjecture." The key was to move readers through the stages of human progress, sketched out by stadialists and confirmed by study of different peoples. "In most cases, it is of more importance to ascertain the progress that is most simple, than the progress that is most agreeable to fact, for paradoxical as the proposition may appear, it is certainly true that the *real* progress is not always the *most natural*"[27]—that is, what one might expect of nature, acting most simply.

Here one might speculate, given our disclosures in the section on racial differences, that the aim ideally and over time was to create social homogeneity across the globe, insofar as it was possible, by eliminating barbarity, pushing humans to establish themselves in moderate climates with healthy waters and productive earth, and other such things to assist human progress and happiness.

"When great evils happen…"
Jefferson's Medialism

Jefferson's 1824 letter to Ludow suggests purchase of linear stadialism, yet numerous other writings, expressive of distinct anticity sentiments and urbanism as decay, suggest otherwise.[28]

---

[26] Colin Kidd, "Subscription, the Scottish Enlightenment and the Moderate Interpretation of History," in *The Journal of Ecclesiastical History*, Vol. 55, No. 3, 2004, 507–8.
[27] Dugald Stewart, "An Account of the Life and Writings of Adam Smith," in *The Theory of Moral Sentiments* (New York, 1966), xli–xlii.
[28] E.g., TJ to Edward Carrington, 16 Jan. 1787, and TJ to James Madison, 30 Jan. 1787.

Was Jefferson a linearist or a cyclicalist?

The answer, I have elsewhere argued,[29] is that Jefferson was neither a linearist nor a cyclicalist. He was a medialist, and in two senses: nomological and naturalistic.

Jefferson made purchase of nomological medialism in that his republicanism was a mean between the sort of small societies, typified by Native Americans, where honor and shame took the place of laws. We find expression of that purchase in *Notes on the State of Virginia* and in letters to Edward Carrington and James Madison.

In *Notes on Virginia*, Jefferson notes lack of "any shadow of government" among Native Americans. "Their only controuls are their manners, and that moral sense of right and wrong." European countries, in contrast, have superabundancy of laws. Is absence of law preferable to nimiety? Appealing to experience and consonant with the utopian sentiments of Thomas More and James Harrington,[30] he states baldly, and unsurprisingly, that nimiety of law is the greatest evil. "The sheep are happier of themselves, than under care of the wolves."[31]

To Edward Carrington (16 Jan. 1787), Jefferson says that the lawless Indians "enjoy in their general mass an infinitely greater degree of happiness than those who live under the European governments." He again appeals to the metaphor of wolves and sheep. Europeans "have divided their nations into two classes, wolves and sheep." Wolves were public officials who had become "inattentive to the public affairs."

To James Madison two weeks later (30 Jan. 1787), Jefferson limns three "sufficiently distinguishable" forms of society. There are societies "without government," exemplified by the Indians; societies "under governments wherein the will of every one has a just influence," exemplified best by the United States; and societies "under governments of force," exemplified by most monarchies and most other republics—governments of "wolves over sheep." Here he states that a society without laws might be the best, but it is "inconsistent with any great degree of population." In the second society, "the mass of mankind under that [form of government] enjoys a precious degree of liberty & happiness," but it tends toward turbulence. Nonetheless, turbulent

---

[29] M. Andrew Holowchak, "Differences of Circumstance, Differences of Fact: Jefferson Medialist View of History," in *American Studies in Scandinavia*, Vol. 47, No. 1: 2015, 3–21.
[30] Thomas More, *Utopia*, trans. Gilbert Burnet (London, 1684), 148, and James Harrington, *The Oceana and Other Works of James Harrington Esq; Collected, Methodiz'd, and Review'd with an Exact Account of his Life*, ed. John Toland (London, 1747), 37.
[31] Thomas Jefferson, Query XI, *Notes on Virginia*, 93.

liberty is much preferable to quiet servitude. Moreover, it prevents complacency and keeps honest elected officials.

Next, there is Jefferson's naturalistic medialism, which concerns proper use of land—*viz.*, eschewal of overuse and underuse of land.

Overuse of land is typified by the suffocation of human thriving that occurs in cities of any noticeable size.

In a letter to Dr. Benjamin Rush (23 Sept. 1800), Jefferson addresses remnants of the scourge of yellow fever in Philadelphia, which had 111,000 people at the time. "When great evils happen, I am in the habit of looking out for what good may arise from them as consolations to us, and Providence has in fact so established the order of things, as that most evils are the means of producing some good. The yellow fever will discourage the growth of great cities in our nation, & I view great cities as pestilential to the morals, the health and the liberties of man. True, they nourish some of the elegant arts, but the useful ones can thrive elsewhere, and less perfection in the others, with more health, virtue & freedom, would be my choice."

To David Williams three years later (14 Nov. 1803), Jefferson notes that want of land to farm in cities leads to "an overcharge in the class of competitors for learned occupation." Jefferson adds, "The general desire of men to live by their heads rather than their hands, and the strong allurements of great cities to those who have any turn for dissipation, threaten to make them here, as in Europe, the sinks of voluntary misery."[32]

For Jefferson, cities are a stark illustration of human enormity due to overreaching—of wanting beyond one's needs. Thus, agrestic living is a means between underuse of land for subsistence living and its exploitation for commercial gain.

Underuse of land is exemplified by wilderness, untouched by human hands.

Jefferson sees husbandmen as those who can make best use of land, when arable. In that, he follows the lead of many utopists whom he read and admired.[33] Thomas More (1478–1535) in *Utopia* describes an ideal state with 54 cities, and numerous farms. The chief occupation is husbandry.[34] Novelist and critic Louis-Sébastien Mercier (1740–1814) in *L'an 2440* offers readers a futuristic view of Paris in which the city, "founded principally on agriculture …

---

[32] See also TJ to Dr. Caspar Wistar, 21 June 1807.
[33] For more on the influence of utopian thinking on Jefferson's political and moral thinking, see M. Andrew Holowchak, *Thomas Jefferson's Political Philosophy and the Metaphysics of Utopia* (London: Brill, 2017), chap. 3.
[34] Thomas More, *Utopia*, ed. Mildred Campbell (New York: Walter Black, 1947), 71–72 and 90.

distributes the most necessary aliments [and] it satisfies the wants of man, but not his pride."[35] Marquis de Condorcet (1743–1794) in *Outlines of an Historical View of the Progress of the Human Mind* lists 10 epochs of human progress. The second epoch is the transitional state from hunting and gathering to agriculture and domestication of animals, and Condorcet throughout the remaining epochs of advance, gives pride of place for "the strong virtues of agricultural nations"—man's moral link to nature.[36] The influence of ancients such as Hesiod (*Works and Days*) and Virgil (*Georgics*) is manifest.

Nomological medialism and naturalistic medialism show that movement to the stage of widespread urbanism for Jefferson is not inevasible. People, he thinks, are able to observe the benefits of mostly agrestic living, through use of their moral sense—note "voluntary misery" in the letter to Williams. Thus, they can steer clear of excessive manufacture and undue laws, characteristic of large-scale urbanism as well as both deficiencies of unlegislated living and poor usage of land, characteristic of Native-American cultures and the under-legislated living of frontiersmen. Urbanism is stoppable, or at least capable of being tethered. As Merrill Peterson says: "It was not so much the farmer or farming that Jefferson … idealized, but a state of life midway between the primitive and the civilized, possessing the virtues of both and the vices of neither. This dreamy state captured his feelings and his hopes for the culture of man in America."[37]

In sum, Jeffersonian medialism acknowledges four stages, but the final stage, despite what he says to Ludow, is not "the most improved state," but indicative of social decay through movement from an agrestic ideal, with its focus on husbandry. Failure to move to the agrestic ideal—wanting less than what is needed for human thriving—is a matter of human under-reaching and symptomatic of human decline. That typifies Native American societies, without science, with little art, without laws, and without scientific use of lands. Movement beyond the agrestic ideal—wanting more than what is needed for human thriving—is a matter of overreaching and symptomatic of human decline. That typifies most European nations, with abundancy of science, but with too much art,[38] too many laws, and poor use of lands.

---

[35] Louis-Sebastien Mercier, *Memoirs of the Year Two Thousand Five Hundred* (Philadelphia: Thomas Dobson, 1795), 311–12.

[36] Jean-Antoine Nicolas de Caritat, *Outlines of an Historical View of the Progress of the Human Mind: Being a Posthumous Work of the Late M. de Condorcet* (London: J. Johnson, 1795), 21–68.

[37] Merrill D. Peterson, *Thomas Jefferson and the New Nation: A Biography* (Cambridge: Oxford University Press, 1970), 257.

[38] A comment, for instance, Jefferson often makes when he and Adams toured the pleasure

Upshot

Following the steady, slow, but sure advances of science, Jefferson could never accept the view that systems of government, grounded in morality, were not advancing. "The ground of liberty is to be gained by inches," he wrote to Rev. Charles Clay (27 Jan. 1790), "that we must be contented to secure what we can get from time to time, and eternally press forward for what is yet to get. It takes time to persuade men to do even what is for their own good." Politics too was forward-moving, though tardigrade. Decay through increased urbanization might have been the tendency of his day, but there was nothing inevasible about it. Jefferson, at various times, saw clearly a future state of the world with nations predominantly agricultural, friendly in commerce, and peace-abiding. That was not to state that he believed in a realizable eschaton. Jefferson likely believed in convergence toward an ideal state, not its actualization. Yet such convergence toward an ideal future state was a medial and not a linear ideal—a delicate balance between under-reaching and overreaching—and just what his republican schema was created to accommodate.

---

gardens of England. Thomas Jefferson, "Tour of Some of the Gardens of England," *in Thomas Jefferson: Writings,* ed. Merrill D. Peterson (New York: Library of America, 1984), 623–28.

Chapter II

Jefferson on the Praxis of History

Problems fronted, at least implicitly, by conjectural historians include the nodi that the many facts that historians typically have at their disposal cannot cohere without a large sum of surmise and that those facts typically concern large figures and large events. There are just too many gaps between incontestable facts and there are just too few documented facts concerning figures and events, less than large. The latter difficulty—said misleadingly by Jack McLaughlin to be the result of the myopia of historians, as "they perceive only what is large and conspicuous"[1]—cannot be reasonably overcome without a commitment to surmise. Yet the former difficulty is tackleable. Historians can aim to eschew it through *reasonable* surmise—by creating one of many possible narratives that fills those gaps—while conjecturalists, we have seen, have utilized that surmise which best advances moral aims.

Jefferson's views on liberty cannot be studied independently of his views on history and its philosophy, since, for Jefferson, if history shows anything through its unfolding, it shows that humans are essentially liberty-loving creatures. In this chapter, I focus on Jefferson's view of the philosophy or meaning of history, which is fundamentally the disinterested study of the movement of humans throughout time. I then turn to the sort of history, interested and morality-enhancing, that he preferred to read. I begin, however, with a needed "digression"—some discussion of the viability of veridical approaches to history with so many historians today, still and for some strange reason, committed to treadmill Postmodernist/Progressivist subjectivism. This digression, as it were, is needed because of the taint of subjectivism in Jeffersonian history today—mostly the result, in my estimation, of the introduction of Peter Onuf as the Thomas Jefferson Foundation Scholar in 1987 at University of Virginia.

"Everyman his own historian"
Yesterday's, Today's, and Tomorrow's History

Historians today with interest in historiography—what is often characterized simply and somewhat misleadingly as the history of history—seem to be in

---

[1] Jack McLaughlin, *To His Excellency Thomas Jefferson: Letters to a President* (New York: W.W. Norton & Company, 1991), xvii.

general agreement that the aims and methods of "historians" over millennia have changed. Study of history, as the argument goes, unquestionably shows that. There was yesterday's history, there is today's history, and there will be tomorrow's history, and there need not to be any thread that any of the three have in common. To complicate matters, the methods used in any epoch are not uniform, standardized. And so, the common-sense notion that the aim of a historian is to craft, at least in approximation, veridical narratives about the past cannot be maintained.

There is today uncritical acceptance by many historians of the notion that professional history is dead—*viz.*, that we are in a phase where we have disavowed the notion that we can know anything about the past and so there is no need of "academic" historians. Even "uncontested" facts cannot be assumed to be true. Moreover, by accessing the past through the lens of the present, we inevasibly import present biases. Those biases are exacerbated by the personal partialities, dictated by the biology and experiences of each historian.

Furthermore, the modern notion that there is a method for history—that history is fact-based, analytical, critical, rigorous, and comprehensive—is ludicrous, and so, anathema. If there is no method to history, then there are no professional historians. In the epigrammatic words of Progressivist Carl Becker, "Everyman his own historian." He adds: "Every generation, our own included, will, must inevitably, understand the past and anticipate the future in the light of its own restricted experience, must inevitably play on the dead whatever tricks it finds necessary for its own peace of mind." By "trick," Becker does not mean "malicious invention," but unconscious effort to grasp what we are doing given what we have done and what we aim to do. And so, we seek to use "Mr. Everyman's mythological adaptation of what actually happened."[2] In short, there is no way for anyone to access the past in the manner of the timeless words of Leopold von Ranke, "*wie es eigentlich gewesen ist.*"[3] We are forever prisoners of the present and of our own constitution and experiences, which shape our perspective of things. Modernism is passé; we are, in today's language, *post* modernism, hence Postmodernist historiography.[4]

---

[2] Carl Becker, "Everyman His Own Historian," in *American Historical Review*, Vol. 37, No. 2, 1932: 235.

[3] "As it actually happened." Leopold von Ranke, *Histories of the Latin and Germanic Nations from 1494–1514*, trans. Wilma A. Iggers (New York: Routledge, 2011), 86.

[4] See M. Andrew Holowchak, "Thomas Jefferson and the Conditions of Good History: Some Implications for Writing about the American Revolution and Early American History," in *Journal of the American Revolution,* https://allthingsliberty.com/2023/03/thomas-jefferson-and-the-conditions-of-good-history-writing-about-the-american-revolution/.

Jeffersonian scholars, at the lead of Peter Onuf, have jumped on the bandwagon of postmodernist subjectivism. In *The Mind of Thomas Jefferson*—"mind" being a malapropism of the first order, because the book does nothing to tell us anything about the mind of Jefferson other than that it is inaccessible—Onuf tells us that "historians who look for disclosures of an authentic self behind these many voices [of Jefferson] and roles will be frustrated." Jefferson was in his letters a brilliant chameleon who pandered to the interests and needs of his varied correspondents.[5] Moreover, Onuf is not shy about disclosure that his approach to Jefferson is postmodernist. For instance, while he praises Conor Cruise O'Brien's "trashing of Jefferson" because O'Brien lays "his cards on the table," Onuf condemns O'Brien's aim of truthful history. "O'Brien's pseudopositivism (his book strings together long quotations from original sources, with a few 'talking head' secondary sources thrown in) clearly signals his alienation from fashionable humanities scholarship: no relativism, no constructivism, no 'invented tradition,' thank you, just the facts."[6] The great historians, for Onuf, concern themselves with what is trendy, what is fashionable, not what is truthful.

Onuf's remonstration—if it can be called "remonstration"—is incredibly vacuous, but it typifies the sort of scholarship that today is fashionable and published. It is astonishing that he repudiates another scholar for grounding claims in "just the facts," as if facts-grounding ought to be some sort of crime. O'Brien it seems is being taken to task for not aiming to avoid fantasy in his account! Yet that in some sense typifies the general landscape of today's Jeffersonian scholarship. The sensational trumps the factual.

Onuf's postmodernist historiography is also manifestly on display in his 1993 collection of off-the-wall essays in *Jeffersonian Legacies*. That comes out cleanly—if expressions of postmodernism are ever clean—in Dan Jordan's foreword in which he describes the conference which gave birth to the book as "an intellectual free-for-all" driven by "revisionist zeal, presentism, and a tint of political correctness."[7] It comes out also in Joyce Appleby's introduction in which she talks about how the present historical commitment to "pluralism, diversity, multiculturalism, relativism" makes difficult our grasp of Jefferson's "scientific gloss" of things. Were he today alive—Appleby writes in 1993—Jefferson, she asserts, would have disavowed his Rankean historical ideals.[8]

---

[5] Peter Onuf, *The Mind of Thomas Jefferson* (Charlottesville: University of Virginia Press, 2007), 33.
[6] Peter Onuf, *The Mind of Thomas Jefferson*, 53–54.
[7] Daniel P. Jordan, Foreword, in *Jeffersonian Legacies*, ed. Peter Onuf (Charlottesville: University of Virginia Press, 1993), vii–viii.
[8] Joyce Appleby, "Introduction," in *Jeffersonian Legacies*, ed. Peter Onuf (Charlottesville: University of Virginia Press, 1993), 15.

There are crippling problems for postmodernists, and I include the early Progressivists among them.

First, historians' acceptance of historiography as a valid discipline creates a complication. The notion that there can be a history of history presupposes some sort of meta-history with its own methods or standards that enable us to categorize the varied and discordant approaches to "chronicling" past events as histories of some form. In sum, historiography requires that all types of history share some common element that enables us to categorize them as histories, otherwise, historiography would be impossible, meaningless—a word without denotation. If there is some essence to the history of history, there too must be some essence to history, and that allows for criteria for excluding some avowed forms of history from categorization as historical. Likewise, if there is no essence to history, then there cannot be historiography other than of an arbitrary sort. In short, the existence of historiography as a valid discipline presupposes that some approaches to the past are not aboveboard histories.

Moreover, the notion that there are phases of history—pre-modern, modern, and postmodern phases, in the words of postmodernist historiographers—strongly suggests intellectual movement of some sort. Recognition that there can be no history "as it actually happened"—more plainly, that history is subjective, not objective—must be an epistemological insight and an advance the likes of which we were not in possession in the modern phase, if it is to be a *substantive* and accurate claim. Yet if the movement from modern to postmodern is for the better—and that is the only way to take the claim, for otherwise it is gibberish—then the postmodern historian crafts a claim that goes well beyond our own "restricted experience." It is a claim that transcends time, and thus, is a trick not just on the dead, but on the living. In short, the assertion that all utterances are essentially subjective cannot be grounded, for it too is suffocatingly subjective. We here find ourselves walking on a treadmill.

Last, there is the strange notion that we can have no access to the actuality of past events. While history cannot chronicle events "as they actually happened"—it is not even clear what that phrase means—that does not mean that it is inescapably subjective and uninformative, as postmodernists claim. That there cannot be any once-and-for-all account of, say, the Revolutionary War, does not imply that we cannot know anything about the Revolutionary War—that to write about it is to engage in drivel. Historians' narratives are fact-guided, and larger access to critical first-hand documents and, for instance, to archeological or biological data, gives historians more raw data from which to work. There is also the indispensability of critical interaction among historians that functions as a corrective to false theses—an interaction that for postmodernists is not profit, but play.⁹

Consequently, we can do away with postmodernism.

"It is compiled ... for an everlasting possession..."
Herodotus versus Thucydides

By "historiography," let us understand "the study of the theory and praxis of history"—the study of the principles guiding historical research and the methods utilized by historians—instead of the inefficaciously circular definition "history of history."¹⁰

Jefferson was fond of ancient history from the Greeks Herodotus and Thucydides to the Italians Livy and Tacitus. He found great comfort and wisdom in the moral lessons they reinforced.

In recommended reading lists on ancient history,¹¹ Jefferson always begins with the Greek Herodotus, commonly referred to as the "Father of History," a title given to him by Cicero,¹² since the Greek is the first person of which we know to aim to chronicle a particularly singular event in world history, the Persian War (490–479 B.C.), and to do so in narration. Of his account of the Persian War, Herodotus writes: "The aim [of my account] is to prevent the erasure of the evidence of obscure human events (*aklea*), and to preserve the glory of the important and remarkable deeds (*erga*) of both Greeks and non-Greeks; among the matters I cover, in particular, there is the provenance of the hostilities between Greeks and non-Greeks."¹³ The disclosure, aiming at impartiality, is moving.

---

⁹ It is astonishing, given the theoretical flexibility that Onufian postmodernism allows for interpretations of Jefferson (an infinity!) that the accounts he endorses only underscore Jefferson's opprobrium.

¹⁰ See M. Andrew Holowchak, "Thomas Jefferson and the Conditions of Good History: Some Implications for Writing about the American Revolution and Early American History," *Journal of the American Revolution*, https://allthingsliberty.com/2023/03/thomas-jefferson-and-the-conditions-of-good-history-writing-about-the-american-revolution/, accessed 20 Nov. 2023.

¹¹ E.g., TJ to Peter Carr, 19 Aug. 1785; TJ to Francis Eppes, 6 Oct. 1820; and TJ to George W. Lewis, 25 Oct. 1825.

¹² Cicero, *On the Laws*, trans. Clinton W. Keyes (Cambridge, MA: Harvard University Press, 1928), I.5.

¹³ My translation here from the Greek. For an English translation, see Herodotus, *The Histories*, Vol. I, trans. A.D. Godley (Cambridge: Harvard University Press, 1920), 2.

While Herodotus, who traveled extensively, offers accounts of famous battles—e.g., Marathon, Thermopylae, and Salamis—and delves into Persian culture, foreign to Greek readers, the work is fraught with digressions, though many are aidful in situating occurrences in his narrative that would otherwise go unexplained. To facilitate accessibility of events by readers, Herodotus includes speeches, dialog, and short stories, and adds among the last, divine retribution for human hubris like that of the Persian king, Xerxes. Assets of his approach to history include his detachment and disinterest, his eye for minutiae, his inclusion of inconsistent accounts of some key event, and his insistence that the events he chronicled be given a sense of unity by being related in narrative form. Liabilities include uncritical acceptance of word-of-mouth accounts, problems that involve insistence on a narrative form, and the moralistic tone at times of the work.

Decades later, Thucydides offers an account of the Peloponnesian War, between Athens against Sparta. The war began in 431 and ended in 404 B.C., though Thucydides' account broke off in 411 B.C., perhaps because of his death.[14] Thucydides' work marks a sharp break with Herodotus' account, where the affairs of humans can be segregated from the interests of the gods—human events for Thucydides are the doing of humans—and where events are not given in a strictly chronological manner. Thucydides works from oral sources, though he fails to disclose them. To give a thread to the events he describes, there is addition of lengthy perorations, like the eulogy for Pericles, by key players throughout his account. There is all throughout no attempt to depict the cultural climate of any of the *poleis* involved in the fighting and, most singularly, no attempt to moralize concerning the goodness or badness of the war or its players.[15]

Human agency, for Thucydides, is reduced to the interplay of chance and necessity, which are deemed to determine human behavior. Having participated in the events of which he writes, Thucydides is a narrator who gives life to the events, not merely a dry chronicler, though he steers clear of the "fantasia" of Herodotus. Thus, he is, in intendment, a veridicalist, not a fabulist.

> To hear this history rehearsed, for that there be inserted in it no fables, shall be perhaps not delightful. But he who desires to look into the truth of actions, and which (according to the condition of humanity) may be done again, or at least their like, shall find enough herein to make him

---

[14] Xenophon's *Hellenica* which begins where Thucydides' account abruptly ends, is a continuation of the work.

[15] Thucydides, *History of the Peloponnesian War*, trans. Richard Crawley (1874).

think it profitable. And it is compiled rather for an everlasting possession than to be rehearsed for a prize.[16]

Much has been made about this "everlasting possession." Thucydides is, unlike Agathon of Plato's *Symposium*, no mere producer of beautiful words for pleasant effect—no orator in competition for a prize on account of his dulciloquy, his sweet words—but offers us what he believes to be a veridical account of the war and its causes. In doing so, he at least implicitly advises that heedfulness of the past can prevent us from repeating the past, should we wish not to repeat the past, for "the condition of humanity" seemingly inclines us to repeat ourselves, unless otherwise instructed. Nonetheless, Thucydides is not a moralist, like Herodotus before him and historians after him. "Thucydides has no political aim in view: he was purely a historian. But it was part of the method of both alike to eliminate conventional sentiment and morality."[17]

One can take Herodotus and Thucydides as harbingers of roughly two distinct approaches to history, though I add that these lines need not be seen as non-overlapping.

Herodotus	**Thucydides**
Interested	*Disinterested*
Didactic	Factual
Entertaining	Rigorous & Uncolored
Discursive	Chronological
Religious	Secular
Cultural	Militaristic

For the purposes of this undertaking, the two approaches to history can be called "Interested History" and "Disinterested History." Most of the Greeks and Romans after the two—Ctesias, Polybius, Diodorus, Plutarch, Livy, and Tacitus—are interested historians, and moralists, and we see today interested history in Marxism, Progressivism, Revisionism, and Postmodernism. In contrast, the disinterested nature of *The Peloponnesian War* centuries later leads to the *realpolitik* of Machiavelli and Hobbes, and profoundly influences German philosophers such as Friedrich Schelling, Friedrich Schlegel, Friedrich Nietzsche, and Leopold von Ranke, and continues today in evidentiary approaches to history, such as neo-Positivism.

---

[16] In short, he eschews the mellifluous prosody of orators. Thucydides, *History of the Peloponnesian War*, I.22.iv.
[17] John Bagnell Bury, *The Ancient Greek Historians* (London, MacMillan, 1909), 140–43.

"The whole of everything said and done there…"
Jefferson, Bolingbroke, & Disinterested History

Jefferson is axially committed to a Thucydidean/Disinterested approach to the praxis of history. Evidence of that occurs early in life in his *Literary Commonplace Book*. There Jefferson commonplaces Lord Bolingbroke (§57), who writes of history, rightly practiced.[18] For history to be authentic, Jefferson, continuing to copy Bolingbroke, adds that "these are some of the conditions necessary" (1–4, numbers mine):

> 1. it must be writ by a cotemporary author, or by one who had cotemporary materials in his hands. 2. it must have been published among men who are able to judge of the capacity of th[e] author, and of the authenticity of the memorials on whic[h] he writ. 3. nothing repugnant to the universal experience of mankind must be contained in it. 4. the principal facts at least, which it contains, must be confirmed by collateral testimony, that is, by the testimony of thos[e] who had no common interest of country, of religion, or of profession, to disguise or falsify the truth.

We may thus sum these needed conditions, according to Jefferson, for sound history:

C_1 **(Proximity Condition):** a historian must either be living at the time of the events he describes or, if not, he must be privy to documents written of the time he describes by witnesses.

C_2 **(Authenticity Condition):** the author must be judged to be capable and ingenuous by others of his day who are capable and ingenuous and his materials must be judged authentic by such persons.

C_3 **(Consistency Condition):** what is described is consistent with what is universally experienced by mankind—e.g., there be no contraventions of the amply verified laws of physical nature.

C_4 **(Confirmation Condition):** the axial facts of the testimony must be confirmed by qualified disinterested others.

---

[18] See M. Andrew Holowchak, "Thomas Jefferson and the Conditions of Good History: Some Implications for Writing about the American Revolution and Early American History," *Journal of the American Revolution*, https://allthingsliberty.com/2023/03/thomas-jefferson-and-the-conditions-of-good-history-writing-about-the-american-revolution/, accessed 20 Nov. 2023.

Bolingbroke's principles, clearly driven by his empiricism, entail sufficient vetting of both persons and material. That Jefferson commonplaces the passage strongly intimates purchase of Bolingbrokean principles of proper history. Jefferson's inclusion of "some" indicates the likelihood of other conditions necessary, not listed by Bolingbroke.

I now proffer textual evidence of Jefferson's purchase of the four axial principles.

First, there is the *proximity condition.* To John Adams (10 Aug. 1815), Jefferson writes of his concern that there can never be a definitive account of the American Revolution because none of the discussions of the Continental Congress has been left to posterity by members of that Congress. "On the subject of the history of the American Revolution, you ask who shall write it?" says Jefferson. "Who can write it? And who will ever be able to write it? Nobody; except merely its external facts; all its councils, designs and discussions having been conducted by Congress with closed doors, and no members, as far as I know, having even made notes of them. These, which are the life and soul of history, must forever be unknown."

To John Adams (10 Aug. 1815), Jefferson writes of his notes on American independence.

> On the questions of Independence, and on the two articles of Confederation respecting taxes and votings, I took minutes of the heads of the arguments. On the first, I threw all into one mass, without ascribing to the speakers their respective arguments; pretty much in the manner of Hume's summary digests of the reasonings in parliament for and against a measure. On the last, I stated the heads of the arguments used by each speaker. But the whole of my notes on the question of Independence does not occupy more than five pages, such as of this letter; and on the other questions, two such sheets. They have never been communicated to any one.

Jefferson adds, however, that there is an account, "the ablest work of this kind," of the debates over the Constitution at the convention in Philadelphia in 1788. "The whole of everything said and done there was taken down by Mr. Madison, with a labor and exactness beyond comprehension."

On June 12, 1823, Jefferson tells William Johnson, "The opening scenes of our present government will not be seen in their true aspect until the letters of the day, now held in private hoards, shall be broken up and laid open to public view." On October 4 of the same year, he tells Hugh Paul Taylor "every good citizen" must do what he can to preserve "documents relating to the history of our country." He is convinced that America, comprising liberty-loving people, has a privileged position in global history.

Next, there is the *authenticity condition*. In some notes he has taken on Christoph Daniel Ebeling (30 July 1795) and his account of the history and geography of America in his *Erdbeschreibung und Geschichte von America* (first published in 1793), Jefferson comments on the American sources of Ebeling's work. There are President Stiles, Dr. Willar, Dr. Ramsay, Mr. Barlow, Mr. Morse, and Mr. Webster. The first is "an excellent man, of very great learning, but remarkable for his credulity." Ramsay, Barlow, and Morse are "men of respectable characters worthy of confidence as to any facts they may state, and rendered, by their good sense, good judges of them." Morse and Webster are "good authorities for whatever relates to the Eastern states, & perhaps as far South as the Delaware." Yet when they talk of states south of Delaware, "their information is worse than none at all, except as far as they quote good authorities." Each traveled once through the South so that they might be considered eyewitnesses. "But to pass once along a public road thro' a country, & in one direction only, to put up at it's taverns, and get into conversation with the idle, drunken individuals who pass their time lounging in these taverns, is not the way to know a country, it's inhabitants, or manners." And so, Ebeling is not entitled "to generalize a whole nation from these specimens."

What then of the newspapers of the country—such as John Fenno's *Gazette of the United States*, Noah Webster's *American Minerva*, Benjamin Russell's *Columbian Sentinel* (Boston), from which Ebeling draws? Those are each Federalist sources, and thus slanted.

Jefferson then recommends Philip Mazzei's *Recherches historiques et politiques sur les Etates-Unis de l'Amerique*—which can be got only from Paris—because "the author is an exact man."

For Jefferson, the greatest illustration of inauthenticity is David Hume's *History of England*. Jefferson writes of the enthusiasm with which he, unaware of its avowed Tory slant, "devoured it when young." Hume, doing backwards history,[19] began with the Stuarts, "became their apologist, and advocated all their enormities," perhaps in some measure to gain fame. "He spared nothing, therefore, to wash them white, and to palliate their misgovernment. For this purpose, he suppressed truths, advanced falsehoods, forged authorities and falsified records." Jefferson continues: "But so bewitching was his style and manner, that his readers were un-willing to doubt anything, swallowed everything, and all England became tories by the magic of his art. His pen revolutionized the public sentiment of that country more completely than the

---

[19] TJ to George Lewis, 25 Oct. 1825.

standing armies could ever have done, which were so much dreaded and deprecated by the patriots of that day." Hume then turned to the Tudors, but then only "selected and arranged the materials of their history as to present their arbitrary acts only, as the genuine samples of the constitutional power of the crown."[20] "It is like the portraits of our countryman [Joseph] Wright, whose eye was so unhappy as to seize all the ugly features of his subject, and to present them faithfully, while it was entirely insensible to every lineament of beauty."[21]

Jefferson's gripe with Hume, he tells George Lewis (25 Oct. 1825), is his pro-monarchy slant. When discussing the reigns of the Plantagenets and Tudors, Hume writes that "it was the people who encroached on the sovereign, not the sovereign who usurped on the rights of the people" and that "the grievances under which the English labored [i.e., whipping, pillorying, cropping, imprisoning, fining, &c.], when considered in themselves, without regard to the constitution, scarcely deserve the name, nor were they either burthensome on the people's properties, or anywise shocking to the natural humanity of mankind." As a Tory historian, Hume derives his understanding of the British constitution from the provenance of the Norman Conquest, while Whig historians derive theirs from the era of the Saxons. I critique Jefferson's account of Hume later in this book.

Third, there is the *consistency condition*. In the manner of Ranke decades after him, Jefferson rails against writers who get right the "great outlines," though "the incidents and coloring are according to the faith or fancy of the writer." He has in mind Judge John Marshall's biography of Washington. "Had Judge Marshall taken half your pains in sifting and scrutinizing facts, he would not have given to the world, as true history a false copy of a record under his eye." The nodus is decupled in subsequent biographies, which draw from sustenance from the first. Historians must begin with facts. "When writers are so indifferent as to the correctness of facts," says Jefferson to William Wirt, who is in the process of a biography of Patrick Henry and enjoining Jefferson for information, "the verification of which lies at their elbow, by what measure shall we estimate their relation of things distant, or of those given to us through the obliquities of their own vision?" To allow for vetted material, it is incumbent on key players in a great historical drama to keep painstakingly records of events.[22]

In a later letter to Wirt (12 Nov. 1816), Jefferson lampoons his friend's finished biography of Henry. "You have certainly practiced vigorously [in the Life of

---

[20] TJ to William Duane, 12 Aug. 1810.
[21] Wright was known for his portraits of American patriots, like Washington and Franklin. He perished in 1793 with yellow fever in Philadelphia. TJ to John Adams, 25 Nov. 1816.
[22] TJ to William Wirt, 14 Aug. 1814.

Patrick Henry] the precept of 'de mortius nil nisi bonum.'[23] This presents a very difficult question,—whether one only or both sides of the medal shall be presented. It constitutes, perhaps, the distinction between panegyric and history." Jefferson is clearly disappointed with Wirt's work. He would list the biography in his library under "Fiction."

It is imperative for Jefferson that chroniclers of persons and events do the digging, as it were, and get right their facts. Travelers to America—like Auberteuil, Longchamps, and Abbé Robin—craft accounts of the Revolution or the jejune country, says Jefferson to the editor of *Journal de Paris* (29 Aug. 1787), that pass as genuine to contemporaries of the persons or events depicted. "How may we expect that future ages shall be better informed? Will those rise from their graves to bear witness to the truth, who would not, while living, lift their voices against falsehood? If cotemporary histories are thus false, what will future compilations be? And what are all those of preceding times?"

Jefferson cites a paragraph concerning John Dickinson's role in the American Revolution. Dickinson is said by a certain M. Meyer to be the sole driving force behind America's independence. Jefferson goes on to give a thorough refutation of that account—a tissue of falsehoods except for one claim. Meyer states that there was a congressional split in the vote for independence; Jefferson notes that the vote was unanimous. After vigorous debate on Jefferson's Declaration, the final document was "approved by an unanimous vote and signed by every member, *except Mr. Dickinson.*" Still, the journal claims that Dickinson, and only Dickinson, declared the independence of the United States.[24]

Finally, there is the *confirmation condition*, which necessitates that even first-hand testimonies, if possible, be vetted by accounts of others—preferably, other first-hand accounts. It is a condition of enumerative inductive which sensibly states that the more testimony we have on behalf of some claim, the more we can be convinced of its truth.

To William Short (8 Jan. 1825), Jefferson recounts a story of which he was fond of relating. In a discussion with John Adams and Alexander Hamilton, the former stated that the British government would be "the most perfect model of

---

[23] "Say only good things about the dead."
[24] "Monsieur Mayer assure qu'une seule voix, un seul homme, prononça l'independance des Etats unis. Ce fut, dit il, John Dickinson, un des Deputés de la Pensilvanie au Congrés. La veille, il avoit vôté pour la soumission, l'egalité des suffrages avoit suspendu la resolution; s'il eut persisté, le Congrés ne deliberoit point, il fut foible; il ceda aux instances de ceux qui avoient plus d'energie, plus d'eloquence, et plus de lumieres; il donna sa voix: l'Amerique lui doit une reconnaissance eternelle; c'est Dickinson qui l'a affranchie. »

government ever devised by the wit of man" if its imperfections were expunged. Hamilton corrected Adams, "With these corruptions it was perfect, and without them it would be an impracticable government." Jefferson adds that the account was confirmable by Henry Knox and Edmund Randolph, who were then also present. Jefferson sums:

> The true history of that conflict of parties will never be in possession of the public, until, by the death of the actors in it, the hoards of their letters shall be broken up and given to the world. I should not fear to appeal to those of Harper himself, if he has kept copies of them, for abundant proof that he was himself a monarchist. I shall not live to see these unrevealed proofs, nor probably you; for time will be requisite. But time will, in the end, produce the truth.

In addition to the four needed conditions of right history, Jefferson also commonplaces a sentence on the worthlessness of circumstantial history.

> A story circumstantially related, ought not to be received on the faith of tradition; since the last reflection on human nature is sufficient to shew how unsafely a system of facts and circumstances can be trusted for it's preservation to memory alone, and for it's conveiance to oral report alone; how liable it must be to all those alterations, which the weakness of the human mind must cause necessarily, and which the corruption of the human heart will be sure to suggest.

Thus, any report that is handed down through the years from mouth to mouth is historically unreliable. In consequence, reports must be first-hand. An excellent illustration of direct testimony occurs in a letter from Thomas Jefferson to James Madison (20 Feb. 1784), concerning Marquis de Chastellux's book, *Travels in North America, Through the Years, 1780, 1781, and 1782*: "He has visited all the principal fields of battle, enquired minutely into the detail of the actions, & has given what are probably the best accounts extant of them. He often finds occasion to criticise & to deny the British accounts from an inspection of the ground."

"It is a good secretion of their matter"

Desiderata of Disinterested History

Inspection of Jefferson's writings shows a commitment to other principles, not as needed principles, but as desiderata.

First, to be a fit historian, one ought to devote a lifetime to the discipline and write down one's experiences before one's faculties have decayed. Josephus Bradner Stuart, to illustrate, bids Jefferson to write his account of his life and the times in which he has lived. "The American People, after all you have done for them, wish one more last & lasting favor from you: that is, that not withstanding your advanced age, your extensive correspondence, your numerous & important duties, you will yet favor them & the world with such history of your own life & times, as your leisure may permit you to compile. For such a work the voice of the nation, as far as I can ascertain it, seems to be loud & united."[25]

Jefferson replies (10 May 1817) that while a public servant, he had the cognitive resources but not the time, while now that he is retired, he has the time but lacks the cognitive resources.

> to write history requires a whole life of observation, of enquiry, of labor and correction. it's materials are not to be found among the ruins of a decayed memory. at this day I should begin where I ought to have left off. the 'solve senescentem equum' is a precept we learn in youth,[26] but for the practice of age; and were I to disregard it, it would be but a proof the more of it's soundness.

Jefferson adds that he would certainly lose the respect of his fellow citizens "by exposing the decay of [his] faculties," were he to attempt such a history. It is, thus, for Stuart and his "brethren of the rising generation to arraign at your tribunal the actions of your predecessors, and to pronounce the sentence they may have merited or incurred."

Second, a historian ought to practice concision and focus. On December 18, 1824, William Short writes to Jefferson of the goings-on of the secret Hartford Convention, held by Federalists from late 1814 to early 1815.[27] Short remarks

---

[25] Josephus B. Stuart to TJ, 25 Apr. 1817.
[26] From Horace, who writes, "Solve senescentem mature sanus equum, ne peccet ad extremum ridendus et ilia ducat" ("Be wise in time, and turn loose the ageing horse, lest at the last he stumble amid jeers and burst his wind [pass gas]"). Horace, *Satires, Epistles, Art of Poetry*, trans. Rushton Fairclough (Cambridge, MA: Harvard University Press, 1926), Book I, Epistle I, lines 8–9.
[27] Meetings at Hartford of Federalists from Massachusetts, New Hampshire, Connecticut, Rhode Island, and Vermont from December 15, 1814, to January 5, 1815, to discuss pressing political issues such as the dreadful War of 1812, the possibility of secession from the union of states, removal of the three-fifths clause, the legality of the Louisiana Purchase, the Embargo of 1807, a requirement to have two-thirds of congress approve declarations of war, restrictions of trade, and admission of new states. Three

on his astonishment on a certain Harper who had written too little on the convention and had not consulted the pamphlet of Harrison Gray Otis. Jefferson replies: "It is impossible to read thoroughly such writings as those of Harper and Otis, who take a page to say what requires but a sentence, or rather, who give you whole pages of what is nothing to the purpose." Jefferson, though he lived in a time when prolixity of written expression was the norm—one sentence, especially in legal documents, could run on for pages—was remarkably economical when writing and always to the point. Jefferson championed concision of expression for all manners of communicating through words. Jefferson was also relevant, not divaricate.

Third, Jefferson militates for some degree of embellishment, so long as a historian does not depart from the facts. We recall that Herodotus wrote his *Histories* to prevent erasure of exceptional events and Thucydides added that in chronicling noteworthy events, one ought not to hyperbolize, but instead ought to stick to the truth, even if the account is dry. Yet given what I have mentioned of concision and given Jefferson's penchant for truthfulness, it might come as a surprise that he was not adamantly against some measure of embellishment to enliven the otherwise dreary, fact-based prose. He writes to John Adams (5 May 1817):

> I am now reading Botta's History of our own Revolution.[28] Bating the ancient practice which he has adopted of putting speeches into mouths which never made them, and fancying motives of action which we never felt, he has given that history with more detail, precision and candor, than any writer I have yet met with. It is, to be sure, compiled from those writers; but it is a good secretion of their matter, the pure from the impure, and presented in a just sense of right in opposition to usurpation.

What exactly is Jefferson here saying? The second sentence seems to be a concession. Jefferson is likely asserting that despite having added speeches that were never uttered in the mouths of Patriots, Botta has still given the most detailed, precise, and candid account of the American Revolution. Drawing from other sources, he has purified their impure accounts, because he has explained the revolution from the perspective of right, not of insurgency for the

---

representatives from the secret meetings were subsequently sent to Washington to discuss their terms, but news of Andrew Jackson's stunning victory in the Battle of New Orleans preceded them and thereby the representatives lost whatever leverage they might have had and returned to Massachusetts.

[28] Carlo Giuseppe Guglielmo Botta, *History of the War of the Independence of the United States of America* (Philadelphia: 1820–1821).

sake of usurpation of power. If so, this is not a blanket endorsement of adding fictive speeches to enliven narrative, but it is clear that Jefferson does not object to the practice.

Upshot

In this chapter, I begin with a philosophical problem: history as a viable science. I turn next to a sketch of Herodotean, interested history as contrasted with Thucydidean, disinterested history. In the remainder of the chapter, I epitomize Jefferson's account of the ingenuous praxis of history, which is a commitment to disinterest, through Jefferson's commitment to four axial principles gleaned from the writings of Lord Bolingbroke.

That noted, Jefferson was not averse to practice of interested history, so long interestedness was in the service of moral advance. That is the subject of the third chapter.

Chapter III

The Argument for Interested History

While in his late twenties, Thomas Jefferson writes to Robert Skipwith (3 Aug. 1771): "Considering history as a moral exercise, her lessons would be too infrequent if confined to real life. Of those recorded by historians few incidents have been attended with such circumstances as to excite in any high degree this sympathetic emotion of virtue." Humans are, however, of such matter that we are moved by the deeds and misdeeds of fictive characters. "The spacious field of imagination is thus laid open to our use, and lessons may be formed to illustrate and carry home to the heart every moral rule of life."

The sentiment is that history, when considered "a moral exercise," offers little stimulation to the moral sense of each person, for history, when done disinterestedly, affords humans too few instances of morality-enhancing lessons. Historians, the introductory participial phrase strongly suggests, are not writing morality plays, but merely leaving to posterity, to the best of their ability, veridical accounts of past events to be used howsoever people wish to use them.

Yet one might counter that no academic discipline is value-neutral. Every academic discipline has some end, presumably for human betterment, and Jefferson more than others of his day was fixated on useful knowledge, not merely knowledge for its own sake—hence, Jefferson's disdain of metaphysics and of metempirical religious squabbles that could be apprehended, if at all, only by the disputants. Hence, there was also his preference for history that not only proffered veridical narratives of the past, but also had agents and events that invited reflection, directly or indirectly, on moral improvement.

In this chapter, I explain Jefferson's preference for interested history, turn to his argument for republicanized history, and end with the question concerning whether interested history is necessarily politicized history.

"A compound of history and morality"

Jefferson's Interest in Interested History

Though Jefferson seems not to have been committed to history being essentially moral, he preferred to read historians—e.g., Plutarch, Tacitus, and Livy—who were moralists. While acknowledging that the essence of history was knowledge of the past, his predilection was for useful history—history in the service of moral improvement—because he, like many other Enlightenment thinkers, was so heavily invested in human progress, of which his republicanism was both an instrument and an effect. A letter to granddaughter Anne Randolph Bankhead (8 Dec. 1808) sums his view. "Middleton's life of Cicero is among the most valuable accounts we have of the period of which he writes; and Tacitus I consider as the first writer in the world without a single exception. His book is a compound of history and morality of which we have no other example." Jefferson praises Middleton for giving a clear snapshot of the time of Cicero; Jefferson praises Tacitus for dexterously combining history—i.e., doing what Middleton was doing—with morality.

As a lifelong and tireless advocate of government of and for the people—government by the will of the majority of the citizenry—Jefferson had a decided personal preference for interested history: history advancing morality and fighting against what he always construed to be the tyranny of monocracy. "The most effectual means of preventing the perversion of power into tyranny," begins Jefferson in his Bill for the More General Diffusion of Knowledge (1779), "are to illuminate, as far as practicable, the minds of the people at large, and more especially to give them knowledge of those facts, which history exhibits, that possessed thereby of the experience of other ages and countries, they may be enabled to know ambition under all its shapes, and prompt to exert their natural powers to defeat its purposes."[1]

So that it does not lapse into bedlam, there are demands on republican governing, which is essentially, for Jefferson, an experiment concerning human will and human goodness. There is no guarantee that the experiment will work and it is not the case, realizes Jefferson, that republicanism is trouble free. Liberty, though an unquestioned value, brings with it turbulence. "Weigh [turbulence] against the oppressions of monarchy, and it becomes nothing," His preference is for turbulent liberty, not quiet servitude. Ever sanguine, he adds that this evil too is "productive of good," as it turns public attention toward public affairs. "I hold it that a little rebellion now and then is a good thing, & as necessary in the political world as storms in the physical. ... An observation of this truth should render honest republican governors so mild in their punishment of rebellions, as not to discourage them too much. It is a medicine necessary for the sound health of government."[2]

To encourage acceptance of republicanism, Jefferson champions useful history—history which not only tells readers about the past but also underscores

---

[1] Thomas Jefferson, Bill for the More General Diffusion of Knowledge, in *The Scholar's Thomas Jefferson: Vital Writings of a Vital American*, ed. M. Andrew Holowchak (Newcastle upon Tyne: Cambridge Scholars, 2021), 279.
[2] TJ to James Madison, 30 Jan. 1787.

the horrors of monocratic governing throughout the millennia. That is why Jefferson relates to William Duane (4 Apr. 1813) his predilection for ancient to modern history. The history of his day banishes "all moral principle from the code which governs the intercourse of nations." Lack of censure by historians for opprobrious deeds of agents sickens his soul to death. At the hand of "a Livy, a Sallust and a Tacitus," the Catilines and Caligulas suffer condemnation. And so, "we are comforted with the reflection that the condemnation of all succeeding generations has confirmed the sentence of the historian, and consigned their memories to everlasting infamy, a solace we cannot have with the Georges and Napoleons but by anticipation." Thus, though a champion of disinterested history, Jefferson himself prefers to read interested history. Interested history can be readily put to use for human betterment, because it inspires.

"Among masterless men, there is perpetual war"

Need of Republicanized History

People, for centuries, have been so accustomed to the abuses of governing by the artificial aristocracy, monocrats especially, that they needed prompting to understand and to enjoy the privileges of republican government. Though the concepts of liberty and equality were not new, they would undergo redefinition in Enlightenment times, and their political application would be a matter of large discussion. That was made achievable by philosophical discussion of the possibility of a new social order, based on individualism and equality, not collectivism and social rank, determined by birth. The people of a society were no longer to be construed as "the masses" or "*hoi polloi*." Each was to be considered a distinct human being of the same stuff and worth of any sovereign, or relatively so.

It is difficult, if not impossible, for us to grasp the revolutionary nature of the concept of human equality—to be further discussed in chapter 5. It is sufficient to say that though many discussed the concept, few, in any visceral sense, believed it to be true. There was the additional botheration of how to put the notion of human equality into political praxis. Equality, for instance, demanded numerous political changes—in Isaiah Berlin's words, positive liberty[3]—so that all citizens could act on their equality. Jefferson, as we shall see, worked ceaselessly throughout his life to institute the sort of changes needed for a politically robust society where all were at liberty to exercise their equality.

Other key acknowledgments of Enlightenment thinking—not all were internally consistent—were the notions that humans could know the cosmos

---

[3] Isaiah Berlin, "Two Concepts of Liberty," https://cactus.utahtech.edu/green/B_Readings/I_Berlin%20Two%20Concpets%20of%20Liberty.pdf, accessed 6 Feb. 2020.

through empirical investigation and use of reason; that to some extent, humans could control their destinies; that there were natural laws governing both human societies and morality to be disclosed through empirical investigation and use of reason; that knowledge of humans and their societies led to human progress; and that trust in traditional authorities like Aristotle or the Church impeded understanding and human progress.

Important Enlightenment thinkers—excluding natural philosophers such as Galileo and Newton, covered in the next chapter—were Thomas Hobbes, John Locke, and Marquis de Condorcet. Their influence on Jefferson is unmistakable, so some discussion of each is profitable.

The influence of Hobbes on Jefferson was the influence of Hobbes on all other liberals of Jefferson's day: A philosopher whose pro-monarchism needed to be refuted. For Thomas Hobbes (1588–1679), individuals were by nature greedy, power-loving, and preoccupied by self-preservation. In the state of nature—for Hobbes, not necessarily a historical state, but a state inferred by reason on account of the nature of humans—those attributes made for a short, brutish, and anxious life. "Amongst masterless men, there is perpetual war, of every man against his neighbor; no inheritance, to transmit to the son, nor to expect from the father; no propriety of goods, or land; no security; but a full and absolute liberty in every particular man." Absolute liberty, for Hobbes, was a "condition of a perpetual war."[4] Thus, humans gladly sacrificed their "freedom" for the security provided by social living, under the auspices of a sovereign. "A *commonwealth* is said to be *instituted*, when a *multitude* of men do agree, and *covenant, every one, with every one*, that to whatsoever *man*, or *assembly of men*, shall be given by the major part, the *right* to *present* the person of them all, that is to say, to be their *representative*; every one, as well he that *voted for it*, as he that *voted against it*, shall *authorize* all the actions and judgment, of that man, or assembly of men, in the same manner, as if they were his own, to the end, to live peaceably amongst themselves, and be protected against other men."[5] Humans gladly sacrificed absolute liberty for the prospect of security.

John Locke (1632–1704), whose influence on Jefferson is obvious, begins his *Second Treatise of Government* with the notion of humans as rational, tolerant, abiding, and cooperative in the state of nature. The state of nature is a "*state of perfect freedom* to order their actions, and dispose of their possessions and persons, as they think fit, within the bounds of the law of nature, without … depending on the will of any other man." That perfect freedom within nature's law is a "*state* also *of equality*, wherein all the power and jurisdiction is reciprocal,

---

[4] Thomas Hobbes, *Leviathan*, ed. Michael Oakeshott (New York: Macmillan, 1962), 162.
[5] Thomas Hobbes, *Leviathan*, 134.

no one having more than another; there being nothing more evident, than that creatures of the same species and rank, promiscuously born to all the same advantages of nature, and the use of the same faculties, should also be equal one amongst another without subordination or subjection."[6] In a sentiment that Jefferson clearly appropriates for his Declaration of Independence, Locke adds that the state of liberty is not a state of license. "The *state of nature* has a law of nature to govern it, which obliges every one: and reason, which is that law, teaches all mankind, who will but consult it, that being all *equal and independent*, not one ought to harm another in his life, health, liberty, or possessions." Moreover, he ought also, when his own self-preservation is not at stake, "*to preserve the rest of mankind.*" By the law of nature, Locke adds, people have the right to punish those who transgress the law of nature.[7]

Marie Jean Antoine Nicolas de Caritat, more commonly known as Marquis de Condorcet (1743–1794), writes *Sketch for a Historical Picture of the Progress of the Human Mind,* which is published posthumously in 1795. It is a book, much concordant with Jefferson's political philosophy, which Jefferson highly recommended to others.[8] The book is a sketch of 10 epochs of human development throughout history in an effort to show "the perfectibility of man is absolutely indefinite."[9] Progress occurs through growth of human faculties to allow for the acquisition of language, extensive moral ideas, and commencement of social order; the attainment of language, of extensive moral ideas, and of social order; and last, the triumph of truth over prejudice; and the linkage of knowledge with liberty, virtue, and respect for the natural rights of man.[10]

From hordes of hunters and gatherers, humans became sedentary and agricultural and gradually learned to garner greater yield with less labor. Science and philosophy began to flourish and men investigated various political systems. With printing presses, there began dissemination of knowledge and movement toward recognition of liberty for and equality of all humans and history became history of all, not merely great men.[11]

---

[6] John Locke, *Second Treatise of Government*, ed. C.B. Macpherson (Indianapolis: Hackett Publishing, 1980), 8.
[7] John Locke, *Second Treatise of Government*, 9.
[8] M. Andrew Holowchak, *Thomas Jefferson's Political Philosophy and the Metaphysics of Utopia* (London: Brill, 2017), chap. 3.
[9] Jean-Antoine Nicolas de Caritat, *Outlines of an Historical View of the Progress of the Human Mind: Being a Posthumous Work of the Late M. de Condorcet* (London: J. Johnson, 1795), 13–14.
[10] Jean-Antoine Nicolas de Caritat, *History,* 12–15 and 18–19.
[11] Jean-Antoine Nicolas de Caritat, *History,* 12–158.

"Baxter has performed a good operation on it"
The Toxin of Hume's *History of England*

David Hume's *History of England*, to which we were introduced in the prior chapter, was a tremendously influential work, and thought Jefferson, a dangerous book because it was a seductive inveiglement. The reason was Hume's felicity of expression and concinnity of composition. Yet Jefferson thought that the book was a clever defense of Toryism. Hume's book is "plausible & pleasing in it's style & manner," and because of those things, it quietly instills "the errors & heresies" of British Toryism into unwary minds.

Jefferson's lengthiest expression of his take on Hume's *History of England* comes in a letter to George Lewis (25 Oct. 1825).[12] "Hume's [*History*], were it faithful," writes Jefferson, "would be the finest piece of history which has ever been written by man. Its unfortunate bias may be partly ascribed to the accident of his having written it backwards." "The whig historians of England, therefore, have always gone back to the Saxon period for the true principles of their constitution, while the tories and Hume, their Coryphæus, date it from the Norman Conquest."

Beginning with the Normal Conquest, Hume's book, says Jefferson, is "an apology for them." Hume "spared nothing, therefore, to wash them white, and to palliate their misgovernment. For this purpose he suppressed truths, advanced falsehoods, forged authorities and falsified records." Adds Jefferson, "So bewitching was his style and manner, that his readers were un-willing to doubt anything, swallowed everything, and all England became tories by the magic of his art. His pen revolutionized the public sentiment of that country more completely than the standing armies could ever have done, which were so much dreaded and deprecated by the patriots of that day." He quotes Hume, "The grievances under which the English labored [i.e., whipping, pillorying, cropping, imprisoning, fining, &c.], when considered in themselves, without regard to the constitution, scarcely deserve the name, nor were they either burthensome on the people's properties, or anywise shocking to the natural humanity of mankind." Consequently, Jefferson could not recommend the book as a viable account of Britain's history.

Acknowledging that the work is not without much merit, despite its slant, Jefferson recommends John Baxter's alternative—a republicanization of Hume's work. "Baxter has performed a good operation on it," says Jefferson to John Norvell (14 June 1807). "He has taken the text of Hume as his ground work,

---

[12] For an early expression of my thoughts on Hume and Baxter, see M. Andrew Holowchak, *Thomas Jefferson, Moralist* (Jefferson City, NC: McFarland, 2017), chap. 5.

abridging it by the omission of some details of little interest, and wherever he has found him endeavoring to mislead, by either the suppression of a truth or by giving it a false coloring, he has changed the text to what it should be, so that we may properly call it Hume's history republicanised." There is the added plus that Baxter has continued the history of England to the year 1800.[13]

There has been, and quite expectedly, great hubbub among all scholars in the secondary literature concerning Jefferson's disavowal of Hume's *History* and patronage of Baxter's expurgation of Hume's work: Baxter's *A New and Impartial History of England*. Jefferson, the doughty champion of freedom of expression, is really a champion of restriction of expression—so goes the animadversion. Works expressive of political ideology inconsonant with his can legitimately be surgically changed.

Though he was accused by Jefferson and others of Toryist leanings, Hume was, he says, fighting not the Whigs of his day, but merely their atavism. The Whigs of his time were aiming to rewrite and politicize British history. The skepticism and impartiality of his philosophical and political works, persons like Jefferson maintain, have been put aside for partiality and a political agenda when it comes to writing history. In his *Autobiography*, Hume writes of the abysmal reception of his book, which he attributed to Whig dominance in "the State and in Literature" and likely their reaction to him, painting the earliest Stuarts as Tories. Hume comments, "It is ridiculous to consider the English Constitution before that Period as a regular Plan of Liberty."[14] The passage has tended to be taken as evidence of Toryism, while it is merely expression of the absurdity, given Hume's commitment to ingenuousness and disinterest in writing, of resisting Whig "clamour"—Whigs painting a picture of early Stuarts as Tories. There were neither Whigs nor Tories at the time. It is, thus, clear that Jefferson's conviction of the Tory slant of *History of England*, if we follow Hume's explanation, is mistaken, and there is no reason not to follow Hume's explanation.

Jefferson's slanted reading of Hume had implications for the curriculum at his University of Virginia. As staunch advocate of intellectual integrity

---

[13] Baxter makes it known that his reasons for writing are political. "We are the more convinced of the propriety and absolute necessity of such an undertaking at this time, because we have seen persons in authority making considerable incroachments on the liberties of the people, and under false or frivolous accusations shutting men up in prison, and attempting their lives, because they had virtue enough to oppose their arbitrary measures." John Baxter, *A New and Impartial History of England, from the Most Warly Period of Genuine Historical Evidence to the Present Important and Alarming crisis* (London: 1796), v.
[14] Ernest Campbell Mossner, "Was Hume a Tory Historian? Facts and Reconsiderations," in *Journal of the History of Ideas*, Vol. 2, No. 2, 225–36.

through intellectual freedom, Jefferson allowed each professor at his university the freedom to choose his own texts. The exception, however, was the professorship in politics. The Federalist antics of the prior Adams' administration had shown Jefferson that the jejune country was still, by the time of opening of University of Virginia, in danger of monocratic contamination. Jefferson fought to militate against that danger by mandating that the School of Law use only texts that fostered republicanism of the Jeffersonian sort—*viz.*, to protect against monocracy. In a memorandum, Jefferson recognizes the vulnerability of the young nation because of its susceptibility to autocratic influences—we have merely to consider the Alien and Sedition Acts and Adams' appointment of the midnight Federalist judges prior to leaving the first office—and so, concerning "the principles of govmt which shall be inculcated therein," Jefferson was especially guarded that "none shall be inculcated which are incompatible with those on which the constitutions of this state and of the U.S. were genuinely based in the common opinion." In that regard, he insisted that only books be used at University of Virginia that reinforced the principles of republicanism. He writes:

> Resolved that it is the opinion of this board that as to the general principles of liberty and the rights of man, in nature, and in society, the doctrines of Locke in his 'Essay concerning the true original, extent, & end of civil govmt,' and of Sydney in his 'Discourses on govmt,' may be considered as those generally approved by our fellow citizens of this, and of the US. and that on the distinctive principles of the govmt of our own state, and of that of the US. as understood and assented to when brought into union 1. The book known by the title of the 'Federalist,' 2. The Resolns of the General assembly of Virga, in 1799 on the subject of the alien and sedition laws, and 3. The Declaration of Independence, ought to be considered as possessing the general approbation of our fellow-citizens. The 1st as an authority to which appeal is habitually made by all, and rarely declined or denied by any, as evidence of the general opinion of those who made and of those who accepted the constitn of the US. on questions as to its genuine meaning. the 2^d as sanctioned by the people of the US. as manifested in the exercise of their rights of suffrage immediately subsequent to that publication; and the 3^d as the fundamental act of union of these states. And that in the branch of the school of Law which is to treat on the subject of government, these shall be used as

the text and documents of the school; and no principles shall be inculcated which do not harmonise with them.[15]

The final statement is brutally clear: Works that are inconsistent with the principles articulated in the three major works will not be considered.

"History, by apprising them of the past…"
Is Interested History Necessarily Politicized History?

I have shown thus far that Jefferson thought that the praxis of history ought to be disinterested in that historians ought not to have a preset agenda. Yet he acknowledges that many historians practice interested history and he unabashedly admits to a preference for interested history of a particular sort— that which is morally enabling and reinforces the significance of liberty in governmental affairs. Is morally enabling and liberal history necessarily politicized or agenda-driven? In other words, are interested history and disinterested history, names notwithstanding, necessarily mutually exclusive? In this final segment, I aim to answer that question.

We have seen in the last section that Jefferson's view that Hume was practicing interested history of a Tory sort was very likely mistaken. Hume was doing the converse: He was trying to rescue British history from Whig interpretations, not painting the Stuarts in Tory strokes. Jefferson, thus, was guilty of the black and white fallacy: Hume's failure to recognize the Saxons as the true creators of the original British constitution (and as Whigs) meant that he must have been painting the Stuarts as Tories. The Saxons were not Whigs and the Stuarts were not Tories.

Yet there was good reason for Jefferson's panic vis-à-vis the monarchist element in the United States. When he returned from his stint as minister plenipotentiary to France, he noted that the American political scene was bitterly divided between monarchists, loyal to Alexander Hamilton and committed to strong and centralized government anchored by a national bank and heavy national debt under the "pollutions of their favorite English model," and republicans, who wanted government by the people.[16] He writes to William Short (8 Jan 1825), "When I arrived at New York in 1790, to take a part in the administration, being fresh from the French revolution, while in its first and

---

[15] Thomas Jefferson, "Principles of Government for UVa, February 1825," *Founders Online*, National Archives, https://founders.archives.gov/documents/Jefferson/98-01-02-5007, accessed 11 May 2022.

[16] Thomas Jefferson, Anas, in *Thomas Jefferson: Writings*, ed. Merrill D. Peterson (New York: Library of America, 1984), 672.

pure stage, and consequently somewhat whetted up in my own republican principles, I found a state of things, in the general society of the place, which I could not have supposed possible." He talks of having been feted at large dinners, where the American and French Revolutions were the topics of conversation. He continues, "I was astonished to find the general prevalence of monarchical sentiments, insomuch that in maintaining those of republicanism, I had always the whole company on my hands, never scarcely finding among them a single co-advocate in that argument, unless some old member of Congress happened to be present." Monarchism, not republicanism, Jefferson relates to Short, was in vogue. What, then, was the point of the American Revolution?

Jefferson's worry, above-board, is that the efforts of the American revolutionists would prove to be abortive, if the same system of governing, from which they fought so ardently to escape, should be put into place. That is why he states in his Declaration of Independence that "governments long established" ought never to be abolished "for light & transient causes."[17] Thus, there is no question that he had an interested commitment to republicanism and representative government. Yet is commitment to republicanism and rejection of Federalism or monarchism necessarily politicized?

The scholarly consensus overwhelmingly condemns Jefferson of the same hypocrisy of which the Federalists were guilty and that seems *prima facie* plausible—that is, until we investigate philosophically the issue.

Despite each person having a moral-sense faculty, Jefferson, appealing to experience, notes that those who govern tend to do so with their self-interest chiefly in mind, or will do so, in time, if not checked. Yet governors, Jefferson believes, are merely stewards of the people, not their betters. As Jefferson says paternalistically to King George III in his 1774 Summary View of the Rights of British America, "kings are the servants, not the proprietors of the people."[18] It is, thus, essential that governors be watched closely by those who have elected them and be removed when they surcease to act as representatives of the people.

How are people to recognize corruption and degeneracy?

That question is answered in Jefferson's thoughts on education. He writes in Query XIV of his *Notes on the State of Virginia*. "Of all the views of this law none

---

[17] Thomas Jefferson, Declaration of Independence, in *The Scholar's Thomas Jefferson: Vital Writings of a Vital American*, ed. M. Andrew Holowchak (Newcastle upon Tyne: Cambridge Scholars, 2021), 26.

[18] Thomas Jefferson, Summary View of the Rights of British America, in *The Scholar's Thomas Jefferson: Vital Writings of a Vital American*, ed. M. Andrew Holowchak (Newcastle upon Tyne: Cambridge Scholars, 2021), 15.

is more important, none more legitimate, than that of rendering the people the safe [sic], as they are the ultimate, guardians of their own liberty." He continues: "In every government on earth is some trace of human weakness, some germ of corruption and degeneracy, which cunning will discover, and wickedness insensibly open, cultivate and improve. Every government degenerates when trusted to the rulers of the people alone. The people themselves, therefore, are its only safe depositories. And to render even them safe, their minds must be improved."[19]

It is here that Jefferson underscores the urgency of ward-school education. Given a basic education, each citizen will be an able participant to some degree in governing. "If every individual which composes their mass participates of the ultimate authority, the government will be safe; because the corrupting [of] the whole mass will exceed any private resources of wealth; and public ones cannot be provided but by levies on the people." The argument here is that there are resources sufficient for corruptors to suborn a small part of the citizenry, the governors, but not the entirety of the citizenry. "The government of Great Britain has been corrupted, because but one man in ten has a right to vote for members of parliament. The sellers of the government, therefore, get nine-tenths of their price clear."

The next step in the educative process is grammar school education, where the focus is on languages, ancient and useful modern. Of those who complete education at a grammar school, where there is no exposure to religious instruction,[20] some will move forward to an institution of the highest level of education, like College of William and Mary. At such an institution, students are to be exposed to such sciences as accord with their interests—thus, their education will essentially be elective.[21]

Upon matriculating at a university, students are to study first history to help to qualify them as participatory citizens. "History, by apprising them of the past, will enable them to judge of the future; it will avail them of the experience of other times and other nations; it will qualify them as judges of the actions and designs of men; it will enable them to know ambition under every disguise it may assume; and knowing it, to defeat its views."[22]

---

[19] Thomas Jefferson, *Notes on the State of Virginia*, ed. William Peden (Chapel Hill: University of North Carolina Press, 1954), 147–48.

[20] Jefferson says that between the ages of eight and 16, the mind is still not "firm enough for laborious and close operations." To pretend that children are men when they are not by exposing them to operations of thought of which they are incapable results in reducing them to children when they are men. Thomas Jefferson, *Notes on Virginia*, 147.

[21] That at least will be the *modus operandi* decades later at University of Virginia.

[22] Thomas Jefferson, *Notes on Virginia*, 147–48.

There is little reason to question whether Jefferson had an agenda when it concerned discussion of advancing the causes of republicanism. He did. Various forms of "aristocracy" for centuries have been tried, but they have always been abusive to the well-being of the general citizenry. There was, he thought, no guarantee that government by the people through elected representatives would work, but it was time to give that "experiment" its turn. If that meant using propaganda to fight the propaganda of monarchism, then he was not averse to that.

Yet there were, for Jefferson, philosophical reasons that confirmed his belief in the workability of republicanism: his commitment to human equality based on each person's possession of a moral sense.

Equality, which I cover more fully in chapter 5, is the most fundamental concept of Jefferson's philosophical system—his political philosophy. Evidence of that occurs in his Declaration—as it is the first of his "self-evident" truths—and especially in the first draft of the document, where he makes it clear that equality is the primary human attribute, from which humans are deserving of these rights: life, liberty, and pursuit of happiness. Human equality at creation is what makes humans deserving of rights, and other truths, as rights, are derivative. "We hold these Truths to be self-evident; that all Men are created equal & independent; that from that equal creation they derive rights inherent & inalienable, among which are the preservation of life, & liberty, & the pursuit of happiness."[23]

In what sense are humans at birth equal? That question has never been given a satisfactory answer in the secondary literature, because Jefferson's answer is that each person, at birth, is in possession of a morality-sensing faculty, and Jeffersonian scholars are too illy acquainted with Jefferson's moral sense and the moral-sense and moral-sentiment philosophers of Jefferson's day to grasp that. Jefferson's moral sense is a faculty much superior to human rationality, because human rationality is given fully to all too few persons. Moreover, among those with the gift of full rationality, many use it in a deviously interested sense: to advance their own ends.[24] I dilate on Jefferson's notions of equality and the moral sense in chapter 5.

---

[23] Thomas Jefferson, "A Declaration by the Representatives of the United States of America in general Congress assembled, 28 June 1776," *Founders Online*, National Archives, https://founders.archives.gov/documents/Adams/06-04-02-0139-0002, accessed 13 Aug. 2022.

[24] See M. Andrew Holowchak, *Thomas Jefferson, Moralist* (Jefferson, NC: McFarland, 2017), chap. 1, and "The March of Morality: Making Sense of Jefferson's Moral Sense," in *Thomas Jefferson and Philosophy: Essays on the Philosophical Cast of Jefferson's Writings*, ed. M. Andrew Holowchak (Lanham, MD: Lexington Books, 2013), chap. 8.

So, all persons for Jefferson at birth are moral equals, and thus, deserving of rights. Moral equality, consequently, grounds Jefferson's political philosophy—the notions of government of and for the people, of elected governors that function as stewards and not betters, and of fullest political participation by all citizens pursuant to their talents and time, inter alia. And so, Jefferson's thoughts on republicanism must not be seen fundamentally, though he often says this, as proffering a political alternative to aristocratic governments, which customarily neglect the *hoi polloi*, but as a political system founded on a morality-grounded assertion—viz., his argument is fundamentally philosophical, not political. Showing that that assertion is false is the surest way to undermine his views on the superiority of republicanism, though that philosophical claim might be false while republicanism might still be preferable to aristocratic systems.

Upshot

We are now in position to answer the question: Is interested history necessary politicized history?

History for Jefferson can be both disinterested and interested. Jefferson's deep interest in preserving the laws of Virginia for posterity is evidence of his commitment to disinterested history. Yet commitment to disinterested history is likely because people never know to what use seemingly adiaphorous actions—actions neither moral nor immoral, like preservation for posterity of Virginia's laws—might someday have. Jefferson was ever committed to useful knowledge, hence his distaste for metaphysics and theological speculations. In other words, yesterday's disinterested history might be tomorrow's interested history—history to be put to moral usage.

Such things noted, Jefferson would not have seen his promotion of republicanism as interested history of the politicized sort—that is, history with a political agenda. The best history is the most useful and the greatest sort of human utility for Jefferson is that which prompts morally correct activity, grounded on human equality and necessitating human liberty for fullest expression.

Part II
The Nature & Civic Possibility of Liberty

Chapter IV

The Advances of Science

Part one has been an attempt to disclose for Jefferson the meaning of "history." The science of history, I argue, is for him essentially disinterested. That, however, does not mean that historians cannot be motivated by matters that are self-serving—*viz.*, an American interested in the American Revolution might begin his research on assumption that Colonists were morally justified in their break with their mother country—only that history, once undertaken, cannot be self-serving—*viz.*, a historian, while researching the American Revolution, must accommodate all relevant available data and shape his findings on all that relevant available data. History, serving moral aims, must itself be practiced ingenuously. That, unfortunately, seldom happens.

There is, Jefferson believes, a method to proper history and that method is essentially, as we have seen, Bolingbrokean. A historian must live at the time of the events he describes or must have ready access to documents of others who have then lived. A historian must be acknowledged to be ingenuous and credible. His findings must be consistent with what is generally known about other commonly accepted things. Last, there must be confirmation of his findings by other historians. There is nothing in such conditions that disallows methodologically a historian to make moral judgments, so long as those judgments are consistent with the reality of the situation, and not motivated politically. Though the rightness or wrongness of an act, for Jefferson, is felt, not intellectually discerned, there is a reality to its rightness or wrongness—the felt universal approbation or disapprobation of a deed in the manner that a person who places his hand over a flickering candle feels heat. There is no historical enormity, for illustration, in stating that Bonaparte has behaved consistently as if he lacks any sense or right or wrong, or more strongly, that Bonaparte lacks a moral sense so long as that assessment accords with reality. An analogy from art is aidful. John Trumbull's depiction of Washington as a modern-day Cincinnatus in his *General George Washington Resigning His Commission* plainly is morally edifying, while it also captures a real event. Trumbull's painting depicts a gallant, humble general, submitting his resignation to members of the Congress, in the manner of a true Cincinnatus, who is about to return to being one of the people.[1]

---

[1] Lucius Quinctius Cincinnatus (c. 519-c. 430 B.C.) was both Roman citizen and general.

Jefferson has a personal preference for history with moral content—it inspires him each day to improve himself and will do the same for others—and he also prefers moral history because it inspires moral, and thus, political advance in social settings.

Study of history done disinterestedly, for Jefferson, shows unmistakably that there is a direction or *telos* of human history: History is the slow unfolding of human thriving through embrace of human liberty—strongly suggestive of cosmic purposiveness and the inevitability of human progress through heightened scientific understanding of the cosmos, and "scientific" entails "political" and "moral," each considered at the time a viable science[2]

"Out of slavery…"

History from Above, History from Below

There is today no commonly accepted notion of "science" and of its divisions, but "science" is sometimes, and reasonably so, broken into Natural Sciences (e.g., physics, astronomy, chemistry, and biology), Human Sciences (e.g., history, law, sociology, and political science), and Formal Sciences (e.g., logic and mathematics)—the first two, empirical; the last, metempirical.

Nonetheless, his catalog of books for his libraries followed the Baconian classification of History (Memory), Philosophy (Reason), and Imagination (Fine Arts) and included many subjects that were not legitimate sciences. The fine arts, grounded on taste for Jefferson, were certainly not sciences. Moreover, disciplines like ethics and religion for Jefferson were not empirically grounded, for the "truths" of morality were sensed or felt, not reasoned, and the principles of natural religion were for Jefferson identical with the fundamental principles of morality, comprising duties to man and duties to God.[3]

Still, the disciplines of politics, morality, and religion[4] were generally regarded as sciences—*scientia* in Latin being "knowledge," "craft," or "science"—in his

---

Livy tells us that Cincinnatus, in his old age, he worked on his small farm until the Romans called for his leadership at the provenance of a war. Having achieved swift victory in only 16 days, he refused to wallow in his success, but merely returned to working his farm. Titus Livius, *The History of Rome*, ed. D. Spillan (London: Henry G. Bohn, 1853), III.26–29.

[2] I cover Jefferson and cosmic purposiveness in *Jefferson's Political Philosophy and the Metaphysics of Utopia* (London: Brill, 2017), preface.

[3] M. Andrew Holowchak, *American Messiah: The Surprisingly Simple Religious Views of Thomas Jefferson* (Abilene: Abilene Christian University Press, 2019), chap. 1.

[4] Religious study was not, like it is today, a comparative study of different religions, but indoctrination, as it was early for instance on at William and Mary, in the state-sponsored religion (e.g., Anglicanism) of the day.

day since they were subjects that were customarily taught at institutions such as College of New Jersey (today, Princeton) and College of William and Mary. Politics for Jefferson was empirical in that aristocratic systems over millennia have proven themselves by experience to be ineffective for the wellbeing of large bodies of people and indifferent to the plight of the general citizenry. Moreover, early systems of government, of the sort described by Aristotle and iterated in Jefferson's day by scholars like Montesquieu, he considered obsolete insofar they have never considered representative government to accommodate governments of large populations or governments covering large expanses of land.[5]

Jefferson was inescapably committed to intellectual, political, and moral human progress. That, in itself, is unremarkable, given the intellectual climate of Enlightenment times. In that, he was no different from others such as Immanuel Kant, Condorcet, and Louis-Sébastien Mercier.

Yet it seems remarkable, because we live in a time of emasculated rationality, to grasp the climate of Enlightenment times, characterized by indescribable intellectual sanguineness and intellectual excitement, but captured today by polarities: hope and fear, optimism and pessimism, vigor and torpor. It was a time of scientific discoveries the uses of which were not always evident, technological inventions aimed at easing the burden of living, and exploration, acquisition, and empire. All but a few of the intellectuals, with an eye to everything that was happening, were swept away by the tsunami which promised intellectual advance and more efficient, easier living.

As I intimate in the first part of this book, it is the task of historians to create what might be dubbed useful "fictions"—the "isms" of history, like colonialism, imperialism, liberalism, stadialism, and medialism.

What is an ism?[6]

Philosopher and psychologist William James is noted for disclosing that an infant's first experiences with the world are essentially "a blooming buzzing confusion." As the infant matures and interacts with adults, he slowly begins to differentiate objects through grouping them into kinds by noting distinctions between "things." A puffin, for instance, much looks like a penguin, but it is not, for the latter is much larger and cannot fly. It is through interaction with things

---

[5] TJ to Isaac H. Tiffany, 6 Aug. 1816.
[6] I follow closely my account in this essay. M. Andrew Holowchak, "Thomas Jefferson and the Conditions of Good History: Some Implications for Writing about the American Revolution and Early American History," in *Journal of the American Revolution*, https://allthingsliberty.com/2023/03/thomas-jefferson-and-the-conditions-of-good-history-writing-about-the-american-revolution/, accessed 20 Nov. 2023.

deemed independent of him and with those others of larger experience with those things that an infant as a youth and then an experienced adult comes to know the world around him.

Yet the isms of historians are much unlike puffins and penguins. They are unwieldy, slippery, and they often answer more to the psychological eccentricities of historians than they do to reality.

Why is that the case?

That is so, as Carl Becker notes, because historians' subject is the past and no historians have direct access to the past. They garner the relevant data that are available—and revisionist historians often have a very pliant view of what makes data relevant (*viz.*, relevant = is not disconfirmatory of my thesis)—and try to create a coherent story, answerable to the facts. It goes without saying that historians tend to write about topics that interest them and so their motivation is not disinterested. Their narratives reflect that.

Jack McLaughlin's *Jefferson and Monticello: The Biography of a Builder* is a fine illustration of a highly successful narrative. McLaughlin culls a subject heretofore never attempted (a biography of Jefferson through his activities as a builder, not architect), narrows his narrative to the building and rebuilding over the decades of Monticello (both to keep from fictive claims and because there is a large amount of data readily accessible to any scholar inclined to undertake such a project), and covers his account with a thoroughness and attention to minutiae that is beyond the ken of lazier scholars. In short, McLaughlin tries not to do too much, and what he does do is thorough, coherent, and highly informative. Moreover, the prose is light and lively.

Peter Onuf's *The Mind of Thomas Jefferson* is a fine illustration of a highly unsuccessful book. The title promises insight into Jefferson's mind, but we are merely told throughout that Jefferson was such an epistolary chameleon that no historian can have access to a "true Jefferson." The best that any historian can do is construct a "possible Jefferson"—an account of Jefferson that seems merely to be guided by one historiographical consideration: consistency. Anything, thus, goes, so long as, in keeping with Onuf's unabashed detestation of Jefferson, that no historian ends with an account that depicts Jefferson as an estimable figure. Moreover, the book is an omnium gatherum—that is, a loose compilation of essays thrown together without much regard for flow or continuity, hence, my reluctance to use the term narrative.

Yet, an ism is not a narrative. It is instead a sort of metanarrative that glues together the narratives of historians on a particular topic. As no narrative, taken as a whole, can be a true account of some person or event, isms as metanarratives are useful fictions, where "usefulness" is not arbitrary, but answerable to correspondence with reality. Thus, it is fair to say that some narratives are "truer" than others, and it is the same with isms. When historians do their job—e.g., in the case of Dumas Malone's six-volume biography of Jefferson—the facts themselves will be suggestive of the sort of glue—i.e., the narrative—needed to bind them. When facts are few or when historians do a poor job of gleaning them—e.g., in the case of Onuf's *The Mind of Thomas Jefferson*—there will be an indescribably large number of narratives consistent with the facts.

When historians approach their discipline with integrity and guilelessness, they begin from below with a compilation of relevant data (facts), and then forge various narratives on some person or event. Those facts-grounded narratives will then strongly suggest certain isms as metanarratives and disallow others. That in effect is realist history—*history from below*.

When historians politicize their history, they begin not with facts, but from above with isms qua metanarratives and frame their narratives in pursuance of that ism. That in effect is postmodernist history—*history from above*.

Consider, for illustration, the vogue of "racism" today in American history. It is a covering term, brought into play from above, and it is seen, at least in American history, to be something that must be invoked in any historical narrative of an American figure or event.

Racism today is in some sense explanatorily "rich" in that it is used to explain many things about American culture. In Jeffersonian scholarship, racism has been invoked to explain why Jefferson freed too few of his slaves throughout his life, why he maintained that Blacks were deficient in imagination and intellect, and (most astonishingly) even why Jefferson employed grids and octagons in his architectural sketches.[7]

Yet while racism is a much-employed term, it does very little etiological work—its richness is façade—because paradoxically it explains too much. Consider this snippet from Joseph Ellis. "[*Notes on Virginia*] contained the most explicit assessment that Jefferson ever wrote of what he believed were the biological differences between blacks and whites, an assessment that exposed the deep-rooted racism that he, like most Americans and almost all Virginians of his day, harboured throughout his life."[8] Again, Jake Silverstein, editor-in-chief of *New York Times Magazine*, says that everything that is uniquely American is grounded on "anti-black racism":

---

[7] Irene Cheng, "Race and Architectural Geometry: Thomas Jefferson's Octagons," in *The Journal of Nineteenth-Century Americanists*, Vol. 3, No. 1, 2015: 121-30.

[8] Joe J. Ellis, "Thomas Jefferson," in *Encyclopedia Britannica*, https://www.britannica.com/biography/Thomas-Jefferson/, accessed 16 Feb. 2023.

Out of slavery—and the anti-black racism it required—[there] grew nearly everything that has truly made America exceptional: its economic might, its industrial power, its electoral system, its diet and popular music, the inequities of its public health and education, its astonishing penchant for violence, its income inequality, the example it sets for the world as a land of freedom and equality, its slang, its legal system and the endemic racial fears and hatreds that continue to plague it to this day. The seeds of all that were planted long before our official birth date, in 1776, when the men known as our founders formally declared independence from Britain.[9]

Here we come to find that the actual founding of the United States was not in 1776, but 1619!

Some comments are in order to show the vacuousness of both Ellis' and Silverstein's claims.

If we return to Ellis' comment, then if "almost all Virginians" and "most Americans" thought that Blacks were racist, then that does no more than to tell us that almost all Virginians and most Americans thought that Blacks were inferior to Whites, and that must include Blacks' perception of themselves. In Query VIII of *Notes on Virginia*, Jefferson notes that the ratio of Whites to Blacks in Virginia at the time of his writing was about 11:10.[10] If we follow closely Ellis' lead, by implication, most Blacks considered themselves inferior to Whites, and I doubt that that is a statement to which Ellis would commit.

To revisit Silverstein's sentiments, all things that have made America what it today is have been caused by its anti-black racism. What then are we to say about South America and the Caribbean, both of which received many more slaves than North America? What are we to say about England, which had been shipping, by the tens of thousands, slaves (both white and black) to the Americas over the decades? What are we to say about black African princes who eagerly engaged in the slave-trade practice and monetized handsomely by such engagement? Those are questions ignored by 1619 true believers.

One might, of course, address Silverstein's wording: "Out of slavery—and the anti-black racism it required—[there] grew…." Is this a causal claim? If not, it is

---

[9] Jake Silverstein, "Why We Published the 1619 Project," in *The New York Times Magazine*, https://www.nytimes.com/interactive/2019/12/20/magazine/1619-intro.html#:~:text=The%201619%20Project%20examines%20the%20legacy%20of%20slavery,1776%20is%20the%20year%20of%20our%20nation's%20birth, accessed 18 Feb. 2023.

[10] Thomas Jefferson, *Notes on the State of Virginia*, ed. William Peden (Chapel Hill: University of North Carolina Press, 1954), 87.

merely a relaxed way of stating temporally that slavery was in North America early in the seventeenth century prior to the United States becoming an economic superpower and then we are invited to consider the argument as an instance of the *post hoc* fallacy: one thing occurred prior to others, so that one thing is the cause of those others—a needed condition for establishing causal efficacy, but not one that is sufficient. If so, and that seems to be the best way to take the slippery claim, then slavery was the seed out of which all the evils of which America is composed. Nothing much, it seems, good came from that seed.

And so, if temporal, the claim becomes irrelevant, since it states merely that some events came after another. Yet if causal, the claim is irresponsibly absurd. I illustrate below.

Let us flesh out causally Silverstein's argument.

1. America is noted for its economic might, industrial power, electoral system, diet, popular music, inequities of its public health and education, penchant for violence, income inequality, global example of freedom and equality, slang, legal system, and endemic racial fears and hatreds.
2. All such things define America.
3. Black slavery has been around America since 1619 and prior to development of the things that define America.
4. So, all such things that define America have been caused by slavery.
5. Slavery is essentially anti-black racism.
6. So, anti-black racism has given rise to everything (or "nearly everything") that defines America.

That argument is perhaps the most absurd and vacuous argument that has ever been made about the United States. Claim 1 is too vague to be helpful. Is claim 2 saying that each of the attributes limned is uniquely American or that they, taken together, define America? If the first, the claim is patently false. Claim 3 is true. Claim 4 is the puzzler. Because black slaves have been around Colonial America prior to the "birth" of the nation and to development of those things that have come to define America, it is *the cause* of America's defining features. Claim 5 too is manifestly false and that is obvious to anyone who takes the time to study slavery across the globe over the centuries of human existence. The conclusion of this paralogism, of course, nowise follows.

The argument insultingly preys on human emotions at the expense of human rationality. The absurdity of 1619 argument is shown by substituting "tobacco" for "racism." It is commonly known that the earliest American settlement at Jamestown suffered numerous calamities and was saved only by businessman John Rolfe's introduction of new tobacco seeds, *Nicotiana tabacum* with its nicotine, to replace the unpopular *Nicotiana rustica*. Rolfe grew the new species of tobacco at his farm, Varina, near Jamestown, and the popularity of that tobacco in England made Rolfe rich and gave Jamestown—a settlement again and again devastated by war, disease, and drought—a new lease on life.[11]

> 1. America is noted for its economic might, industrial power, electoral system, diet, popular music, inequities of its public health and education, penchant for violence, income inequality, global example of freedom and equality, slang, legal system, and its love of growing tobacco.
> 2. All such things define America.
> 3. Tobacco has been around America at least since 1612 (at Jamestown) and prior to development of the things that define America.
> 4. So, all such things that define America have been caused by tobacco.
> 5. Growing tobacco strips soil of key essential nutrients.
> 6. So, growing tobacco is essentially destruction of soil.
> 7. So, destruction of soil has given rise to everything (or "nearly everything") that defines America.

The silliness of this argument should be all too obvious to all. However, the silliness of the 1619 argument should be equally as obvious. It is not, and that is frightening!

The claims of Ellis and Silverstein are illustrations of an explanation explaining too much—postmodernism or use of isms or metanarratives to drive history. Postmodernist historiography, thus, is essentially presentist—it explains events and personages of the past through contemporary concerns—and historically unavailing to those persons who believe that writing history is not writing creative fiction for the purpose of entertainment.

"Sapere aude!"

Science in Jefferson's Day

"The Enlightenment" or "Enlightenmentism" is a commonly employed "useful fiction." Yet that "ism," I maintain, has been gleaned from below, not from above. It is customarily understood as an epoch in which humans began to move from the darkness of ignorance to the light of knowledge, generated by the free exercise of rationality. It was a period of escape from the prison of authority—Aristotle and the Catholic Church—to the openness of early scientific inquiry, guided by renewed experience of the world through rational

---

[11] M. Andrew Holowchak and David Holowchak, *A "Biography" of Lynchburg, Virginia: City with a Soul* (Newcastle upon Tyne: Cambridge Scholars, 2021), 21–22.

inquiry and positing and testing hypotheses. I offer a brief and selective precis of the excitement and illumination generated by the Enlightenment.

In his tour de force works in the 1960s, *The Rise of Modern Paganism* and *The Science of Freedom*, Peter Gay delineates three periods: that of Voltaire; that of Diderot, Alembert, and Rousseau; and that of Lessing and Kant. It is a story, begun from interest but written with disinterest, of the unfolding of human progress through embrace of human liberty and exercise of human rationality. Yet that period was not exclusive to Europe, for the progressivism, liberalism, and rationalism spilled over into Colonial America, with personages such as Benjamin Franklin, Thomas Jefferson, Joel Barlow, Benjamin Rush, Francis Kinlock, and numerous others.[12]

In *The Enlightenment in America* (1976), Henry F. May argues that the Enlightenment in America was not that of Europe, as conditions of living in America—e.g., large parcels of uncultivated land, existence of Native Americans, and biotic dissimilarities—gave the American Enlightenment a parochialism that its European counterpart did not have.[13]

So far, we have some account of the Enlightenment, generated by history from below.

The historical excitement generated by the progressivism,[14] liberalism, and rationalism of early accounts of the Enlightenment were counterbalanced by democratic socialists like Michel Foucault and Jürgen Habermas, who pushed for history from above and historical derationalization.

Foucault is today often categorized as "the great modern counter-Enlightenment philosopher and historian" because he assaults the universalism implicit in the works of many of the Enlightenment thinkers. In *The Order of Things*[15] (1966) and *The Archeology of Knowledge* (1969), Foucault maintains that there is no possibility of knowledge, for ideas cannot simply agree or disagree with what they are supposed to represent—*viz.*, the correspondence theory of truth—and each historical epoch has its own criteria of truth, which dictates scientific discourse, and those criteria change over time. For Foucault, the driving force in human affairs is power: sovereign power (one or a few over many), disciplinary power (bodily movements to reconstruct wishes and thoughts of others), and biopower (internalized norms influencing populations). We live

---

[12] Peter Gay, *The Enlightenment: An Interpretation: The Rise of Modern Paganism* (New York: W.W. Norton, 1966) and *The Enlightenment: An Interpretation: The Science of Freedom* (New York: W.W. Norton, 1969).
[13] Henry F. May, *The Enlightenment in America* (Oxford: Oxford University Press, 1976).
[14] Not in Becker's sense.
[15] Originally *Les mots and les choses*, which is literally *Words and Things*.

today in the era of biopower which regulates most aspects of human behavior. A person is free, for Foucault, only when he has full awareness of his circumstances, shaped by the various forms of power. It is a state of being in relation to oneself, others, and the world, and that state is ever under construction toward heightened or lessened awareness. The aim is existential situatedness, not knowledge.[16] The influence of Marx on Foucault is obvious.

Habermas too de-universalizes rationality by claiming it is found merely in the forms of human communications, aiming at understanding. His work—typified in books such as *The Logic of the Social Sciences* (1967), *Technology and Science as Ideology* (1968), and *Philosophical Discourse of Modernity* (1985)—is not a complete dismissal of Enlightenment ideals, but a corrective to them. Through speech, humans work toward greater humanity, justice, and equality.[17] Rationality, thus, is specific to humans and in the service of human aims.

How did those living in that singular epoch—*viz.*, Jefferson's day—think of the time in which they lived?

To answer that question, I turn to a contemporary of Jefferson. In "What Is Enlightenment?" Immanuel Kant (1724–1804), one of the largest spokespersons of Enlightenment times, proffers this answer.

> Enlightenment is man's emergence from his self-incurred immaturity. Immaturity is the inability to use one's own understanding without the guidance of another. This immaturity is self-incurred if its cause is not lack of understanding, but lack of resolution and courage to use it without the guidance of another. The motto of enlightenment is therefore: Sapere aude! "Have the courage to use your own understanding!"[18]

For Kant, enlightenment is an attitude, a way of being. It is the freedom, generated by courage, to use reason in both private and public matters. Neglect of that use is a form of immaturity that is the "most pernicious and disgraceful."[19]

Kant's motto, I think, can be taken as a way of understanding in gist how those intellectuals who lived in his day thought and behaved.

---

[16] Michel Foucault, *The Order of Things*, trans. Alan Sheridan (New York: Harper and Row, 1970) and *The Archeology of Knowledge*, trans. Allan Sheridan (New York: Harper and Row, 1972).

[17] Jürgen Habermas, *The Logic of the Social Sciences* (1967), *Technology and Science as Ideology* (1968), and *Philosophical Discourse of Modernity* (1985)

[18] Immanuel Kant, "An Answer to the Question: What Is Enlightenment," in *Perpetual Peace and Other Essays*, trans. Ted Humphreys (Indianapolis: Hackett, 1983), 41.

[19] Immanuel Kant, "What Is Enlightenment," in *Perpetual Peace and Other Essays*, trans. Ted Humphreys (Indianapolis: Hackett, 1983), 42.

Intellectual progress was evident to all who were willing to observe the extraordinary movement in humans' understanding of the cosmos. Aided by usage of telescopes and microscopes, natural scientists disclosed a macroscopic universe much beyond the scope of anything hitherto humanly imagined. They also disclosed a microscopic world of animalcules that hitherto escaped detection due to their minuscular size.

Those disclosures just prior to and in his day inevasibly led to abandonment of Aristotle's proper-place cosmos, accepted by most as true for some 2,000 years. Aristotle (384–322 B.C.) left to posterity a model of the cosmos and all existents in it that was telic—everything had its proper place—and static. There were two main realms, separated by the sphere of the moon: a superlunary realm in which there was no change, and a sublunary realm, in which all change occurred.[20]

In the sublunary realm, all existents are composites of fire, air, water, and earth, each of which has an active principle, heat and coldness, and a passive principle, wetness and dryness. There is an ever conversion and blending of those elements in the entities in that realm: cumulous clouds, limestone, sulfuric brooks, Northwestern wolves, Icelandic puffins, Tiger grasses, wild white poppies, and even Anglo-Saxon humans. With the death of a wolf, for Aristotle, the fire and water in its blood and flesh will be converted to earth and water, and that water will soon convert to earth—perhaps later to be worked up into as nutriment for a prickly pear cactus. Two of the elements (Gr., *stoicheia*), water and earth, are naturally heavy and move toward their proper place at the center of the cosmos. Water being less heavy than earth, water tends to sit atop earth. The other two elements, fire and air, are naturally light and move toward their proper place away from the center of the cosmos, but are limited from further motion by the sphere of the moon. Fire, lighter than air, tends to rise above and settle atop air.

In the superlunary realm, there are only bodies deemed divine—e.g., planets and stars—in that their natures never change and they move in circles around the earth, fixed at the center of the cosmos. Aristotle posits some 55 divine bodies, from the moon and sun, nearest the lower realm, to orbs of stellar bodies at the outskirts of the cosmos, and all move through a tenuous matter called *aether*. Incapable of considering perpetual motion without a sustaining cause—that would be for Aristotle like a person continually walking without tiring—he posits a prime mover, comprising pure thought, just outside of the

---

[20] For a fuller account of Jefferson and science, see M. Andrew Holowchak, "Jefferson as Scientist," in *The Cavernous Mind of Thomas Jefferson, An American Savant* (Newcastle upon Tyne: Cambridge Scholars, 2019), 93–124.

outermost superlunary orb and originative of motion through the circular orbs, striving to emulate its divinity, through moving circularly, the most perfect motion.

There were numerous nomological disclosures in astronomy, physics, optics, and chemistry that led to overthrow of Aristotle's telic cosmos, accepted roughly for 2,000 years by most intellectuals.

The revolution in astronomy begins with Nicolaus Copernicus' (1473–1543) assertion of a sun-centered universe in his 1543 work *De revolutionibus orbium coelestium (On the Revolutions of the Celestial Orbs)*. The overall influence of the work at first was not profound—it could not claim to explain observable phenomena any more simply that Ptolemy's (b. 100 A.D.) geocentric model—but it was consistent with observation[21] and it did slowly prompt others, like Kepler and Galileo, to adopt it as veridical.

Tycho Brahe (1546–1601) studied the nighttime sky like no other prior to his day and left behind celestial observations of the sixteenth century that were astonishing and that led to discovery of three laws of planetary motion by pupil Johannes Kepler. Brahe also noted a nova without parallax that appeared in 1572 and he showed it to be beyond the sphere of the moon, and that was indicative of change in the cosmos beyond the superlunary realm—inconsistent with Aristotle's cosmology. Kepler (1571–1630), through painstaking study of Brahe's data of planetary movements, came up with three laws of planetary motion—planets were discovered to follow elliptical, not circular, patterns, and that was another astonishing blow to Aristotle's model—that showed, following Kepler's incredible doggedness, that God was indeed a geometer. He published the first two laws in *Astronomia Nova (New Astronomy,* 1609) and, the last, in *Harmonices Mundi (Harmonies of the World,* 1619).

Galileo Galilei (1564–1642), in his early seventeenth-century book, *Siderius Nuncius (Starry Messenger)*, made further discoveries that were inconsistent with Aristotle's cosmos. Galileo built a telescope and studied the nighttime sky. He discovered that Jupiter had satellites revolving around it, thereby disproving Aristotle's dictum that all things revolved around the earth; that the moon was craterous (he called those craters "*maria*" {seas}), thereby challenging the notion that all bodies in the superlunary realm were perfect; and that Venus, when seen through a telescope, exhibited a full set of phases, inconsistent with it orbiting the earth, though consistent with both it and the earth in the orb around it, orbiting the sun. Moreover, Galileo, by rolling balls down planes of varied inclinations and observing their rate of "fall," also came up with the Law

---

[21] The apparent movement of the sun across the sky during the day is readily explained by the earth rotating on its axis.

of Falling Bodies ($d \approx kt^2$, distance of fall is proportionate to the square of the time of fall). Galileo also nearly came up with the Principle of Bodily Inertia, as he stated that one body moving on a frictionless plane, would continue its motion without abatement. Galileo also unabashedly championed the independency of scientific practice from the authority of the church. In his letter to Grand Duchess Christina, he writes, "The intention of the Holy Spirit is to teach us how one goes to heaven and not how heaven goes."[22] That, of course, was something that the large and powerful dignitaries of the church did not wish to hear. Because of the difficulties he caused the Church, he would live out the remainder of his life under house arrest.

At the end of the seventeenth century, Isaac Newton (1643–1727) synthesized the disclosures of predecessors in *Philosophiae Naturalis Principia Mathematica* (*Mathematica Principles of Natural Philosophy*, 1687). Newton discovered the Universal Law of Gravitation ($F \approx M_1 M_2/d^2$), which posited that there was an attractive force, gravity, determined by the masses of any two bodies, considered as mass points, and the distance between them. He then gave three laws of bodily motion that governed all bodies in the universe.

> 1. Every body continues in its state of rest or of motion in a straight line unless it is compelled to change that state by force impressed on it;
> 2. The change of motion is proportional to the motive force impressed and is made in the direction of the straight line in which that force is impressed ($F \approx ma$).
> 3. To every action there is always opposed an equal reaction: or, the mutual actions of two bodies upon each other are always equal.

The power of Newton's dynamical system was that it subsumed, thus explained, other disclosures: e.g., Kepler's laws and Galileo's Law of Falling Bodies and even Boyle's Law (below).

There were also discoveries in other sciences: e.g., optics and chemistry.

In optics, Kepler and Newton were pioneers. Kepler, in *Astronomiae Pars Optica* (*The Optical Part of Astronomy*, 1604), explained vision via refraction within the eyes. He also studied pin-hole cameras, designed eyeglasses for defects of vision, showed how both eyes were critically involved in depth perception. Newton's great contribution to optics was his prism experiment, which showed that white light, entering a prism, was separated into its constituent colors.

---

[22] Galileo Galilei, "Letter to the Grand Duchess Christina," in *The Essential Galileo*, trans. Maurice A. Finocchiaro (Indianapolis: Hackett, 2008), 119.

In chemistry, there were, among others, Boyle and Lavoisier. Robert Boyle (1627–1691) discovered the Ideal Gas Law, which posited an inverse relationship between pressure and volume of a gas in an enclosed space. He also advocated a mechanical philosophy, in which he maintained that all bodies comprised particles of one matter, though of different shapes and motions. Antoine Lavoisier (1743–1794) rightly explained combustion by oxidation, showed that respiration was an intake of oxygen, and proved that water was composed of hydrogen and oxygen.

There were also advances in biological taxonomy, mathematics, medicine, zoology, geology, and mineralogy, as well as countless inventions that aimed to ease the toil of human labor or lead to greater yield with similar labor (e.g., spinning jenny, carding machine, and cotton gin), that could be put to immediate human usage (e.g., dictionary, thermometers, timepieces, eyeglasses, and the guillotine), that held the promise of future usage (e.g., steam engines, submarines, and balloons), or merely that led to greater human flourishing (e.g., vaccination, invention of piano, and machine for sheets of paper).

The abundant successes of the sciences of the time were perpetuated at scientific academies and societies—like the Royal Society of London (1662), Académie Royale des Sciences of Paris (1666) and American Philosophical Society of Philadelphia (1743), founded by Benjamin Franklin—and the growth of the number of societies was quick. The findings of such societies were published in journals such as *Philosophical Transactions of the Royal Society* and *Transactions of the American Philosophical Society* as well as numerous smaller periodicals. New discoveries required new terminology, that is neology,[23] and so scientific encyclopedias and dictionaries were created. Esoteric works, like Galileo's *Sidereus Nuncius* and Newton's *Principia Mathematica*, written in Latin, were then translated into English, French, and other languages to reach a wider audience. The overwhelming successes of those sciences were due to the freeing of human rationality—to the human embrace of liberty.

"He who receives an idea from me…"

Jefferson as Patron of the Sciences

The seeming excursus of the section prior, the chary reader will recognize, is no divagation, but needed background information. Too few Jeffersonian scholars, who focus on Jefferson's political thinking, know much about the scientific climate of the Enlightenment times, and thus they cannot fully see just how the

---

[23] For Jefferson on neology, see TJ to John Waldo, 16 Aug. 1813, and TJ to John Adams, 15 Aug. 1820.

advances in the sciences shaped Jefferson's political philosophy. There were numerous new discoveries about the world through study of it, and those discoveries greatly excited science-minded intellectuals like Jefferson. As much as any American of his day, Thomas Jefferson was a patron of the sciences and a champion of scientific progress.[24] Patronage and championing were due to his ineluctable belief that republican government, freedom-loving, had to be partnered with science. For people to be empowered with the task of governing, they had to have full access to knowledge and the scientific disclosures of their day. Tyrannical governments "worked" only because the citizenry was kept ignorant.

Jefferson was passionate about Natural Philosophy and Natural History in a manner that he could never have been about politics or law. He was a politician from necessity, not choice, as his disposition was taciturn, conciliatory, and withdrawn, though he had one trait that would have made him as successful a scientist as he was as a politician: an uncanny capacity to focus on pressing issues, with generally exceptional results (e.g., Summary View on the Rights of British America, 1774; Plan for Establishing Uniformity in the Coinage, Weights, and Measures, 1790; and First Inaugural Address, 1801).

Robert Faulkner says, "At home and abroad, ... Jefferson was the inveterate inquirer, inventor, tinkerer, and improver. ... He was the information center for observations and information on both sides of the Atlantic, the President most informed ever about the sciences, and the first to provide government support of science."[25] Though he was a practicing scientist of some distinction, Jefferson was, because of not having the luxury of time, a dilettante, though an impassioned one, more than a true scientist. Of that he was aware, as he frequently referred to himself as a "zealous amateur."[26] Nonetheless, the contribution of this dilettante to science in the budding republic was enormous. More than any other politician of his stature in his day, Jefferson recognized the importance of patronage and free practice of science in America. His ardent and indefatigable aegis of science throughout his life was largely responsible for the rapid growth of the nation—a large claim, but one that I believe is true. He is the single most significant patron of the sciences of the political representatives of the early republic.

---

[24] His political obligations, always pressing, disallowed him any capacity for sustained attention to scientific nodi, such as the existence of fossils in the foothills of Blue Ridge Mountains, though he did attend carefully to some problems, like the Native American barrows near him.

[25] Robert Faulkner, "Spreading Progress: Jefferson's Mix of Science and Liberty," in *The Good Society*, Vol. 17, No. 1, 2008: 26.

[26] Edward T. Martin, *Thomas Jefferson: Scientist* (New York: Henry Schuman, Inc., 1952), 9.

Jefferson's obsession with science was a result of his obsession with self- and other-edification for scientific advance. In his *Autobiography*, as I note at the beginning of chapter 1, he mentions his practice of jotting down during his perambulations anything that he thinks might be of future use for the advance of his country.[27] The result, of course, was his estimable *Notes on the State of Virginia*, a veritable American classic. In *Thomas Jefferson: Psychobiography of an American Lion*, I write of Jefferson's obsession with observing, measuring, recording, and even critiquing phenomena that are of possible use for human betterment.[28] In much of what follows, I draw from chapter 4, "Jefferson as Scientist, of my book, *The Cavernous Mind of Thomas Jefferson, An American Savant*.[29]

Jefferson's world had to be neat and ordered, and Jefferson's life was a quest to discover in or even impose on the world neatness and order. Science was his primary tool. In botany, Jefferson classified plants into the overlapping categories "medicinal," "ornamental," "useful," and "esculent." He ever fidgeted with the most productive means of sewing and reaping farmed goods. Jefferson experimented with crop rotation, enhanced corn grains, searched for a method for training grape vines, introduced contour plowing for hilly lands to prevent soil erosion, and introduced a new rice mill, a Carolina drill (to sow four rows, not one row, of wheat at a 12-inch distance), a Scotch threshing machine, a wind-powered saw mill, and a one-horse-powered hemp break (to do the work of 10 men). He also brought to America seeds of Malta grass, cork-oak acorns, Italian rice, and olive trees.[30] Besides his improved plow mold board, his extant sketches indicate that he tinkered with inventions of machines for shelling corn, an apple press, and a cider mill. His successes, and failures, over the decades, he shared with fellow farmers and men of scientific societies.

In part to refute Comte de Buffon's notion that biota in the New World were inferior due to its climate being cooler and wetter than that of Europe, Jefferson began in 1776 to conduct meteorological readings at Monticello, or wherever he chanced to be. That habit he conducted till he died. Finding 4 a.m. to be (roughly)

---

[27] Thomas Jefferson, *Autobiography*, in *Thomas Jefferson: Writings*, ed. Merrill D. Peterson (New York: Library of America, 1984), 55.
[28] For more, Silvio Bedini, *Jefferson and Science* (Thomas Jefferson Foundation: Monticello Monograph Series, 2002), 71; Edward T. Martin, *Thomas Jefferson: Scientist* (New York: Henry Schuman, Inc., 1952), 38; and E. Shalhope, "Agriculture," in *Thomas Jefferson: A Reference Biography*, ed. Merrill D. Peterson (New York: Charles Scribner's Sons, 1986), 391.
[29] M. Andrew Holowchak, "Jefferson as Scientist," in *The Cavernous Mind of Thomas Jefferson, An American Savant* (Newcastle upon Tyne: Cambridge Scholars, 2019), 93–124.
[30] John W. Oliver, "Thomas Jefferson—Scientist," in *The Scientific Monthly*, Vol. 56, No. 5, 1943, 461–65.

the coolest time of day and 4 p.m., the warmest, he would record both readings, each day, into a meteorological booklet. In addition to his measurements, he would include observations concerning weather in the morning and the afternoon as well as certain miscellanea like "the appearance of birds, leafing and flowering of trees, frosts remarkeably [sic] late or early, Aurora borealis, &c." Jefferson devised a system with letters: "*a*, is after: *c*, cloudy: *f*, fair: *h*, hail: *r*, rain: *s*, snow," And so, *f a r* designated "fair after rain," while *c a s* designated "cloudy after snow." Finally, "cloudy" meant that the sky was at least half covered with clouds, while "fair" meant not cloudy.[31] In his Garden Book, Jefferson was in the habit of noting, for each vegetable, where it was planted, when it was sowed, when it was transplanted, when it came to the table, when its seeds could be gathered, and certain other miscellanea concerning it.

Jefferson was also in inventor of some note. He created his ivory-leafed notebook in which to pencil observations while he traveled, glasses with interchangeable lenses, a portable music stand, a lap-desk for writing while traveling, a swivel chair, an adjustable bookcase, and a cipher wheel for masking certain information in letters, *inter alia*.[32] He invented a greatly improved plow-moldboard,[33] which he refused to patent, because he wished it to be serviceable to his fellow men, and an invention for which he received a gold medal from France.

Jefferson was also greatly interested in the inventions of others which could prove useful to humankind, as he ever had a wish "to see new inventions encouraged, and old ones brought again into useful notice."[34] He purchased a polygraph machine for duplicating important writings. He took a lively interest in hot-air or hydrogen-filled balloons and even speculated on their practicality. He also supported David Bushnell's "excellently contrived" submarine as well as Watt and Boulton's steam-powered grist mill.[35]

As the scientific discoveries and inventions of his time showed, science thrived only in such a political climate where there was no hostility to new ideas—where ideas could be freely expressed and exchanged. "The thinking power called an idea," says Jefferson to Isaac McPherson (13 Aug. 1794), "forces itself into the possession of every one," once it is divulged. Lost of its provenance through divulgement, it yet remains whole in its creator and whole

---

[31] See http://www.monticello.org/site/research-and-collections/weather-observations. See also TJ to Giovanni Fabbroni, 8 June 1778.
[32] John W. Oliver, "Thomas Jefferson—Scientist," 463.
[33] "A good instrument of this kind is almost the greatest desideratum in husbandry." TJ to John Taylor, 29 Dec. 1794.
[34] TJ to Isaac McPherson, 13 Aug. 1813.
[35] Edward T. Martin, *Thomas Jefferson: Scientist*, 68–80.

in those to whom it is communicated. "He who receives an idea from me, receives instruction himself without lessening mine; as he who lights his taper at mine, receives light without darkening me."[36]

Beneficial ideas, Jefferson continues to McPherson, ought not to be monopolized for personal profit. "That ideas should freely spread from one to another over the globe for the moral and mutual instruction of man, and improvement of his condition, seems to have been peculiarly and benevolently designed by nature, when she made the, like fire, expansible over all space, without lessening their density in any point, and like the air in which we breathe, move, and have our physical being, incapable of confinement or exclusive appropriation." Consequently, an invention is no proper subject of property, though a society may wish to allow pecuniary rights to them to encourage production of ideas for further benefit. A man may claim to be the provenance of an idea, but he cannot claim ownership.

Upshot

America was, for Jefferson, a country that celebrated the freedom of ideas—a condition needed for continued scientific advance. Jeffersonian republicanism, thus, partnered with science and the advances of science were appropriated by those governing, thereby leading to political and moral maturation. Governments that shunned or stymied science were backward, or retrograde. Hence, Jefferson found laughable the common animadversion that he was unfit for political office due to his passion for science.[37] He greatly distrusted filiopietistic politicians, ever looking backward, who believed "that government, religion, morality, and every other science were in the highest perfection in ages of the darkest ignorance, and that nothing can ever be devised more perfect than what was established by our forefathers"[38]—accordingly, Jefferson's commitment to periodic changes in any constitution.

One consequence of his recognition of the need for scientific advance in America was that he corresponded with some of the foremost scientists of his day—e.g., physicians Benjamin Rush, Vine Utley, and Philip Turpin; botanists John Bartram, William Bartram, and Benjamin Barton; naturalist Alexander von

---

[36] See M. Andrew Holowchak, "'The thinking power called an idea': Thomas Jefferson, the Right to Patents, and Some Ideas on Ideas," in *History News Network*, http://historynewsnetwork.org/article/172970.

[37] Says TJ to Charles E. Wells (3 Dec. 1809): "Of all the charges brought against me by my political adversaries, that of possessing some science has probably done them the least credit. Our countrymen are too enlightened themselves, to believe that ignorance is the best qualification for their service."

[38] See also TJ to Elbridge Gerry, 26 Jan. 1799, and TJ to John Adams, 15 June 1813.

Humboldt; anatomist Caspar Wistar; chemists Joseph Priestley and Pierre Samuel Du Pont de Nemours; physiologist Pierre J.G. Cabanis; immunologist Edward Jenner; physicists Benjamin Franklin and Benjamin Thompson; astronomer David Rittenhouse; ornithologist Alexander Wilson; and agriculturalist Sir John Sinclair. He also became a member of the American Philosophical Society in 1780 and served as its president in 1797—a service he rendered until January of 1815. As a member of the APS, he had several publications in their *Transactions* during his tenure.[39] That correspondence was possible because of the liberty the correspondents enjoyed to express freely their ideas on science without the meddlesome intervention of intrusive political or religious institutions.

---

[39] Silvio A. Bedini, *Jefferson and Science*, 41–43.

Chapter V

The Nature of Humans

Thomas Jefferson's empiricism—his commitment to ground knowledge on the evidence of the senses—drove him and countless others of his day to embrace the notion that they were living in a time of large intellectual illumination, given numerous advances in all the sciences. The most outstanding advances in the science of politics were reconceptualization and purchase of liberty in service of what we today consider democratic ends. For Jefferson, liberty was the chief instrument of his republicanism. Human thriving, human happiness—the true *telos* of all political bodies—was possible only with fullest instantiation of liberty within the social system to grant citizens freedom from governmental intrusions in their life for the sake of fullest expression of their abilities.

The notion of each person being in desert of liberty, and thus of equal rights, was possible only through recognition that each person was in some fundamental sense the equal of all others, and that was a singularly radical notion in the history of human thinking—a notion that theretofore had never been seriously entertained. For Jefferson, as I show in this chapter, liberty might have been the most recognizable concept in his political philosophy, but it was likely derivative, not axial. The axiom of that philosophy was human equality—the focus of this chapter.

I begin this chapter with a precis of Jefferson's materialism, turn to the axiality of "equality," and end with an account of how human material creatures, each equal and free, are of such stuff to be responsible moral agents.

"I feel: therefore I exist"

Feeling, & Thinking, Matter

Jefferson was a complete physicalist in the manner of the Greek philosopher Epicurus and the great atomist Sir Isaac Newton. Standing on the shoulders of giants such as Johannes Kepler and Galileo Galilei, Newton declared that the cosmos itself was a physical system, comprising atoms swimming in empty infinite space and amenable to inviolable laws, which Newton himself disclosed.

Jefferson's admiration of Newton was inestimable. To David Rittenhouse (19 July 1778), Jefferson speaks of Newton's fathomless genius, and the injustice to the world that would have occurred had Newton been "thrown away … upon the occupations of a crown." To John Trumbull (15 Feb. 1789), he asks for a picture of Bacon, Locke, and Newton—"the three greatest men that have ever lived, without any exception," as they have "laid the foundation of those superstructures which have been raised in the Physical and Moral sciences"[1]—to be made "into a knot on the same canvas, that they may not be confounded at all with the herd of other great men."[2] To John Adams (24 Jan. 1814), Jefferson writes, "Placed along side of Newton, every human character must appear diminutive."

In *Thomas Jefferson's* Notes on the State of Virginia: *A Prolegomena*, I note that Jefferson was indebted to Newton not only because of the latter's discoveries of the laws of the physical universe, but also because of Newton's "Rules of Reasoning in Philosophy"—that is, Newton's methods of scientific research—which Jefferson rigorously applied when he did science.[3] Those principles were not unique to Newton. Some can be traced back to Aristotle.

Newton's triumph in subsuming other discovered laws of science—e.g., Boyle's lay concerning the inverse relationship between pressure and volume of gases in an enclosed space, Galileo's law of falling bodies, and Kepler's laws of planetary motion—under his universal law of gravitation and his three laws of bodily motion was unconditionally lauded by scientists throughout Europe and elsewhere and was adjudged sufficient proof of the veridicality of his dynamical system. There was for the first time a mathematical explanation for the movements of all of the universe's physical bodies, each considered mathematically as a point of mass. What the Greeks called *kosmos*—meaning "order," "arrangement," or "regularity"—was indeed a cosmos.

Yet that unconditioned triumph quickly led to a weighty philosophical problem. There was for the first time an explanation for the movement of all physical bodies and humans too were not exceptions to the laws of the universe. Comprising bones, blood, skin, hair, phlegm, and other material substances, humans were also points of mass. Yet were not humans unique in the cosmos? Were they not masters of their own destiny pursuant to the dictates of their will and deliberations of their intellect? Moreover, how did God fit into

---

[1] See also TJ to Benjamin Rush, 16 Jan. 1811; TJ to Donald Fraser, 8 Jan. 1813; and TJ to Walter Jones, 2 Jan. 1814.

[2] On 10 Mar. 1789, Trumbull replies: "I have given your Commission for the three pictures: but I cannot say I think you will like the arrangement you propose when you see it executed: The blank spaces between the three ovals will have a very awkward look." He suggests three separate pictures. Jefferson (15 Mar. 1789) agrees to have three separate pictures made. Three separate pictures, near to each other, hang now in Monticello.

[3] M. Andrew Holowchak, *Thomas Jefferson's 'Notes on the State of Virginia': A Prolegomena* (Wilmington, DE: Vernon Press, 2023), chap. 10.

the mechanistic explanatory picture? Was there even the need of God, as the system itself seemed self-explanatory?

Jefferson, as I have elsewhere noted fully in several publications, was a dyed-in-the-wool physicalist. He maintained flatly that all existents, even mind and God, were matter. "'I feel: therefore I exist,'" says Jefferson to John Adams (15 Aug. 1820). "I feel bodies which are not myself: there are other existencies then. I call them *matter*. I feel them changing place. This gives me motion. Where there is an absence of matter, I call it *void*, or *nothing*, or *immaterial space*. On the basis of sensation, of matter and motion, we may erect the fabric of all the certainties we can have or need."[4] He adds to Adams: "To talk of *immaterial* existences is to talk of *nothings*. To say that the human soul, angels, god, are immaterial, is to say they are *nothings*, or that there is no god, no angels, no soul. I cannot reason otherwise."[5]

In an earlier letter to Francis Adrian Van der Kemp (9 Feb. 1820), Jefferson writes:

> nothing is known to us but Matter. we percieve in it solidity, extension, and activity. this last property manifests itself 1. by it's constant effort to descend vertically towards the center of the earth, called, gravitation; 2. by the energy with which it clings to contiguous particles of matter, in every direction, called attraction of Cohesion. 3. in some combinations of matter by the faculty of thought, with which they are endowed. the modes in which these different faculties are exercised are unknown to us. we see the facts only.

An apple freed of its stem, Jefferson continues, "immediately descends towards the centre, until some obstacle arrests it's course." A stone appears to find rest on the ground, but one has only "to interpose [one's] hand, and [one] immediately feel[s] it's efforts to proceed in it's course of descent." With a stem of elastic wood, forcibly bent from its habitual form, "the cohesive attraction of it's parts is immediately in a state of exertion to return to the position in which their mutual attractions were *in equilibrio*." It is the same with artifacts. If you wind the spring of a watch, "there commences instantly, within itself, a nisus to

---

[4] The sentiments are clearly influenced by Tracy, who writes solipsistically, "*I think, I feel, or I perceive, that such a thing is in such a manner, or that such a being produces such an effect*," and "I feel because I feel: I feel because I exist; and I do not exist but because I feel." Existence and sensibility of it are "one and the same thing" or "identical beings." A.L.C. Destutt de Tracy, *A Treatise on Political Economy*, ed. Thomas Jefferson (Georgetown: Joseph Milligan, 1817), 3 and 27.

[5] See also TJ to Francis A. Van der Kemp, 9 Feb. 1818, and TJ to John Adams, 14 Mar. 1820.

expand, and return to it's prior state." Those principles of activity, disclosed by Newton, are themselves invisible to humans, yet their activity is undeniable, and so too is their existence. It is the same with animal matter and thought. It might be inconceivable that some sorts of matter have the capacity for thought, but the difficulties of positing thinking immatter—that is, mind or soul, which can à la Descartes mysteriously act on matter—are decupled, and as Newton notes, one ought always to adopt as true the simpler of any two hypotheses. Immaterialism, thus for Jefferson, explains nothing. Immatter cannot act on matter.

The notion of thinking matter is strongly suggestive that Jefferson considered the brain to be the organ of thought. That is confirmed by key late-in-life letters—TJ to John Adams (14 Mar. 1820 and 8 Jan. 1825) and TJ to Francis Adrian Van der Kemp (11 Jan. 1825)—when Jefferson discusses the work of Dugald Stewart, A.L.C. Destutt de Tracy, Pierre Jean George Cabanis, and especially Jean Pierre Flourens concerning thought and the human brain. Flourens' experiments on animals' brains show unquestionably that the cerebrum enables animals to sense, think, and remember and that the cerebellum is the fount of regulated motion.[6] Thus, by virtue of their brain, encephalated animals move, perceive, remember, and think; destroy the brain, and then the animal, to all intents and purposes, ceases to exist. The inescapable conclusion is that mind just is the physical brain.

"All men are created equal & independant"

Jefferson & the Axiality of Human Equality

"All men are created equal," I aim to show, is the axial "self-evidence truth" that Thomas Jefferson expresses in his Declaration of Independence. What, then, is one to make of that curious, unobvious claim?[7]

That cannot be answered until one expiscates what Jefferson means by "equality." Yet it is first profitable to look at Virginia and the other colonies in Jefferson's day, for Colonial America would prove a perfect stage to test the notion of some measure of human equality.

---

[6] For fuller discussion, see M. Andrew Holowchak, *American Messiah: The Surprisingly Simple Religious Views of Thomas Jefferson* (Abilene: Abilene Christian University Press, 2020), chap. 4.

[7] See M. Andrew Holowchak, "Jefferson and Equality," at Abbeville Institute, https://www.abbevilleinstitute.org/jefferson-and-equality/, and M. Andrew Holowchak, "Did Jefferson Really Write the Declaration of Independence?" at *History News Network*, accessed 9 Nov. 2023. https://historynewsnetwork.org/article/169462.

"The republican revolution was the greatest utopian movement in American history," asseverates Gordon Wood.[8] Though a weighty claim, it is true, and it might even be true if one excises the term American. The links that kept together European societies were links forged of inequality—hierarchies (e.g., king and subject, noble and commoner) that existed and were accepted, if only because people knew no better—and they did not exist in Colonial America. Many if not most of the earliest "settlers" were white dependents: prostitutes, vagabonds, urchins, prisoners from the Irish, Scottish, Welsh, Germans, and British in the form of indentured servants or indentured apprentices, who while in England were generally treated no better than beasts to be sold or bought as the market dictated, so the opportunity to leave their condition had large appeal.[9] In this salmagundi of humanity in Colonial America, there was never a strong sense of those British "outcasts" being British. The earliest settlers were merely guinea pigs. Thomas Jefferson, for instance, believed his ancestry on his father's side was linked to Wales, given some evidence of a "Jefferson" or "Jeaffreson" being a plaintiff or defendant in a law report in Wales, though that information has never been confirmed. The first confirmed evidence of an ancestor is of his grandfather in Chesterfield County, Virginia— toward the east of present-day Virginia.[10] From what can be ascertained of his heritage, he likely did not come from noble blood.

Yet bonds of dependency in Colonial America could readily be broken—say, through serving one's tenure as a servant or proving one's worth through work—but not so with bonds of blood, which for the most part did not exist in Colonial America, at least, not as they did in England. Colonists, in deciding the fate of Colonial America, worked from the axiom of some sense of human equality, if only the crude senses of no one being any worse than any other and of all having roughly an equal opportunity to improve their lot. By the time of the First Continental Congress, Colonists were hell-bent on obliterating the notions of superiority and inferiority and of the king being favored by God. As Jefferson, following John Locke, notes poignantly in Summary View of the Rights of British America, freedom of thought and speech are not gifts of kings, but parts of the "laws of nature," and "kings are the servants, not the proprietors of the people."[11]

---

[8] Gordon Wood, *The Radicalism of the American Revolution* (New York: Vintage Books, 1991), 229.
[9] Bernard Bailyn, *Voyagers to the West* (New York: Alfred A. Knopf, 1986), 292.
[10] Thomas Jefferson, *Autobiography*, in *Thomas Jefferson: Writings*, ed. Merrill D. Peterson (New York: Library of America, 1984), 3.
[11] Thomas Jefferson, Summary View of the Rights of British America, in *The Scholars' Thomas Jefferson* (Newcastle upon Tyne: Cambridge Scholars, 2021), 15.

Those two Jeffersonian sentiments, which doubtless struck a chord with many Patriots, were sockdolagers and could only have infuriated King George III, whose authority was not only being undermined, but also questioned. The first challenged the Hobbesian notion that kings spoke on behalf of God. Subjects who disobeyed their king thus disobeyed God. Jefferson's words imply that God, through nature, speaks directly to all persons, without need of any intermediary. That claim was, to many traditionalist thinkers, sheer bombast. It demanded a reversal of the centuries-grounded view of the relationship of a king and his people. The people, says Jefferson, were not servants of the king; the king was the servant of the people. The people were not in their actions answerable to their king; the king was in his actions answerable to the people.

Jefferson's disavowal of the notion of the king as proprietor is also worth analysis. No king owned his people or lorded over them as a superior. Kings were allowed to rule by being given sanction by those persons over whom they ruled.

The bloodline of the *bon ton* in Europe did not exist in Colonial America. There were no nobles in Colonial America, and those of noble blood who formed the first colonies of North America were soon disabused of their belief in their own superiority. Many of noble blood were part of early Jamestown. Many came for land, because they were not first-born and were destined not to inherit any land, but at least three noblemen were first-born, and so their reasons for leaving England were other: say, adventure or profit. The first list of inhabitants shows that gentlemen far outnumbered laborers, yet they were taught by Captain John Smith that there could be no freeloading in their volatile situation. "He who works not, eats not," said he[12]—a sentiment that set the stage for the equalitarianism of Colonial America.

It is in that milieu, without different classes of persons based on worth, that Jefferson was nurtured, and that is why he was able to craft so persuasively his Summary View in 1774 and Declaration of Independence two years later. In that milieu, Jefferson could articulate a notion of human equality that supported a robust notion of human liberty for human happiness.

In Summary View of the Rights of British America, Jefferson writes of "complaints" due to "unwarranted encroachments and usurpations" of "those rights which God and the laws have given equally and independently to all."[13] The wording here suggests that rights and laws are afforded all humans equally and independently and that intimates that all humans are equal and, in some

---

[12] "History," *Jamestown Rediscovery,* https://historicjamestowne.org/history/history-of-jamestown/first-settlers/, accessed 1 June 2022.
[13] Thomas Jefferson, Summary View of the Rights of British America, 3.

fundamental sense, free at birth. That, if correct, is consistent with many other Enlightenment thinkers of Jefferson's day—e.g., John Locke and George Mason. In his Second Treatise on Government, Locke asserts that the state of nature is a state of perfect freedom and equality. In that state and created by an "omnipotent and infinitely wise maker," men are the servants of and subjects of that maker, and subjects of his will. And so, one cannot authorize the destruction of another or seek his own extermination.[14] In his Virginia Declaration of Rights, Mason begins, "That all men are by nature equally free and independent and have certain inherent rights, of which, when they enter into a state of society, they cannot, by any compact, deprive or divest their posterity; namely, the enjoyment of life and liberty, with the means of acquiring and possessing property, and pursuing and obtaining happiness and safety."[15]

What did Jefferson think?

Examination of Jefferson's first draft of his Declaration of Independence strongly intimates the axiality of equality in Jefferson's political philosophy—that is, that liberty is derivative. This original draft is prior to the cosmetic edits of Adams and Franklin and the heavy edits of the Congress, and I suspect, offers us the best barometer of Jefferson's intentions. That is, at least, what I shall argue.

First, the first paragraph is Jefferson's opening salvo, which lays open to all men the reason for construction of the document. It has been preserved fully in the final version.

> When in the course of human events it becomes necessary for a people to advance from that subordination in which they have hitherto remained, & to assume among the powers of the earth the equal & independant station to which the laws of nature & of nature's god entitle them, a decent respect to the opinions of mankind requires that they should declare the causes which impel them to the change.

That salvo is an appeal to the good judgment of mankind for the causes of the colonists' push for separation. It is framed as a conditional (if-then) claim, but

---

[14] John Locke, *Second Treatise on Government*, ed. C.B. Macpherson (Indianapolis: Hackett Publishing, 1980), II.4–6. It is an argument that goes back to Plato. In *Phaedo*, Socrates, in prison, entertains the analogical argument that human life is like being in a prison with the gods as guardians. Plato, *Phaedo*, trans. Harold North Fowler (Cambridge, MA: Harvard University Press, [1914], 1990), 62b.

[15] George Mason, "Virginia Declaration of Rights," at *National Archives: America's Founding Documents,* https://www.archives.gov/founding-docs/virginia-declaration-of-rights, accessed 31 Oct. 2022.

the sentence can be taken as an implicit argument (formally, *modus ponens*: If A, then B; A; so, B), with brackets below indicative of claims implicit:

> 1. When in human events it is necessary for one people to separate from another due to subordination and to form a separate people, equal and independent (entitled them by nature), respect for the opinions of mankind requires that they limn the causes for such separation.
> [2. The North American colonists have separated from their mother country.]
> [3. So, North American Colonists must limn the causes of their separation.]

We note here that in the antecedent of the lengthy conditional claim includes the natural entitlement of the equal and independent station of any group of people that has been subordinated to the will of another group. The sentiment seems to be, given inclusion of "independent," that humans are equal and independent by nature.

Yet that interpretation is challengeable by the second paragraph, which strongly suggests that it is wrong to equate "independence" and "liberty," for Jefferson then turns to certain truths, which are dubbed in this original draft to be "sacred & undeniable" (numbers, mine), but "self-evident" in the final version:

> We hold these truths to be sacred & undeniable, (1) that all men are created equal & independent, (2) that from that equal creation they derives rights inherent & inalienable, among which are the preservation of life, & liberty, & the pursuit of happiness, (3) that to secure these ends, governments are instituted among men, deriving their just powers from the consent of the governed; (4) that whenever any form of government shall become destructive of these ends, it is the right of the people to alter or to abolish it, & to institute new government, laying it's foundation on such principles & organising it's powers in such form, as to them shall seem most likely to effect their safety & happiness.

First, we see that there are four "thats," each separated by a semi-colon (the first comma should be a semi-colon), and each "that" introduces a key proposition.

Claim 1, concerning the equality and independence of all men, is axial and an ingemination of what was said in the opening paragraph. In claim 2, Jefferson states that the three listed rights—liberty being one—are derivative of equal creation. The significancy of that is we have the rights of life, liberty, and pursuit of happiness, our sacred and undeniable rights, only because we are, in some fundamental sense, equal. The questions here are these: How do "life," "liberty," and "pursuit of happiness" follow from "equality"? and if "independence" is not the same thing as "liberty," then what does Jefferson mean by "independence"?

Claim 3 shows that life, liberty, and pursuit of happiness are rights that governments are instituted to preserve—suggestive that "liberty" differs from "independence" in that liberty is the sort of independence one has in a society, while independence is merely a sort of generic freedom humans have *qua* being human. That is the view that Jean-Jacques Rousseau, as we shall see in the next chapter, holds.[16] The final draft reads, "We hold these truths to be self-evident, that all men are created equal, that they are endowed by their Creator with certain unalienable Rights, that among these are Life, Liberty and the pursuit of Happiness." Here we do not have the explicit derivation of liberty from equality, but that is not Jefferson's doing.

To simplify matters concerning Jefferson's first draft, we might merely isolate "equality" and "liberty." What Jefferson says is that "from that equal creation" we are deserving of liberty; not the converse, that from human liberty, we deserve equality. Etiological directionality here is critical. One cannot derive with deductive certainty "equality" from "liberty" other than in a tautologous sense: that is, on assumption that people are equal in that each has in some sense equal freedom in nature. One might then claim that the lion in the gazelle upon which the lion preys are equal in that both enjoy freedom in nature. This line of thinking seems unpromising. Yet "liberty" as a derivative of "equality" and as a political notion of freedom does make sense, at least for humans, and perhaps even for other social animals: Because humans are in some manner equal, they deserve civic liberty.

The third claim—that every government derives its powers to govern from the consent of the governed and it is the task of government to secure the life, liberty, and pursuit of happiness of its citizens—was highly controversial in Jefferson's day, a topic of vibrant discussion. The received view, believed for hundreds of years and framed boldly by Hobbes in *Leviathan*, was that kings were answerable only to God.

Finally, the last claim, like the opening salvo, is conditional. When a government turns a blind eye to the rights of its citizens, then its citizens have a right to (a) alter or abolish it and (b) to institute a new government, based on what the citizens deem most likely to promote their safety and happiness.

---

[16] This is not to suggest that Jefferson follows Rousseau. There is no evidence that Rousseau's *Social Contract* had any influence on Jefferson. Jefferson had Rousseau's *Collected Works* in his library, but says little about Rousseau in his letters and other writings.

Jefferson immediately offers a caveat. "Governments long established should not be changed for light & transient causes," and so citizens ought to suffer abuses while they are sufferable. Nonetheless, "when a long train of abuses & usurpations, begun at a distinguished period, & pursuing invariably the same object, evinces a design to subject them to arbitrary power, it is their right, it is their duty, to throw off such government & to provide new guards for their future security."

Next, Jefferson lists some 24 grievances (there are more, as many plaints are compound claims)—"facts ... submitted to a candid world"—which aim to show King George III's behavior, when it comes to ignoring their rights, to be discretionary, and thus, tyrannical. The longest, placed at the end, concerns the opprobrium of slavery, and was excised by the Congress, as it was an issue with which Southern states did not wish at the time to grapple.

Finally, there's the ending paragraph which proffers the ultimate conclusion. "We therefore the representatives of the United States of America in General Congress assembled do, in the name & by authority of the good people of these states, ... declare these a colonies to be free and independant states, and that as free & independant states they shall hereafter have power to levy war, conclude peace, contract alliances, establish commerce, & to do all other acts and things which independent states may of right do."

Thus, the Declaration is a lengthy argument, given in gist mostly in the second paragraph. All people are created equal. All people are endowed with certain rights (life, liberty, and the pursuit of happiness) to enable them to live peaceably among each other in a social setting, given their equality. Governmental power is derived from the consent of the people. The main task of a government is to secure its citizens' rights. When any government fails to secure its citizens' rights, the citizens have a right to abolish it and institute a new government. King George III has abusively violated the British colonists' rights (24, or so, grievances). In consequence, the colonists have a right to form their own government in keeping with their own notions of their safety and happiness.

In sum, if my reasoning here is cogent, by following the anfractuous path of reasoning in Jefferson's original rough draft of his Declaration, the argument for the right to revolution is fundamentally based on the axial notion of human equality. Liberty, as a right, is, in its social sense, derivative.

"He who made us would have been a pitiful bungler..."
Warrant for the Axiality of Human Equality

There was, we have seen, a rough sense of human equality in Colonial America, which did not have the social stratification of European countries. Yet the

Colonists embraced the institution of slavery, where people, Whites and Blacks, were indentured for fixed periods or for life, so there was some sense of stratification. Did Jefferson believe that slaves were not equals of non-slaves?[17]

The abuses Jefferson limns in his original draft of the Declaration are many, at least 24, and he lists last and devotes the most ink, 168 words, to the introduction of slavery into the colonies.

> he [King George III] has waged cruel war against human nature itself, violating it's most sacred rights of life & liberty in the persons of a distant people who never offended him, captivating & carrying them into slavery in another hemisphere, or to incur miserable death in their transportation thither. this piratical warfare, the opprobrium of **infidel** powers, is the warfare of the Christian king of Great Britain, determined to keep open a market where MEN should be bought & sold, he has prostituted his negative for suppressing every legislative attempt to prohibit or to restrain this execrable commerce: and that this assemblage of horrors might want no fact of distinguished die, he is now exciting those very people to rise in arms among us, and to purchase that liberty of which he has deprived them, & murdering the people upon whom he also obtruded them; thus paying off former crimes committed against the **liberties** of one people, with crimes which he urges them to commit against the **lives** of another.

We note Jefferson's use of capital letters for the word men. Nowhere else in his draft does he do use capitals. That shows unequivocally that Jefferson considered slaves as men, not as chattel, and that argues decisively against the naïve view, articulated by too many in the secondary literature, that the Declaration was not meant to include Blacks, who were the lion's share of the slaves at the time imported into the Colonies. Slaves, Blacks among them, qua men, are deserving of the same axial rights as all other men.[18]

Yet what precisely does Jefferson mean concerning the at-birth equality of all persons? What does he mean by "equal creation?"

One way to understand the term is pragmatically and politically. There are no reasons to see constitutional differences in people at birth. The children of the

---

[17] M. Andrew Holowchak, "Jefferson and Moral Equality," at Abbeville Institute, https://www.abbevilleinstitute.org/jefferson-and-moral-equality.

[18] It has typically gone unnoticed that often when Jefferson rails against the institution of slavery, he does not make it an issue of color (race), as is always done today. Note, e.g., his argument against slavery in Query XVIII of his *Notes on the State of Virginia*. He argues against men oppressing men, not Whites oppressing Blacks.

wealthy and wellborn are constitutionally indistinct, or relatively so, from those who are not, but they have opportunities that others do not have—among them, readier access to medical care and education. Level the playing field by affording equality of opportunities through, for instance, change of inheritance laws and educational reforms, then the children of those not wealthy or wellborn will perform as well as those of the wealthy and wellborn, so thinks Jefferson. That is a matter of creating equality of opportunity—a historical or empirical notion. It realizes, says John Smith, the differences between persons—e.g., talents, prior social status, education, and wealth—and seeks to "neutralize these differences by providing a homogeneity of living conditions within which everyone will have an equal opportunity in relation to everyone else to pursue his own well being"[19]—what is tantamount to positive liberty. Jefferson's efforts to reform the laws of Virginia, undertaken in 1776, show manifestly a commitment to equality of opportunity. That is what I mean when I write elsewhere, "Jefferson's assertion of the equality of all persons is not a categorical truth, known to be true by the light of intuition, but one of many claims whose truth or untruth would be brought to light by the success or failure of the great political experiment he was proposing."[20]

Yet equality of opportunity is reasonable only if it is warranted—*viz.*, it can be shown that all are deserving of it. If there is no sense in which persons are at-birth equals of all others, then what is the point of creating a climate of equality of opportunity?

Scholar John Smith has an answer: equality of status—a philosophical notion. It recognizes that each human, considered *qua* human, is deserving of equal status in personhood and citizenship.[21] The equality of the Declaration is chiefly equality of status, though Jefferson's great political experiment is also, to some extent, about creating equality of opportunity.

Equality of status seems reasonable, yet one might reasonably ask these questions: What is "status" and why are people, for Jefferson, deserving of equality of status? On account of what, precisely, are humans deserving of equality of status—that is, equal rights?

"Status," of course, refers to the standing (e.g., natural, social, or political) of one person vis-à-vis all others. What sort of status have all persons to enable them to deserve equality of opportunity? Smith sidesteps that question.

---

[19] John Smith, "Philosophical Ideas Behind the 'Declaration of Independence,'" in *Revue Internationale de Philosophia,* Vol. 31, 1977: 374–75.
[20] M. Andrew Holowchak, *Dutiful Correspondent: Philosophical Essays on Thomas Jefferson* (Lanham, MD: Rowman & Littlefield, 2013), 32.
[21] John Smith, "Philosophical Ideas Behind the 'Declaration of Independence,'" 375.

The Nature of Humans 83

Thomas Kidd proffers a theological solution: the Argument from Divine Creation. Jefferson and others of the Enlightenment of his day believed in a created world, which of course implies a creator. Sums Kidd, "Equality by creation, because it was so widely assumed, was the most powerful basis on which to argue for equal rights. For observers such as Jefferson, equality by creation did not mean equality of condition or talents. It did mean that all people had basic dignity before God, because all people were created 'in God's image,' as Genesis puts it."[22] In sum:

1) All people were created in God's image.
2) Those created in God's image had basic dignity before God.
3) So, people had basic dignity before God.
4) That basic dignity is warrant for equal rights.
5) So, all people are deserving of equal rights.

Jefferson, of course, nowhere assents to humans being created in God's image. He would have found that notion laughably absurd. So, the argument is unavailing.

Yet let us examine a weaker, more viable sense of this Argument from Divine Creation, as Jefferson did believe in a deity as Creator:

1) God created all humans.
2) All humans have a God-given essence that distinguishes them from and makes them superior to other beings.
3) That God-given essence makes each the equal of all other humans.
4) So, that essence entitles them to equal rights.

The pitfall of this argument is that Jefferson did not think that humans occupied a privileged position in the cosmos, though they were unique in possession of rationality. The reason for this I shall shortly show.

We are left to consider an even weaker version of the Argument from Divine Creation:

1) God created all humans.
2) All humans have a God-given essence that distinguishes them from other beings.
3) That God-given essence makes each the equal of all other humans.

---

[22] Thomas Kidd, *Thomas Jefferson: A Biography of Spirit and Flesh* (New Haven: Yale University Press, 2022), 54.

4) So, that essence entitles them to equal rights.

The nodus with this "Weakest" Argument from Divine Creation is that premise 3 merely begs the question. One needs only to plug in *mosquitos* or *puffins* for *humans* and work on assumption that God created all things that exist to see that the argument is a non-sequitur. One might certainly object that fleas have a right to happiness, conditioned on a choice of a certain manner of living. One might even object that the flea, now situated and nibbling on my forearm, has a right to life. One wants to know what it is about humans, distinct from all other animals, that makes them and only them deserving of equal rights.

Nonetheless, the answer, for Jefferson, is perhaps not so difficult.

All persons, except for freaks, are born with a moral sense, capable of perceiving or feeling right action in a set of circumstances. He writes to nephew Peter Carr (10 Aug. 1787):

> He who made us would have been a pitiful bungler, if he had made the rules of our moral conduct a matter of science. For one man of science, there are thousands who are not. What would have become of them? Man was destined for society. His morality, therefore, was to be formed to this object. He was endowed with a sense of right and wrong, merely relative to this. This sense is as much a part of his nature, as the sense of hearing, seeing, feeling; it is the true foundation of morality, and not the … truth, &c., as fanciful writers have imagined. The moral sense, or conscience, is as much a part of man as his leg or arm. It is given to all human beings in a stronger or weaker degree, as force of members is given them in a greater or less degree. It may be strengthened by exercise, as may any particular limb of the body.

The existence at birth of a moral sense is not to say that all persons immediately can see the right thing to do, prior to doing it. Children at birth see, but they do not know what they see until they interact with objects of perception and are schooled by others who have been seeing much longer. It is likely the same with the moral sense, which needs cultivation over time.

The moral sense also needs maturation through exposure to a wide variety of experiences over time. A comparison with vision is aidful. A person who has spent his life in a hot Caribbean climate will be taken aback when he, visiting a friend in Michigan's Upper Peninsula, first sees snow, though he has often seen pictures of it. Seeing snow for the first time also involves, for instance, feeling the cold on one's skin and intake of cold air into one's lungs—an unfriendly experience for one who has never experienced it. Thus, moral maturation demands moral exposure to events of varied sorts. A person, thus, who has much experience of varied cultures will be in the best position to perceive morally correct action. He will at least understand why persons in some cultures are moral laggards. That shows that reason, to some extent, does come into play.

The moral sense also needs coaxing over time, for humans are disposed to laziness. One can perceive that something is the right thing to do, but be disinclined to do it, because of hebetude and the right thing to do requires effort and expense. To donate a pint of blood when many people need blood requires that one transports oneself to a donation center, and one might merely be too slothful to do that. One might also not be disposed, for the nonce, to leave oneself minus a pint of blood.

And so, Jefferson's statement of the at-birth equality of all people, construed as a conditional claim, has moral support in Jefferson's eyes. Jefferson believes all persons are at-birth moral equals inasmuch as the moral sense at birth is given to all in the same way that seeing or hearing is given to all.[23] Each person, consequently, has the same at-birth capacity for moral discernment, given proper maturation.[24]

Does at-birth possession of a moral sense make humans unique in the cosmos—special to the creator?

There is a fly, or flea, in the ointment. To John Adams (14 Oct. 1816), Jefferson writes: "I believe that [the moral sense] is instinct, and innate, that the moral sense is as much a part of our constitution as that of feeling, seeing, or hearing; as a wise creator must have seen to be necessary in an animal destined to live in society." The appendage, "in an animal destined to live in society," is troublesome. It makes it probable that, for Jefferson, all social animals— vertebrates such as puffins, penguins, bats, crows, hominids, elephants, dolphins, horses, lions, and hyenas, and invertebrates such as ants, bees,

---

[23] TJ to Thomas Law, 13 June 1814, and TJ to Peter Carr, 10 Aug. 1787.
[24] Jefferson, however, did not think that persons are in any sense at-birth equals *vis-à-vis* talents and ambition. That much is obvious by experience. Yet he did seek to neutralize those differences by providing equal living conditions based on possession of a certain minimal amount of property for each citizen so that each person could live pursuant to his own needs. Hence, he mandated that each Virginian should have 50 acres of property in his proposed constitution for Virginia to promote opportunities for all Virginians and he proposed a certain friendly infrastructure for the fledgling country in his Second Inaugural Address. Thomas Jefferson, Draft Constitution for Virginia and Second Inaugural Address, in *The Scholar's Thomas Jefferson: Vital Writings of a Vital American*, ed. M. Andrew Holowchak (Newcastle upon Tyne: Cambridge Scholars, 2021), 16–26 and 57–63.

termites, and wasps—because of their sociability, have their own sense of "morality," species specific.[25] That is not such a ludicrous claim, if we consider that the moral faculty for humans is sensory, not rational. If so, then morality is something about the physical make-up of certain types of social animals that explains their sociability, not something God gave only to humans to segregate them from other animals.

On this reading, does that mean that all social animals, equipped with some sense of morality to suit their species, are deserving of rights?

The human moral sense, for Jefferson, is unique among social creatures. As Jefferson says in his 1820 letter to Adams (Aug. 15), humans, through their moral sense, feel or perceive God, and it is doubtful that Jefferson thought the same about the "moral" sensibility of other social creatures, like penguins. Thus, through moral sensitivity, humans have a cosmic connectivity that other social creatures likely do not. Humans too also possess the rudiments of rationality: e.g., the capacity to read, write, and calculate. In both ways, humans are unique among social creatures, and deserving equal rights.

"*Liberty*, and *necessity* are consistent"

The Possibility of Human Agency

Jefferson also very likely believed that individuals are freely willful and rational—the two, for Jefferson when it comes to humans, being materially equivalent. An important corollary of this proposition relates to human happiness or flourishing. If humans are freely willful and rational, then they are essentially choosing organisms. Choosing organisms are happiest, when they are doing what they are best suited to do: choosing, without constraints—e.g., political constraints. It follows that individuals are happiest, Jefferson believes, when they are allowed to choose their own path in life, and governments are best when they are structured to do just that.

What does it mean that "freely willful" and "rational" are materially equivalent terms?

Material equivalence means simply that the material conditions needed for a human to actuate rationality, R, are the exact conditions needed for a human to actuate free will, F. That means that rationality, in a given cosmos, implies freedom; freedom implies rationality—that is, that R implies F and F implies R, or in formal terms, R if and only if F ($R \equiv F$). As we saw in the prior chapter,

---

[25] M. Andrew Holowchak, "Did Jefferson Think Humans Occupied a Privileged Position in the Cosmos," in *Thirty-Six More Short Essays, Plus Another, on the Probing Mind of Thomas Jefferson* (Newcastle upon Tyne: Cambridge Scholars, 2020), 88.

liberty is fundamentally a moral category for Jefferson, not a political category, for political liberty is meaningless without personal liberty. "For Jefferson," writes Henry May, "political philosophy could never long be separated from moral philosophy; the nature of government depended on the nature of man"[26]—a very Aristotelian sentiment. That neatly captures Jefferson's belief that no person is naturally superior to another by birth or by wealth—i.e., that there is no natural aristocracy, *pace* John Adams, based on birth or wealth.[27]

Jefferson's conception of rationality is complex. Following fellow empiricists, reason is for Jefferson the faculty of comprehending sensory impressions, which involves analytic and synthetic functions. Yet as an empiricist, Jefferson is not an infalliblist about reason. Reason has its flaws. First, reason is dependent on sensation for its materials and the senses sometimes are deceived. Second, consistent with Hume, reason is beholden to the passions. One has only to consider Jefferson's celebrated anodyne, "If feel, therefore I exist," in his letter to Adams (15 Aug. 1820). Thinking is conspicuously absent. Third, and this attends on the other points, the assertions of reason, vociferated with utmost certainty by various persons, are of the most varied sort. Of reason's fallibleness, Jefferson says to Abigail Adams (11 Sept. 1804): "I tolerate with the utmost latitude the right of others to differ from me in opinion without imputing to them criminality. I know too well the weakness and uncertainty of human reason to wonder at its different results." Last, reason, unlike moral sensitivity, is given fully to too few persons to be a defining feature of human beings. Consequently, reason has been of inestimable aid in moving humans from the darkness of pre-Enlightenment times, but that movement has been due to the actions of men—like Pascal, Bacon, Locke, Boyle, Kepler, Galileo, and Newton—with singular rational capacities. The successes of such intellectual Titans have been greatest when there have been no governmental intrusions inhibiting their activities.

At this juncture, we anticipate a large problem for Jefferson: If all the vital human functions, will included, are brain-based, and if the brain is mere matter, how then is human activity will-driven, and freely so? That is not a trite question, for "liberty," if it is the robust concept that Jefferson's writings show it to be, must imply a capacity for an agent in a particular set of circumstances to be able to have done other than he has done, and Newton's mechanistic and materialistic universe does not seem to allow for that. Humans, as chunks of matter of a unique sort, obey the same laws of the physical cosmos as do all

---

[26] Henry F. May, "The Enlightenment," in *Thomas Jefferson: A Reference Biography*, ed. Merrill D. Peterson (New York: Charles Scribner's Sons, 1986), 51.
[27] TJ to John Adams, 28 Oct. 1813. See also J.W. Cooke, "Jefferson on Liberty," *Journal of the History of Ideas*, 34, 1973: 565-71.

other chunks of matter. No human, pushed from a promontory that juts over the sea, can merely will that he not fall, and then not fall, by virtue of willing. He falls.

There are three reasonable answers that Jefferson could have entertained, because he was acquainted with them—Stoicism, Hobbesianism, and Kamesianism—and a fourth, put forth by Immanuel Kant that addressed cleverly the prickly nodus, but one with which Jefferson was not acquainted.

Let us first look at Stoicism. Like Jefferson, the Stoics of Greek and Roman antiquity were complete physicalists. They believed that the cosmos was a wholly determined system and so, the behavior of all material entities in it, humans among them, was wholly determined. The cosmos was itself deemed to be a god, sometimes called *Zōon* (Gr.; Animal) or Zeus, and it unfolded in accordance with a strict divine plan. As an organic entity, it was united by a cosmic *pneuma* and a certain tension (*tonos*) between all its parts. The Stoic Chrysippus likened the cosmos to a web, on which a disturbance of one part is felt, to a greater or lesser extent, by every other thing on the web. All things, humans too, were parts of a complex causal network.[28]

There was no notion of free human will for the Stoics. That however did not mean that humans were "exculpable" when it came to their actions. The Stoic Chrysippus (c. 279–c. 206 B.C.) posits that some actions are within an agent—that is, their explanation is to be found within the human organism. Though an agentive action is incited by an impression, an agent's response is unique to that impression, given the unique physical nature of each person. That is not assumption of some faculty of willing, causally generative of human action and causally independent of material antecedents. It is merely recognition that human constitutional factors—and with humans those factors are complex—are large contributors to our deeds. When one strikes a large, weighty cube on a surface, it moves little due to its large cubic size, structure, and weight. When one strikes a small, light ball on a surface, it moves much due to its small cubic size, sphericity, and lightness. Yet when one strikes another human being on the face, the response might be a strike returned, recoil and retreat, or merely an unkind remark, but there is for Chrysippus only one possible response, which will be dictated by the precise physical circumstances of the slap and the physical constitution of the sufferer. For Chrysippus, we do what we do, and it is not that we could have done otherwise.

For Stoics, there is rational control not of physical actions, but there is rational control of our mental disposition toward all physical events. There is our then

---

[28] M. Andrew Holowchak, *The Stoics: A Guide for the Perplexed* (London: Continuum, 2008), chap. 1.

capacity to assent to things that must naturally be and to do that habitually, as does a sage, or to assent to things capriciously or to fail to assent, as does someone who is not a sage—these last two being a signal of a diseased soul.[29] The greatest human good is thus a matter of choosing what is in accordance with nature, and rejecting what is contrary to it, and of shaping our desires both to want the things that are properly our own and to want things to be as they will turn out to be.[30] We can, it seems, dispose our mind to the way things will turn out and then be in concord with nature, or dispose our mind otherwise by mentally fighting nature. How that is possible, given that mind is matter, is unclear.

Second, Thomas Hobbes in *Leviathan* proffers a mechanistic conception of freedom. "Free" and "liberty" are applicable only to bodies capable of motion, hence it is nonsense to apply otherwise those terms, for instance, when we talk of the freedom of a path, of a gift, or of speaking. The last implies no freedom of voice, but freedom of the person with voice. For Hobbes, to be free means to be capable of doing what one can do by strength and will and to be "not hindered to do what [one] has a will to."[31]

Yet there is nothing magical about Hobbes' will. "From the use of the word *free-will*, no liberty can be inferred of the will, desire, or inclination, but the liberty of the man; which consisteth in this, that he finds no stop, in doing what he has the will, desire, or inclination to do." Human motion, like other bodies capable of motion, is explicable completely in mechanistic terms. "*Liberty*, and *necessity* are consistent: as in the water, that hath not only liberty, but a necessity of descending by the channel; so likewise in the actions which men voluntarily do: which, because they proceed from their will, proceed from *liberty*; and yet, because every act of man's will, and every desire, and inclination proceedeth from some cause, and that from another cause, in a continual chain, whose first link is in the hand of God the first of all causes, proceed from *necessity*."[32] Liberty, here, means unconstrained. The account is essentially deterministic.

Third, there is the view of Lord Kames (1696–1782), whose views are similar to those of Hobbes, in *Essays on the Principles of Morality and Natural Religion*. Kames, an older contemporary of Jefferson and much read by Jefferson, begins his explanation of human agency by noting that humans have appetites and passions, "which move us to action," and that the moral sense governs our passions. "We are impelled to motion by the very constitution of our nature;

---

[29] M. Andrew Holowchak, *The Stoics*, 45–47.
[30] M. Andrew Holowchak, *The Stoics*, 30 and 38.
[31] Thomas Hobbes, *Leviathan*, ed. Michael Oakshott (New York: Macmillan, 1962), 159.
[32] Thomas Hobbes, *Leviathan*, 159–60.

and to prevent our being carried too far, or in a wrong direction, conscience is set as at the helm."[33]

Humans for Kames have conceptions of a material world and of a moral world. In the former—and here the influence of Newtonianism is obvious—all events proceed "in a fixed and settled train of causes and effects." In the latter, man is an agent, and "this necessary chain of causes and effects appears not so clearly." Agentive man does not seem to be a part of the material world's physical necessity. "In consequence of his deliberation he chuseth: and here, if any where, lies our liberty."[34]

A human motive, i.e., "the will to act," Kames concedes, determines non-reflexive human activities, yet motives are fixed, not free, for every motive is rooted in desire. We desire some end and then act to bring about that end. Still desire is "not under our own power," and "if our desires are not under our own power, neither can our actions be under our power."[35]

"Liberty [however], if it have any meaning, must signify a power to act in contradiction to desire; ... a power to act in contradiction to any view, purpose, or design, we can have in acting." Such a conception, though, he finds absurd. Humans do act not according to liberty, but according to moral necessity. They choose what they desire, but desire is not up to them.[36] Though I might strongly desire to eat the pie of pizza that sits before me when I am famished, I might choose not to eat the pie, but that is not an act contrary to desire, but a triumph of one desire, stronger (a desire, say, to punish myself), over another, less strong (a desire to indulge in the pie). This is today known as "compatibilism": the view that humans can choose what they wish to do, but their choices are determined by desires, which are not free.

What, then, are we to make of the strong sense of contingency apparent in human actions? Deity, Kames states, formed humans not that they could readily grasp the nature of things *per se*, but that their impressions and the notions of them are of utmost use. The senses are not so much for "discovery of the intimate nature and essences of things," but more for "the uses and conveniences of life." Humans perceive color in objects, but, following Newton, it is not a property of objects, but of light. They believe the precise moment of their death is unfixed, but it is strictly determined. Hence, "contingency in this view may justly be considered as a secondary quality, which hath no real

---

[33] Henry Home, *Essays on the Principles of Morality and Natural Religion*, ed. 2 (London: 1758), 55–56.
[34] Henry Home, *Morality and Natural Religion*, 121–22
[35] Henry Home, *Morality and Natural Religion*, 130.
[36] Henry Home, *Morality and Natural Religion*, 130–31.

existence in things; but, like other secondary qualities, is made to appear as an attribute of events, in order to serve the purposes of human life." Kames says, "To make way ... for the sense of contingency, the necessary connection betwixt desire and will is kept out of sight; and by this contrivance it is, that we are not sensible of being necessary agents." Consequently, liberty and necessity are reconciled. Though humans are necessitated animals, they perceive themselves to be free, for that is how deity saw fit for humans to be.[37]

A fourth option is the deontological view of Immanuel Kant, whose thoughts on morality many philosophers today still find mystifyingly attractive in some effort to allow for human willfulness in what is otherwise a deterministic macroscopic world. An older contemporary of Jefferson, Kant (1724–1804) aimed to reconcile moral inculpation with the determinism of Newton's dynamical universe. To do so, Kant, similar to Kames, posited both phenomenal and noumenal worlds—the world of experience, or things as they appear to be, and the world of reason, or things as they are behind their appearances.

In *Grounding for the Metaphysics of Morals*, Kant begins with the notion of the possibility of "good without qualification," which he takes to be a good will—*viz.*, something good through its willing and, thus, good in itself.[38] That takes Kant to consideration of all actions that are done from duty (hence deontology) and from no other inclination: e.g., the principles to preserve one's life; to be beneficent, when possible; to speak truthfully; and to secure one's happiness.[39] Any action performed only from duty has worth not from any end secured or the completion of the action, but from "the principle of volition according to which ... the action has been done." If it is the product of a good will, then it has moral worth.

Why, however, ought anyone to act ever to preserve one's life or to act beneficently? Kant's answer is another principle: a grounding principle. Any action (e.g., telling the truth) is willfully done from duty when one can will that that maxim (e.g., always tell the truth) ought to become a universal moral law—a law binding of any creature capable of rationality.[40] It is by that method that humans discover the universal moral laws. Thus, humans through willing from duty are both legislators *and* discoverers of universal moral truths. Through willing from duty, will becomes good will. Kant, thus, aims to do for morality what Newton did for physics.

---

[37] Henry Home, *Morality and Natural Religion*, 113–14, 152–53, and 162.
[38] Immanuel Kant, *Grounding for the Metaphysics of Morals,* trans. James W. Ellington (Indianapolis: Hackett Publishing Company, 1981), §§393–96.
[39] Immanuel Kant, *Grounding for the Metaphysics of Morals*, §§397–99.
[40] Immanuel Kant, Grounding for the Metaphysics of Morals, §402.

What for Kant are will, reason, and natural necessity? "The will is a kind of causality belonging to living beings insofar as they are rational; freedom would be the property of this causality that makes it effective independent of any determination by alien causes"; and "natural necessity is the property of the causality of all non-rational beings by which they are determined to activity through the influence of alien causes." In short, will for Kant is a "law to itself"—that is, freedom is an essential presupposition of the will of each rational being.[41]

We return here to the phenomenal and noumenal worlds. The phenomenal world, being the world as it seems to be, as we experience it to be, is ever in flux and appears to be different to different observers. The noumenal world, being the reality behind the appearances and "the basis of the former," is ever the same. Each rational belong—and Kant makes no attempt to single out humans as the only rational beings in the universe—belongs to the "world of sense," and yet each is an "intelligence and each is subject to the law of the intelligible world." He sums, "The moral *ought* is, therefore, a necessary *would* insofar as he is a member of the intelligible world, and is thought by him as an *ought* only insofar as he regards himself as being at the same time a member of the world of sense." While the idea of a free will is questionable on the grounds of experience, the notion of all things being naturally necessitated is, for Kant, opprobrious to reason.[42]

And so, Kant reconciles the determinism of Newton's material universe with freedom of the moral world in a sort of Platonic manner: There is for rational beings a world of reason and will, where humans are volitionally free, behind the veneer of the world of appearances, where humans are necessitated mass points that swim in the flux of matter. In some sense, he turns Kames on his head. For Kames, the moral world is how things seem to be to humans; for Kant, the moral world is the reality behind the amaranthine flux of the world of experience.

Where now do we stand? How did Jefferson, who always expressed disdain of philosophizing, reconcile human liberty with Newton's deterministic dynamical system?

The first difficulty is human progress, to which Jefferson was inescapably committed.

Jefferson, with advent of printing presses and dissemination of information, was committed to human progress in the sciences, not excluding morality and politics. Each generation, on average, would move beyond, if only slightly, that

---

[41] Immanuel Kant, *Grounding for the Metaphysics of Morals*, §448.
[42] Immanuel Kant, *Grounding for the Metaphysics of Morals*, §§455–56.

of the prior generation in intelligence and moral sensitivity, and the result was that politics too was progressing. People, having advanced intelligently and morally, would of necessity figure out better ways to live in social settings. The key to all advances was embrace of liberty, and Jefferson, more than others of his day, had a very robust notion of liberty, as it was the catalyst for human thriving, human happiness.

Was Jefferson on agentive human activities influenced by the Stoics, for whom human inculpation was merely a matter of grounding non-reflexive human actions in some sense in the material disposition of an organism; by Hobbes, for whom humans acted on will, which was itself necessitated; by Kames, whose work on morality and natural religion was large in the formation of Jefferson's own views on moral activity; or did he stumble on something similar to Kant's moral views in his decades of reflection on moral activity?

We can speedily answer "no" to the last question. His access to Kant was only through secondary literature and there is no evidence that he was aware of Kant's moral views. Had he been aware of them, he certainly would have found them unattractive, given Jefferson's own views that moral "judgments" were sensory and relatively immediate, not rationally grounded. For Jefferson, reason was seldom involved in morality, and when involved, always indirectly and typically harmfully. It aided the moral sense only when doing the right thing might have facinorous consequences: e.g., when pushing too early and too hard to eliminate slavery when the "moral" disposition of the American citizenry was not readied for that event.

We can also quickly rule out Hobbes inasmuch as Jefferson, whose references to Hobbes are few, flatly rejected Hobbes' notion of right and wrong being discretionary. Jefferson writes to Francis Gilmer, (7 June 1816): "I lament to see that he [Destutt de Tracy] will adopt the principle of Hobbes, so humiliating to human nature, that the sense of justice & injustice is not derived from our natural organisation, but founded on convention only. I lament this [all] the more as he is unquestionably the ablest writer living on abstract subjects." In short, Jefferson was doubtless attracted to Hobbes' materialism, but put off by Hobbes' moral conventionalism. For Jefferson, morality is grounded in the physical nature of humans, which is sensory and (roughly) the same for all men.

Next, there is Kames. Though Jefferson was abundantly influenced by Kames on morality, there is no evidence that Jefferson embraced Kamesian determinism. In a letter to nephew Peter Carr (22 June 1792), Jefferson agrees with Carr that "Ld. Kaims ... is too metaphysical." *Pace* Kames, Jefferson likely did not believe that all human actions were determined and that the notion of will, freely choosing, was merely an *ignes fatui*, a will-o'-the-wisp. Jefferson, unfortunately, left no thoughts on freedom of the will, perhaps because it was merely too metaphysical.

Finally, Jefferson there are some nuggets in Jefferson's writings that strongly suggests a commitment to Stoicism. He writes Maria Cosway (12 Oct. 1786) that there is "no rose without it's thorn; no pleasure without alloy. It is the law of our existence; & we must acquiesce." Jefferson writes to John Adams (8 Apr. 1816) about the goodness of the world: "I think … that it is a good world on the whole, that it has been framed on a principle of benevolence, and more pleasure than pain dealt out to us. There are indeed … gloomy and hypochondriac minds, inhabitants of diseased bodies, disgusted with the present, and despairing of the future; always counting that the worst will happen, because it may happen. To these I say How much pain have cost us the evils which have never happened?" To Abigail Adams (11 Jan. 1817), he says: "Perhaps … one of the elements of future felicity is to be a constant and unimpassioned view[er] of what is passing here. … On the whole however, perhaps it is wise and well to be contented with the good things which the master of the feast places before us, and to be thankful for what we have, rather than thoughtful about what we have not." The sentiment is likely drawn from the *Handbook*, where Epictetus writes of a banqueter not reaching out for food, but merely taking food from what is handed to him, when it is handed to him.[43] In 1819, he states to William Short (Oct. 31): "My business is to beguile the wearisomeness of declining life, as I endeavor to do, by the delights of classical reading and mathematical truths, and by consolation of a sound philosophy, equally indifferent to hope and fear." Monticello overseer Edmund Bacon described Jefferson's temperament as Stoical: "His countenance was always mild and pleasant. You never saw it ruffled. No odds what happened [sic], it always maintained the same expression."[44] Those nuggets cleanly express a commitment to acceptance of things that happen to oneself that are beyond one's control, not to acceptance of all things being beyond one's control. Nonetheless, there is nothing that expressly indicates a commitment to Stoic determinism, with its notion of assent somehow being a free capacity of mind, though all behavior being strictly determined.

There is another possibility. Let us take a closer look at A.L.C. Destutt de Tracy's (1754–1836) views on will in his *Elements of Ideology*. Jefferson was handed the translated manuscript which he "carefully revised and corrected," such that the meaning of the French is captured in English and "uniformity of

---

[43] Epictetus, *Handbook*, trans. W.A. Oldfather (Cambridge: Harvard University Press, [1928], 2000), #15.
[44] James A. Bear, Jr., *Jefferson at Monticello: Recollections of a Monticello Slave and of a Monticello Overseer* (Charlottesville: University of Virginia Press, 1967), 71.

style is returned." Jefferson strangely saw the work, titled in French *Éléments d'idéologie,* essentially as one of political economy, which Jefferson titled *A Treatise on Political Economy,* while Tracy saw his work, later expanded to many volumes as a treatise on human willing and its effects. Emmet Kennedy states that for Tracy ideology was "a superscience that would tie political, economic, and social issues together through the universal application of its insights into human behavior."[45] It was, for Tracy, essentially a treatise on will.

Tracy in his *magnum opus* writes that man is a being "*willing* in consequence of his impression and of his knowledge, and *acting* in consequence of his will." Will, he continues, "is really and properly the general and universal faculty of finding one thing preferable to another—the faculty responsible for love or attraction and hate or revulsion. He adds, "We cannot will without a cause, (this is a thing very necessary to be remarked, and never to be forgotten)."[46] Therefore, Tracy's view of willing seems not to be substantially different from Kames', if not identical to it, and is thus unavailing.

Later in his work, Tracy turns to the relationship of will and liberty. Liberty—"the power of executing our will, of acting conformably with our desire"—is birthed from the faculty of willing. Liberty is "the accomplishment of all our desires, the satisfaction of all our wants, and consequently the first of all our goods, that which produces and comprehends them all. It is the same thing as our happiness," at least inasmuch as "our happiness cannot have either more or less extension than our liberty; that is to say than our power of satisfying our desires."[47]

Tracy illustrates this by considering the value of liberty. The "sum of liberty" is "the power of using [a man's] faculties according to his will." Considering liberty as a totality, if some portion is detracted, the value of that portion is equal to the "value of the faculties, from the exercise of which he is debarred." The value of that liberty that remains is, consequently, equal to the "value of the faculties, the use of which he still preserves." Moreover, the loss of all liberty, even for a person of feeble animation, "is the extinction of every possibility of happiness" as well as "the loss of the sum total of his being."[48] Liberty, then, seems to be a power to bring about what we value—what we desire. It actuates will, which seems to be a faculty of pure potency. Yet it can be diminished in its capacity. Tracy's language is consistent with mechanistic materialism and it

---

[45] Emmet Kennedy, *A Philosopher in the Age of Revolution* (Philadelphia: American Philosophical Society, 1978), 45–47.
[46] A.L.C. Destutt de Tracy, *A Treatise on Political Economy,* ed. Thomas Jefferson (Georgetown: Joseph Milligan, 1817), 23–24.
[47] A.L.C. Destutt de Tracy, *A Treatise on Political Economy,* 44.
[48] A.L.C. Destutt de Tracy, *A Treatise on Political Economy,* 46–47.

seems likely that he is no expositor of a will, free in the Kantian sense insofar as it is independent of the material world. Of Tracy's sense of moral agency, Emmet Kennedy writes:

> [Tracy] is not a moral agent in the classic or Christian sense, but rather stresses mechanistic inducements to civic morality. His moral theory is thus both functional and materialistic—functional in that he sees the reproduction of morality as a function of something else like taxes or property arrangements; materialism because he believes human beings do not do so much what they ought, as what they perceive to be in their interests. These interests are for the most part material so that if you want to create industries, for instance, you should make laws against fast speculation, rather than teach the virtue of moderation. This approach to morality presumes that human beings do not have free will and we know from his *Mémoire sur la faculté de penser* that Tracy did not go beyond Locke's famous formulation that the individual will is free to execute his will but not to create it. If individuals do not have free will, exhortation is useless.[49]

In short, will, determined by desire, actuates its "choice" through liberty, which seems to be nothing other than the faculty, somehow "birthed" by will, for doing what is willed. If the choices of will are determined, it follows that what is birthed by will is also determined. So, Tracy's "liberty" amounts to nothing. Therefore, in spite of Jefferson calling Tracy "the most correct metaphysician living"—Jefferson's attraction to Tracy qua metaphysician is because the latter "prostrates the visions of Malebranche, Berkeley, and other skeptics, by resting the question on the single basis of 'We Feel'" (TJ to Francis Eppes, 27 June 1821), that is, he enables us to avoid stultifying skepticism—there is no good reason to believe he thought all that much of Tracy's metaphysical views, if indeed he correctly apprehended them, for as we can see, they seem ferhoodled, confused. To John Adams (14 Oct. 1816), Jefferson writes of later editions of Tracy's work on ideology. "His three 8vo. Volumes on Ideology, which constitute the foundation of what he has since written, I have not entirely read; because I am not fond of reading what is merely abstract, and unapplied immediately to some useful science."

---

[49] Emmet Kennedy, "The Secularism of Destutt de Tracy's 'Ideology,'" https://www.geisteswissenschaften.fu-berlin.de/v/grammaire_generale/Actes_du_colloque/Textes/Kennedy/Emmet_Kennedy.pdf, accessed 14 Oct. 2022.

Upshot

In this chapter, heavily philosophical, I have aimed to expiscate the notion of human progress, articulated in the prior chapter, by expiscation of the notion for Jefferson of the nature of humans. For Jefferson, we are deserving of liberty because we are moral equals—that is, each person has an inborn moral faculty capable of sensing morally correct activity—and to some extent, rational equals.

However, how do we act on what we sense to be correct action?

Rationality and will here have in some sense to come into play, yet Jefferson never anywhere tells us just how they do so. Jefferson could have adopted, to explain how one goes from sensing what is right to acting on what one senses to be right, one of four views with which he was acquainted: Chrysippean Stoicism as well as the views of Hobbes, Kames and Tracy—and one view, Kant's, with which he was unacquainted, but might have anticipated. Yet there is no evidence of Jefferson adopting any of those views. At day's end, Jefferson is content to leave unexplained the matter. It is enough to know that humans have a moral sense and that that sense somehow incites the lion's share of humans' actions. How it materially incites human activity is something beyond human apprehension, and something to be consigned to agnosticism. As he writes to John Adams (14 Mar. 1820) concerning the nodus of how some matter is capable of thought: "when I meet with a proposition beyond finite comprehension, I abandon it as I do a weight which human strength cannot lift: and I think ignorance, in these cases, is truly the softest pillow on which I can lay my head." Yet his answer certainly would be physicalist, perhaps compatibilist. He continues to Admas in the manner of Lockean materialism:

> I ... prefer swallowing one incomprehensibility rather than two. it requires one effort only to admit the single incomprehensibility of matter endowed with thought; and two to believe, 1st that of an existence called Spirit, of which we have neither evidence nor idea, and then 2dly how that spirit which has neither extension nor solidity, can put material organs into motion.

Chapter VI

The Lexical Ambiguity of "Liberty"

In *On Liberty*, one of the most singular works of the nineteenth century, John Stuart Mill takes up the issue of civil liberty: "the nature and limits of the power which can be legitimately exercised by society over the individual." That is not a new issue, he states. It has been extant for millennia. Yet it is become in his day, because of human civil advances, differently cloaked, and thus, requires "a different and more fundamental treatment."[1] The different treatment required is on account of the emergence and implementation of representative government.

Mill begins with "one very simple principle," articulated to regulate "the dealings of society with the individual"—"the sole end for which mankind are warranted, individually or collectively, in interfering with the liberty of action of any of their number." That is "to prevent harm to others." When his actions concern himself, and only himself, "the individual is sovereign"; when his actions concern others, his sovereignty ends.[2] Of his robust account of personal liberty, Mill sums: "Each is the proper guardian of his own health, whether bodily or mental and spiritual. Mankind are greater gainers by suffering each other to live as seems good to themselves than by compelling each to live as seems good to the rest."[3]

Mill does not ground his argument on "abstract right," but on utility—"the ultimate appeal on all ethical questions." This utility, however, must be "grounded on the permanent interests of man as progressive being."[4]

Yet Mill's focus is on civil liberty, not "liberty of the will," which he states is unfortunately often contrasted with "philosophical necessity." Nonetheless, expiscation of civil liberty can only be fully grasped after some account of the slippery concept of liberty of the will.

While Jefferson, like Mill, generally eschewed analysis of conceptions of "liberty" other than civil liberty—philosophical inspection of liberty of will was merely one of those bootless, because metaphysical, enterprises—he did have,

---

[1] John Stuart Mill, *On Liberty*, ed. Elizabeth Rapaport (Indianapolis: Hackett, 1978), 1.
[2] John Stuart Mill, *On Liberty*, 9.
[3] John Stuart Mill, *On Liberty*, 12.
[4] John Stuart Mill, *On Liberty*, 10.

I have elsewhere argued, a rich, multifaceted conception of liberty,[5] which is the aim of this chapter. As with Mill, my focus will be Jefferson's conception of civil liberty.

"The perpetual intestine struggle"
Politics & Liberty

Prior to Mill, the thinkers of the Enlightenment, in setting up liberty in its civil sense as an ideal for human flourishing, were proposing a radical reconceptualization of the concept—for Jefferson, to be of especial service for representative government, a novelty in Enlightenment times. In this section, I take a selective look at Hobbes, Trenchard, Gordon, Hume, and Rousseau on liberty—each an author who was widely read and discussed in Jefferson's day and each of whom had an influence on Jefferson's thinking on the concept.

Thomas Hobbes, whom we have seen in the prior chapter, was a complete mechanist and his mechanism, of course, had implications for his conception of liberty. In its most generic sense, liberty for Hobbes was merely the capacity for a body capable of motion to be unimpeded in that motion. Thus, a chunk of coal, kept from motion to the ground by a human holding it in his hand, can be freed to fall to the earth. It is the same with a human who desires and wills to fight with an antagonist, but he is physically restrained by friends. In a mechanistic universe, humans are not by nature free any more than the chunk of coal is free.

In the state of nature, men, like other animals, are free to do as they please to do, but because of the primitiveness of nature, they therein exist in a state of perpetual war. They escape that uncertain state by voluntarily entering a commonwealth under the rule of a sovereign, whose promise is to provide security for his subjects, to whom they award full powers for that security. Personal freedom humans gladly trade for security.[6]

In the social state, liberty for Hobbes is a seductive, yet dangerous concept—a misappropriation from the lessons of Greek and Roman authors. "It is easy for men to be deceived, by the special name of liberty," says Hobbes. That deception is highlighted by reading Western Greek and Roman writers like Aristotle, who talk of men being free in democracy, and Romans like Cicero, who has been "taught to hate monarchy." Hobbes sums, "And by reading of these Greek, and Latin authors, men from their childhood have gotten a habit, under a false show of liberty, of favouring tumults, and of licentious controlling

---

[5] M. Andrew Holowchak, *Thomas Jefferson: Uncovering his Unique Philosophy and Vision* (Amherst, NY: Prometheus, 2014), Chap. 3.
[6] Thomas Hobbes, *Leviathan*, ed. Michael Oakshott (New York: Macmillan, 1962), 162.

the actions of their sovereign, and again of controlling those controllers; with the effusion of so much blood, as I think I may truly say, there was never any thing so dearly bought, as these western parts have bought the learning of the Greek and Latin tongues."[7]

Though they grant their sovereign relatively unlimited powers and pledge obedience to them, subjects in a commonwealth are still not without certain rights, based on the acknowledged nisus for self-preservation. They have a right to self-preservation: to defend their bodies, even if others lawfully threaten them. They have a right to disobey commands directing a subject to harm, even kill, himself. They have the right to refuse participation in warfare, which must be voluntary, given the right to self-preservation. They have a right to break their covenant with their sovereign, when that sovereign can no longer protect them. Finally, there are other liberties, dictated by "the silence of the law." Says Hobbes, "In cases where the sovereign has prescribed no rule, there the subject hath the liberty to do, or forbear, according to his own discretion.[8] Though by no means a liberal, Hobbs sets the stage for liberalism through acknowledging that the security afforded them in a commonwealth cannot compromise their right to protect their life.

Englander John Trenchard (1662–1723)—who gained fame through co-authorship of *Cato's Letters*, largely read and enormously influential in its day, with much younger friend Thomas Gordon—offers a more expansive conception of liberty than Hobbes. While for Hobbes, liberty is reducible to certain rights appertaining to the preservation of each person's life in a commonwealth, for Trenchard, liberty is that, plus the power of directing his affairs as he sees fit. He writes that all living creatures have implanted in them a love of liberty, which entails the instincts for self-preservation and "of satisfying their desires in the manner which they themselves choose and like best." He says, "By liberty, I understand the power which every man has over his own actions, and his right to enjoy the fruit of his labour, art, and industry, as far as by it he hurts not the society, or any members of it, by taking from any member, or by hindering him from enjoying what he himself enjoys." It is, he adds, "the parent of all the virtues."[9]

Trenchard gives a definition of individual liberty, the power of a man over his own actions, or liberty of will, and also of political liberty, the power to enjoy the fruit of one's labor in a social setting so long as one allows by one's actions the same opportunity for enjoyment for all others. Trenchard adds vis-à-vis

---

[7] Thomas Hobbes, *Leviathan*, 163.
[8] Thomas Hobbes, *Leviathan*, 166–67.
[9] John Trenchard and Thomas Gordon, *Cato's Letters*, ed. Ronald Hamowy (Indianapolis: Liberty Fund, 1995), 427 and 429–30.

civil liberty that government is in the business of protecting the rights of its citizens, not directing their affairs. For Trenchard, liberty is in some sense more fundamental than the particular virtues. It is their "parent."

Thomas Gordon (c. 1691–1750) was an even more zealous advocate of liberty. It was for him not only the parent of the virtues, but it is also the parent of pleasure, plenty, and security. He writes:

> Can we ever over-rate it, or be too jealous of a treasure which includes in it almost all human felicities? Or can we encourage too much those that contend for it, and those that promote it? It is the parent of virtue, pleasure, plenty, and security; and 'tis innocent, as well as lovely. In all contentions between liberty and power, the latter has almost constantly been the aggressor. Liberty, if ever it produce any evils, does also cure them: Its worst effect, licentiousness, never does, and never can, continue long. Anarchy cannot be of much duration: and where 'tis so, it is the child and companion of tyranny; which is not government, but a dissolution of it, as tyrants are the enemies of mankind.[10]

Even though it often gives rise to licentiousness and ochlocracy (mobocracy), liberty stays by the side of anarchy, ever short-lived, and readies itself to succeed it. Gordon's distrust of power is expressed brachylogously and efficiently in a later letter, "No man ought to be trusted with what no man is equal to."[11]

In Letter 63, Gordon continues his paean to liberty in a manner consistent with Trenchard. "All civil virtue and happiness, every moral excellency, all politeness, all good arts and science, are produced by liberty." In contrast, tyranny gives birth to wickedness, baseness, and misery. With liberty established, there is equality of justice for all and just distribution of property. "As rapine is the child of oppression, justice is the offspring of liberty, and her handmaid; it is the guardian of innocence, and the terror of vice; otherwise, like beauty without wealth, she may be praised, but more probably will be calumniated, envied, and very often persecuted; while vice, when it is gainful, like rich deformity and prosperous folly, will be admired and pursued." The sentiment is that liberty needs to be safeguarded by justice, otherwise, its excellence will not be recognized. It is likewise with virtue. Virtue, when marketed to the people as its own reward, will attract few buyers, for "few will buy that for a great price, which will sell for none." Virtue requires endowment; "her credit is best secured by her interest." That interest comprises "publick

---

[10] John Trenchard and Thomas Gordon, *Cato's Letters*, ed. Ronald Hamowy (Indianapolis: Liberty Fund, 1995), 185.
[11] John Trenchard and Thomas Gordon, *Cato's Letters*, 240.

encouragements" and "publick laws."[12] Public encouragements and laws, the former especially, must constantly remind the people concerning how things would be without liberty.

Gordon's praise of liberty is pitched as an encomium.

Consider Letter 23. Though liberty has the effect of licentiousness, which is anarchic, licentiousness, being unstable, quickly degenerates into anarchy, which is not a form of government, but perhaps a species of anti-government. That aids us little, as Gordon states that tyranny is never long-lived, and that, appeal to experience shows, is not the case.

In Letter 63, Gordon ingeminates the notion that liberty births all public goods; its lack, all public evils. Yet as such a fecund mother, it is an invisible mother. The good it ever does ever goes unnoticed. Hence, to secure the numerous benefits of liberty, it needs to be publicly encouraged and legally safeguarded. In this letter, there is no downside to liberty. It is described as an unqualified good, and it is queer that an unqualified good would need to be promoted and peddled.

That strangeness is perhaps not so strange. An analogy is aidful. It is today understood that drinking copious amounts of water while working or playing outdoors on a hot day is essential for health and that when the heat and humidity are dangerously high, it is best to forego outdoor activities. Yet numerous persons each year are hospitalized from heatstroke, due to dehydration. Thus, it is no large disclosure to note that people often know that certain things need to be done, or eschewed, and yet they still fail to do, or eschew, them.

Gordon had a Hobbesian view of human nature, and one that John Adams would later adopt, not a Jeffersonian view. Despite the fickleness of human behavior, Gordonian humans are self-interested, not other-interested. While "government [is] but a trust committed by all, or the most, to one, or a few, who are to attend upon the affairs of all, that every one may, with the more security, attend upon his own," those entrusted with governing often are inclined "to increase their power, than to make it useful." And so, this trust is secured only by "many and strong restraints."[13] The key to public encouragement and good legislation is to promote the golden rule, and to honor and advantage those obeying it, while punishing those disobeying it. Public interest, thus, will become private interest.[14]

Yet if people, due to their propensity for self-advantage, need public and legislative encouragement to promote justice and equity, it is difficult to grasp the

---

[12] John Trenchard and Thomas Gordon, *Cato's Letters*, 435–36.
[13] John Trenchard and Thomas Gordon, *Cato's Letters*, 267.
[14] John Trenchard and Thomas Gordon, *Cato's Letters*, 436.

viability of government by consent of the governed, and Gordon is clear that free countries have magistrates, the prince foremost among them, who "must consult the voice and interest of the people." In that, they essentially differ from "enslaved countries." Elsewhere he writes, "No man ought to be the director of the affairs of all, without their consent."[15] Yet given the posit of human selfishness, who then is to establish the encouragements and laws, aiming at squaring public and private interests? How are we to know that such persons will not be acting toward their own advantage? That nodus is compounded by human foolishness. Humans, it seems, cannot see the beauty of beauty without there also being wealth; cannot grasp the worth of virtue without attendant utility; cannot apprehend the fecundity of liberty without prodding. Being fundamentally foolish, it would seem to be relatively facile for guileful governors to acquire the consent of the governed and then act on behalf of themselves, without the beguiled governed knowing of their governors' guile. In short, if every society is a society of fools, what then is the worth of consent of the governed?

Despite apparent inconsistencies in the sentiments articulated in the letters of Gordon, the corpus of letters by John Trenchard and Thomas Gordon, comprising 144 letters, which began to be published in London in 1619, quickly found a large audience in London and in other British cities, and were collected and published in 1724. They also had a marked influence on the growing hostility of American colonists to their mother country, as they were written for common consumption, and the general public was indifferent to their internal inconsistencies. Clinton Rossiter writes that it was Trenchard and Gordon, not Locke, who had the largest influence on the budding liberalism of Colonial America[16]—a weighty claim that might be true, because of the relative inaccessibility of Locke's writings by most Colonists and the relative accessibility of *Cato's Letters*. There is no evidence that *Cato's Letters* had any direct influence on Jefferson, but it is impossible to think that the widely dispersed sentiments from the writings in the colonies did not often reach Jefferson's ears.

The Scottish philosopher and historian David Hume (1711–1776) offers perhaps the most nuanced account of liberty and government in his day. The end of government, says Hume succinctly, is "the distribution of justice." For there to be justice, equity must be grounded on allegiance, which as a form of obedience, must become habitual. Every government, thus, is "the perpetual intestine struggle, open or secret, between Authority and Liberty," and justice is served only when there are concessions to each. "A great sacrifice of liberty must necessarily be made in every government; yet even the authority, which

---

[15] John Trenchard and Thomas Gordon, *Cato's Letters*, 272 and 439.
[16] Clinton Rossiter, *Seedtime of the Republic* (New York: Harcourt, Brace and Company, 1953), 141.

confines liberty, can never, and perhaps ought never, in any constitution, to become quite entire and uncontroulable."[17]

Governments, though of three sorts (monarchic, aristocratic, and democratic, and here he follows Aristotle), are either free or absolute. The ancients, Hume says, note that the arts and sciences arose and flourished in free nations. It is the same with the arts and sciences in modern Italy and France.[18] Moreover, commerce seems to flourish in free governments.[19] Still, Hume thinks, while free government is the "proper Nursery" of the arts and sciences, a civilized monarchy is most favorable to the growth of the "polite [fine] arts,"[20] appreciated in and of themselves.

Hume expiscates the key flaws of "absolute governments" and "free governments." While absolute governments depend critically on the administration put into place, free governments depend critically on the "checks and controuls" of the constitution. Both rely much on skill and honesty.[21]

Preference for one or the other is generally dictated by political partisanship—whether one is a Whig or a Tory. "A Tory ... [is] *a lover of monarchy, though without abandoning liberty; and a partisan of the family of* Stuart." In contrast, "a Whig may be defined to be *a lover of liberty though without renouncing monarchy; and a friend to the settlement in the* Protestant *line.*"[22]

For Hume and against the virtue-ethics line of thought from antiquity, it is not good people who make for good governing, but good laws. Governments founded on good laws keep in line the "humours and tempers of men" so that "consequences almost as general and certain may sometimes be deduced from them, as any which the mathematical sciences afford us." It follows that one part of a republic may be wisely governed, while another, poorly, by the same governors, if they are regulated differently.[23]

---

[17] David Hume, "Of the Origin of Government," in *Essays: Moral, Political, and Literary* (Indianapolis: Liberty Fund, 1987), 37–40.
[18] He elsewhere adds that only in free governments can there be birthed the arts and sciences. David Hume, "On the Rise and Progress of the Arts and Sciences," in *Essays: Moral, Political, and Literary* (Indianapolis: Liberty Fund, 1987), 115.
[19] David Hume, "Of Civil Liberty," in *Essays: Moral, Political, and Literary* (Indianapolis: Liberty Fund, 1987), 89–94.
[20] David Hume, "On the Rise and Progress of the Arts and Sciences," 124.
[21] David Hume, "That Politics May Be Reduced to a Science," in *Essays: Moral, Political, and Literary* (Indianapolis: Liberty Fund, 1987), 15–16.
[22] David Hume, "Of the Parties of Great Britain," in *Essays: Moral, Political, and Literary* (Indianapolis: Liberty Fund, 1987), 71.
[23] David Hume, "That Politics May Be Reduced to a Science," 16 and 24.

Yet Hume merely proffers his observations. He has no preference for free governments over absolute governments, or the converse. Both have undergone in modern times "a great change for the better." Monarchies, "that are a government of Laws, not of Men," Hume concedes, "seem to have made the greatest advances towards perfection." Nonetheless, monarchies are still inferior "in gentleness and stability." He observes that popular governments seem to be degenerating, while monarchical governments seem to be improving, such that time will bring the two "nearer in equality." Democracies seem too freely to be "contracting debt, and mortgaging the public revenues," so that the nation's properties might eventually fall into the hands of the public. In contrast, an absolute prince can become bankrupt, but that bankruptcy can never suffocate the people. Unless popular governments curb public spending, they will be reduced "by the multiplicity of taxes" or impotency apropos of defense. In that case, the people will "curse our very liberty" and wish for the servitude of the nations around England.[24]

For Hume, there are advantages and disadvantages of absolute and free governments. His preference for the former might exist merely on account of their relative fiscal stability.

I finally offer Rousseau's view of liberty, which was commonly known and discussed in Jefferson's day and highly influential. French philosopher Jean-Jacques Rousseau (1712–1778) writes "Discourse on the Origin of Inequality" in 1754. In it, he writes of civil liberty, "Liberty is like those solid and tasty foods or those full-bodied wines which are appropriate for nourishing and strengthening robust constitutions that are used to them, but which overpower, ruin and intoxicate the weak and delicate who are not suited to them."[25] Through study of man, we have become "incapable of knowing him."[26]

Rousseau begins by disambiguation of "inequality" and "equality." One is natural and physical; the other, moral or political. He aims to analyze that juncture where nature became subject to law.[27]

In the state of nature, humans, neither as strong as others nor as lissome as others, are nevertheless "the most advantageously organized of all."[28] He is, in that state, free. Once domesticated, a man becomes a slave: "weak, fearful, and

---

[24] David Hume, "Of Civil Liberty," in *Essays: Moral, Political, and Literary* (Indianapolis: Liberty Fund, 1987), 94–96.
[25] Jean-Jacques Rousseau, "Letter to the Republic of Geneva," in *Basic Political Writings of Jean-Jacques Rousseau,* trans. Donald A. Cress (Indianapolis: Hackett, 1987), 27
[26] Jean-Jacques Rousseau, "Discourse on the Origin of Inequality," in *Basic Political Writings of Jean-Jacques Rousseau,* trans. Donald A. Cress (Indianapolis: Hackett, 1987), 33.
[27] Jean-Jacques Rousseau, "Discourse on the Origin of Inequality," 38.
[28] Jean-Jacques Rousseau, "Discourse on the Origin of Inequality," 40.

servile" and "soft and effeminate."²⁹ He cultivates reason to compensate for his unhappy state, the result, *pace* Hobbes, of "the need to satisfy a multitude of passions which are the product of society and have made laws necessary." In society, he is introduced to thralldom. "It is impossible to enslave a man without having first put him in the position of being incapable of doing without another." They know no virtue because they are ignorant of vice. "I ask if anyone has ever heard tell of a savage who was living in liberty ever dreaming of complaining about his life and killing himself."³⁰

The fall of man began with the first act of civil liberty. "The first person who, having enclosed a plot of land, took it into his head to say *this is mine* and found people simple enough to believe him, was the true founder of civil society." Then there began crimes, wars, and murders. That usurper forgot that "the fruits of the earth belong to all and the earth to no one." With liberty lost, there began the softening of man. With liberty lost, the imperceptible natural inequalities among men become perceptible and "more permanent in their effects."³¹

In *On the Social Contract,* published in 1762, Rousseau begins famously, "Man is born free, and everywhere he is in chains."³² The aim is a more refined look at the notion of socialization as augmentation of human inequality. The work, unlike his "Discourse," is not dystopian.

The axial problem for Rousseau in a social setting is this: to find an association that "defends and protects" the person and goods of each associate so that each associate can form a bond with all others while he remains as free as he was in the state of nature. With each giving himself to all, to the general will, the association is for all equal. Since the association is for all equal, there is no motivation for any to exploit another. Harm to another is harm to the whole. Refusal to obey the general will must lead to coercion to follow it, hence, "[man] will be forced to be free."³³

Rousseau here disambiguates "natural liberty" and "civil liberty." The former is limited by the force of the individual; the latter is limited by the general will. In nature, a person has possession by force or right; in society, a person has proprietary ownership based only on positive title to allow him all that he needs. Sovereignty for Rousseau is merely exercise of the general will and that

---

[29] Jean-Jacques Rousseau, "Discourse on the Origin of Inequality," 43.
[30] Jean-Jacques Rousseau, "Discourse on the Origin of Inequality," 52–53 and 59.
[31] Jean-Jacques Rousseau, "Discourse on the Origin of Inequality," 60 and 67.
[32] Jean-Jacques Rousseau, "On the Social Contract," in *Basic Political Writings of Jean-Jacques Rousseau,* trans. Donald A. Cress (Indianapolis: Hackett, 1987), 141.
[33] Jean-Jacques Rousseau, "On the Social Contract," 148–50.

is inalienable and indivisible. Yet in the civil state, each has moral liberty, which is obedience to the civil will and which curbs appetite. Moral liberty is thus a substitution: Natural liberty is supplanted with moral liberty.[34]

To get clearer on the notion of general will, which "is always right and always tends toward the public utility," there is the will of all, which is not always right and publicly useful. General will comprises merely the general interest, while the will of all is merely the sum of private wills. One can get at the general will through the will of all, in effect, by elimination of the fringe views—"the pluses and minuses that cancel each other out"—and what remains will be the general will. To prevent corruption of the general will, there cannot be "partial associations"—what we today call special-interest groups. Each must think for himself, otherwise the populace can be easily buffaloed.[35]

It follows that in the civil state, "natural independence is exchanged for liberty; the power to harm others is exchanged for their own security; and their force, which others could overcome, [is exchanged] for a right which the social union renders invincible."[36]

In nature, all men have common liberty or independence, and no one is master over another. In civil society, all men have civil liberty, inasmuch as all persons follow the general will, insofar as natural liberty is surrendered, and moral liberty is adopted.

Consequently, slavery for Rousseau is absurd and unjust. "These words, *slavery* and *right*, are contradictory. They are mutually exclusive. Whether it is the statement of one man to another man, or one man to a people, the following sort of talk will always be equally nonsensical. *I make a convention with you which is wholly at your expense and wholly to my advantage; and, for as long as it please, me, I will observe it and so will you*"[37]—a sentiment with which Jefferson certainly agreed.

Rousseau's two works were widely read, and his "Social Contract" is today one of the largest political works in human history. The tension he addresses is that of Hobbes: Why should I obey, and if so, whom? His solution, contractarian, is that one finds civil liberty in surrendering to the general will. Howsoever nuanced are Rousseau's views, and Jefferson was certainly familiar with them, Jefferson's own views were not in any direct sense influenced by them.

---

[34] Jean-Jacques Rousseau, "On the Social Contract," 151–54.
[35] Jean-Jacques Rousseau, "On the Social Contract," 155–56.
[36] Jean-Jacques Rousseau, "On the Social Contract," 158.
[37] Jean-Jacques Rousseau, "On the Social Contract," 146–47.

"Under the law of nature, all men are free"
Jefferson on "Liberty"

The prior section is given to show the polysemy of "liberty" in Enlightenment times. Irrespective of its polysemy and independent of its philosophical use in the etiology of human activity, liberty of will, civil liberty has become one of the most prominent topics of politicians and political philosophers.

What did Jefferson mean by "liberty"? We have touched on that topic in the last chapter. It is time for expiscation.

Jefferson means by "liberty" is a matter of considerable debate among scholars. The discussion is ever limited to understanding civil liberty.[38]

Bernard Bailyn says that Jefferson saw "sensible, hard-working, independent folk secure in their possession of land, free of the corruptions of urban poverty and cynicism, free of dependence on a self-indulgent aristocracy of birth, responsible to the common good as well as to personal betterment, educated in the essentials of free government and committed to the principles of freedom—peaceful, self-reliant, self-respecting, and unintimidated people."[39] Civil liberty, in a climate of equality of opportunity, unyoked individuals' potentials.

Merrill Peterson says that liberty for Jefferson concerned private power—a code of restraint on sovereignty, exercised by a few or many, in order to maximize individuals' self-sufficiency. "He was the first to see that strength, the progress, even the splendor, of the nation might come, not from the consolidation of loyalties, not from the vastness of governing power, but from the release of its myriad individual talents and energies."[40]

Civil liberty, J.W. Cooke states, required a milieu congenial to human thriving. "Jefferson ... sought to create an atmosphere congenial to liberty by stressing the need to consider all relevant circumstances—population density, geography, the level of literacy, experience in self-government, virtue, and the

---

[38] I follow and expand on the account I give in another book, M. Andrew Holowchak, *Thomas Jefferson: Uncovering his Unique Philosophy and Vision* (Amherst, NY: Prometheus, 2014), Chap. 3

[39] Bernard Bailyn, "Jefferson and the Ambiguities of Freedom," in *Proceedings of the American Philosophical Society*, Vol. 137, No. 4, 1993: 502–3.

[40] Merrill Peterson, "Thomas Jefferson and the National Purpose," in *Proceedings of the American Philosophical Society*, Vol. 105, No. 4, 1961: 517–20.

like—in determining the type of government best suited for Americans."[41] The sentiment smacks of political relativism.

Robert Faulkner says that Jeffersonian liberty is rational and seeks what is useful. It is not spontaneous, but planned, and it serves to engender useful power—i.e., the rights to life, liberty, and happiness. It uncages ingenuity by finding beneficial expression of human passions. It disencumbers persons from fear of death and useless desires.[42]

Gordon Wood proffers an account of Jeffersonian liberty as "enlightened conventional radicalism, ... so eager was he to possess the latest and most liberal of eighteenth century [sic] ideas that he could easily get carried away." Wood's Jefferson is a radical who saw the American Revolution as the harbinger of a global movement to "burst the chains ... of monkish ignorance and superstition" in his lifelong effort "to promote the spread of freedom and democracy throughout the world."[43]

Forest McDonald dubs Jefferson the "apostle of abstract liberty," and adds, "whatever that elusive word may mean." Jefferson, McDonald says, "never wrote a systematic treatise on the subject, and he never thought it through as a concept." Jefferson's political philosophy, "or rather his mytho-historical conception of the ideal life that served him as a substitute for a philosophy," was patterned according to his manner of living. His thinking was Bolingbrokean.[44]

All those scholars capture something of the essence of Jefferson on civil liberty. Yet there is still polysemy. Bailyn and Peterson write of liberty of will and civil liberty; Cooke writes of what is today called positive liberty; Faulkner adds that liberty must be aided by rationality to serve useful ends; and Wood cashes out Jeffersonian liberty as a personal investment in an ideology that guided him throughout life. This sampling shows some confusion due to failure to distinguish different Jeffersonian conceptions of liberty. In what follows, I aim for riddance of that confusion through disambiguation of "liberty" for Jefferson.

Liberty for Jefferson is not a simple, but a complex, concept. One can, I think, tease out at least four senses of liberty for Jefferson, two of which make up civil

---

[41] J.W. Cooke, "Jefferson on Liberty," in *Journal of the History of Ideas*, Vol. 34, No. 4, 1973, 574–75.

[42] Robert Faulkner, "Jefferson and the Enlightened Science of Liberty," in *Reason and Republicanism*, ed. Gary L. McDowell and Sharon L. Noble (Lanham, MD: Rowman & Littlefield, 1997), 31–52.

[43] Gordon Wood, *Revolutionary Characters: What Made the Founders Different* (New York: Penguin, 2006), 110.

[44] Forest McDonald, *The Presidency of Thomas Jefferson* (Lawrence, KS: University of Kansas Press, 1976), 31–32 and 53.

or political liberty and two of which, voluntary liberty or liberty of will. Because for Jefferson the political is grounded in the moral, I begin with personal liberty.

Personal liberty or voluntary liberty (liberty of will) is the freedom to make and act on choices. It presupposes that humans are in some sense free-choosing organisms that can deliberate on possible courses of action and decide among them. This notion, called by Jefferson personal liberty, finds full expression in Jefferson's defense of slave Samuel Howell in April 1770 in the case of Howell v. Netherland. Jefferson states in defense of Howell's freedom: "Under the law of nature, all men are born free, every one comes into the world with a right to his own person, which includes the liberty of moving and using it at his own will. This is what is called personal liberty, and is given him by the author of nature, because necessary for his own sustenance."[45] Jefferson here maintains that Howell, though of black blood, has the same right "to his own person" as all other men, and here Jefferson echoes a sentiment that he will express, though the sentiment will be excised by the Congress, in his first draft of his Declaration of Independence on the unrighteousness of slavery. Voluntary liberty exists both in the state of nature and in civil society.

As I have noted in the prior chapter, Jefferson nowhere ever comes clean on how will generates human action, as do compatibilist thinkers such as Hobbes and Kames, for he is loathe to speculate on metaphysics, "a region of fog."[46] To grandson Francis Wayles Eppes (27 June 1821)—we saw this letter in the prior chapter—Jefferson rails against metaphysics. "To pursue the science further is following a will-of-the-wisp, and a very useless waste of time, much better given to sciences more palpable, and more useful in the business of life."

Personal liberty, of course, requires some amount of knowledge to assist in making meaningful, useful choices. Thus, education and purposeful life experiences are needed. However, it is not government's job to promote purposeful life experiences, only to allow for their possibility. For that, a government must promote general and higher education.

As a species of personal or voluntary liberty, there are for Jefferson *moral liberty*, which might be in the interim grasped as a capacity to "sense" or "feel" right action as right action and act on it because of that, and *amoral liberty*, which might be grasped as a capacity to engage in actions without moral implications—adiaphorous actions. Thus, personal liberty can be broken into

---

[45] For more on the case and on Jefferson's willingness to defend slaves' efforts at emancipation without compensation, see M. Andrew Holowchak, *The Cavernous Mind of Thomas Jefferson, an American Savant* (Newcastle upon Tyne: Cambridge Scholars, 2019), chap. 1.
[46] TJ to John Pickering, 27 Oct. 1825

moral actions and adiaphorous actions, which are mutually exclusive and mutually exhaustive of personal liberty.

Adiaphorous actions are those actions that have no moral implications. The engagements of science—e.g., squaring the circle, tracing the orbit of a comet, or investigating the arch of greatest strength or the solid of least resistance, as Jefferson says in his Head-and-Heart letter to Maria Cosway (12 Oct. 1786)—are not moral activities, but strictly affairs of reason, though they certainly might have moral implications in unique circumstances. Boondoggling or loafing—e.g., counting the number of limes on a tree or the number of freckles on a face to pass the time—is also not a moral action so long as one is not boondoggling to eschew moral action.

Yet most human actions are moral actions for Jefferson, for almost all, if not all, human actions have moral consequences. From his 1786 letter to Cosway, Jefferson's decision to bypass a "poor weathered soldier," who pleads to be taken up on Jefferson's coach at Chickahomony is, he admits, a moral failing—a judgment of reason against the moral sense. His purchase of the Louisiana territories and work on the University of Virginia are, for him, moral accomplishments.

For Jefferson, as noted earlier, discernment of correct moral action is in the main, independent of reason. Rationality and moral sensibility are separate faculties. "When nature assigned us the same habitation, she gave us over it a divided empire," Jefferson says in the same letter to Cosway. "[Reason or Head was] allotted the field of science; [Heart or the moral sense] that of morals." Discernment of morally correct action is visceral and immediate, not ratiocinative.

By *civil liberty* for Jefferson, let us understand the sorts of liberties granted by political institutions and grounded in human rights—for Jefferson, rooted in nature. Under that category and following the useful lead of philosopher Isaiah Berlin, we have negative liberty and positive liberty—each of which Jefferson acknowledged to be operable.[47]

First, there is what is today commonly called *negative liberty* or liberal atomism—the capacity to live as one wants to live, without the intervention of others, especially of the state. This is the sense to which Jefferson refers most often when he uses "liberty." Jefferson writes to Monsieur de Meusnier (29 Apr. 1795) that he is "a warm zealot for the attainment & enjoiment by all mankind of as much liberty, as each may exercise without injury to the equal liberty of his fellow citizens."

---

[47] Isaiah Berlin, "Two Concepts of Liberty," in *Four Essays on Liberty* (Oxford, Oxford University Press, 1969), 118–72.

For there to be a civil state, there must be government. For there to be government, some citizens must sacrifice their own well-being for the well-being of the state. In a civil state where all are considered equals, each must give equally of his time to participate in governmental affairs. In sum, for each to be promised time to himself, each must participate to some extent in governing. In short, the guarantee of governmental non-interference requires some amount of political participation, for governors too want time to do as they please. What citizens do when they are not politically involved neither concerns the state nor concerns anyone else, so long as their actions bring no discernible harm to others. That entails freedom to choose one's own path in life and one's own religion and freedom of conscience and speech.[48]

The surest way of preventing government from interfering in the lives of its citizens is to disempower it—to allow it to have only such powers as it needs as a federative entity. The most fundamental powers of the federative government are foreign affairs and protection of citizens' rights. For Jefferson, a government at any level is generally acting justly when it is least visible. With assumption of powers it does not constitutionally have, it becomes toxic and the citizens suffer. The antitoxin for the corruptions of strong, centralized government is weak, demassified government in the hands, and under the watchful eye, of the citizenry. Yet even with demassification and watchfulness, there is still the possibility of governmental corruption, so Jefferson ever advocates rotation in governmental offices, especially the presidency, and periodic constitutional renewal.

The second sort of civil liberty for Jefferson is what today is called *positive liberty*, which in some measure acts as a complement to negative liberty. That entails some degree of governmental involvement in helping its citizens to choose the lives they wish to pursue. To Dutch minister and patriot Francis Adrian Van der Kemp (22 Mar. 1812), Jefferson states, "The only orthodox object of the institution of government is to secure the greatest degree of happiness possible to the general mass of those associated under it." For that, negative liberty is not sufficient. A woman who enters a market only to find that it sells nothing but dragon fruit and desiccated puffin meat is not really free to choose, for though she is free to choose, there are too few options from which to choose. And so, it is not sufficient for happiness that one is left alone to do as one pleases. There must be options from which one can choose to do as one pleases. It is, for Jefferson, in some measure the task of government to secure citizens' happiness through allowing the creation of social settings in which citizens can thrive. I offer illustrations.

---

[48] TJ to Samuel Smith, 22 Aug. 1798 and TJ George Washington, 9 Sept. 1792.

In his 1776 Draft Constitution for Virginia, Jefferson proposes that every male citizen of full age and either without property or owning property in deficiency of 50 acres will be given property to bring them to 50 acres.[49] Ten years later, Jefferson asks James Monroe (July 9), "How may the territories of the union be disposed of so as to produce the greatest degree of happiness to their inhabitants?" The suggestion here is that cities, towns, and land in general ought to be zonated in a manner best suited to promote human thriving. In his Sixth Annual Message as president, Jefferson speaks of a surplus of governmental revenue and suggests spending that money on internal improvements such as public education, roads, rivers, canals and "such other objects of public improvement as it may be thought proper to add to the constitutional enumeration of federal powers." The aim is "new channels of [interstate] communication" so that "lines of separation will disappear, [states'] interests will be identified, and their union cemented by new and indissoluble ties." Jefferson here is writing about lines of communication between the several states to facilitate economic ties and amicable intercourse as well as, without doubt, improved communication for trade with Natives.

In short, the government must sometimes intrude upon citizens' affairs through certain mild "interventions" to allow for full expression of humans' capacities, and thereby allow for the possibility of human thriving. Like Plato in *Republic*, it is not the function of a thriving republic to guarantee the happiness of all persons in it, but the greatest amount of total happiness of those in it. For Jefferson, however, it is only the task of government to allow for the possibility of human thriving—i.e., the pursuit of human happiness—not for happiness itself.

Upshot

No concept has been more discussed in Jeffersonian scholarship than "liberty," because of Jefferson's fixation on the concept. That comes as no surprise. Liberty was the flagship notion of Enlightenment thinkers in Europe and America.

Yet there is still considerable confusion among today's scholars concerning the meaning of "liberty" for Jefferson. While all note that Jefferson's concern was ever with civic liberty, there has been little agreement about just what Jefferson meant by "civic liberty" and how it subserved human thriving, human happiness. That subservience, I show, is a philosophical, not a political, matter—hence, historians' reluctance to penetrate too deeply on this matter.

Jefferson, I say in the introduction, was not merely a political philosopher who much utilized "liberty." He also unflinchingly believed in the improvement

---

[49] Thomas Jefferson, Draft Constitution for Virginia, in *The Scholars' Thomas Jefferson*, ed. M. Andrew Holowchak (Newcastle upon Tyne: Cambridge Scholars, 2021), 16–26.

of the human condition to a medial ideal: all countries across the globe, at some distant time, being Jeffersonian republics, being relatively agrarian and self-sufficient, and being engaged in peaceful commerce of essential surplus goods with other nations.

The inevitability of that movement is best explained metaphysically: Jefferson's hypostatization of "liberty": He makes it a thing. Liberty for Jefferson is a sort of cosmic driving force, like gravity, that invisibly drives humans to a state of moral, and political, perfection, though awareness of that force can help humans to expedite that process. The force of liberty enables them to leave their independence in their small tribal societies and enter large republican societies, where liberty of the civic sort predominates, where rationality can be put in service of enhanced knowledge of the cosmos, and where there will be few retardations of benevolent actions. The movement of humans throughout history is the story, thus, of the slow unfolding of liberty as humans advance from independency in tribal hordes toward the stability of large, echeloned republics with the aim of human happiness.

Part III
Liberty as Pandemic

Chapter VII

Jefferson on the American Revolution

In an extraordinarily long missive Jefferson writes to son-in-law John Wayles Eppes (6 Nov. 1813), who has earlier in 1813 been elected to the Thirteenth U.S. Congress, on the subjects of paper money and a national bank, Jefferson discretionarily slips in the sentiment, "If ever there was a holy war, it was that which saved our liberties and gave us independence." Study of the context of the statement about the "holy war" shows plainly that it adds nothing to what preceded or followed it. It merely chanced to be something that entered Jefferson's mind that needed to find expression through his quill. Jefferson pens letters that day also to Thomas Law, John Barnes, and Wilson Cary Nicholas, but there is nothing in those letters about "liberty" or the "American Revolution," so it is unclear why Jefferson finds need of slipping in the notion that the American Revolution was a holy war. Yet he does, and that the sentiment was prompted by nothing ascertainable is singular. It is also noteworthy that he never elsewhere uses that metaphor, parturient in meaning. It is, thus, a singular, but significant remark, and it is the reason for crafting this undertaking.

"Holy war" implies war fought at the injunction of deity or for a great religious reason. That discretionary epithet speaks loudly on behalf of Jefferson's deepest thoughts on the matchlessness of the American Revolution. It was, for him, a singular event in global history, and one, we shall see, not fought by Americans just for Americans, for by Americans for mankind. It was a revolution fought on behalf of the notions of human freedom and human equality.

In this chapter, I flesh out the American Revolution from Jefferson's perspective. Why were Colonists goaded into revolution? Was Jefferson's view of "revolution" different from others' views? Why did Jefferson consider republicanism as an experiment? By gleaning answers to those, and other, questions, I also descant on the notion of the American Revolution as a "holy war"—a concept, I admit, which was the motivation for this book.

"The lamp of experience"
The Prize of Liberty

Two of the driving concepts of the Enlightenment were equality, covered in the penultimate chapter, and liberty, covered in the prior chapter. The two were inseparable, and much ink was used in writings which praised both, especially liberty.

The most significant spokesperson for liberty in encouragement of the American Revolution was arguably Patrick Henry (1736–1799). Henry's fiery speeches on behalf of the perceived injustices on behalf of the crown did more than any other Patriot to encourage revolution.

Members of Second Virginia Convention met on March 20, 1775, in what is today St. John's Church in Richmond, to discuss a possible plan of defense of Virginia by a soon-to-be-raised militia. At that convention, Patrick Henry, perhaps the Revolution's most perlocutionary figure, gave an agitable speech on behalf of forming a militia in readiness for British aggression.

Henry's speech, "captured" by William Wirt, is by many considered to be an oratorical classic. Henry begins conciliatory, but quickly dismisses formal procedure. "This is no time for ceremony." The predicament is prodigious: "a question of freedom or slavery." He adds, "Should I keep back my opinions at such a time, through fear of giving offence, I should consider myself as guilty of treason towards my country, and of an act of disloyalty toward the majesty of heaven, which I revere above all earthly kings."[1]

Appealing to "the lamp of experience," Henry acknowledges that the British response to Colonists' petitions has been "the implements of war and subjugation." Moreover, what is "this accumulation of navies and armies"? Henry has a ready answer. He asseverates, "They are sent over to bind and rivet upon us those chains which the British ministry have been so long forging."[2]

What then is to be done to unshackle Colonists from those despotic chains?

Henry continues. "We have done everything that could be done, to avert the storm which is now coming on. We have petitioned; we have remonstrated; we have supplicated; we have prostrated ourselves before the throne, and have implored its interposition to arrest the tyrannical hands of the ministry and Parliament." Yet everything that has been done has led to nothing of consequence. "Our petitions have been slighted; our remonstrances have produced additional violence and insult; our supplications have been disregarded; and we have been spurned, with contempt, from the foot of the throne. In vain, after these things, may we indulge the fond hope of peace and reconciliation."[3]

The Colonists, for Henry, were left in a condition of hopelessness. If they wished to have freedom and "to enjoy the inestimable privileges for which we

---

[1] William Wirt, *Sketches of the Life and Character of Patrick Henry* (Philadelphia, 1836), 92.
[2] William Wirt, *Sketches*, 93.
[3] William Wirt, *Sketches*, 93.

have been so long contending," then there was nothing left to do but fight. "We must fight! I repeat it, sir, we must fight! An appeal to arms and to the God of Hosts is all that is left us!" Henry sums: "Is life so dear, or peace so sweet, as to be purchased at the price of chains and slavery? Forbid it, Almighty God! I know not what course others may take; but as for me, give me liberty or give me death!"[4] That final sentiment, though certainly a fabrication by Wirt, is one of the most popular quotes from an American patriot in defense of the American Revolution. The security of life and the sweetness of peace without liberty are not worth having without freedom.

Henry was noted in his day for his large presence and masterly elocution. The problem is that his biographer, William Wirt, was born in 1772. Wirt was three years of age at the time of Henry's speech and did not undertake Henry's biography until 1808, and Henry died in 1799. Hence, Wirt was dependent on whatever documents he could find as well as the testimonies of persons, like Thomas Jefferson, who had personally known Henry. Wirt and Jefferson had a lengthy correspondence on Henry, and Jefferson was so dissatisfied with the result of Wirt's efforts that he eventually kept the book in his library under "Fiction." After many polite words on Wirt's finished product, Jefferson sums thus to Wirt (12 Nov. 1816) the latter's approach to history, "You have certainly practised rigorously the precept of 'de mortuis nil nisi bonum.'[5] this presents a very difficult question, whether one only, or both sides of the medal should be presented. it constitutes perhaps the distinction between panegyric and history." There is nothing in subsequent letters to show that Wirt grasped that Jefferson's comments were a paternalistic dig.

Despite that Wirt's account of the life of Patrick Henry was more panegyric than history—today's historians confirm that assessment—what is beyond question is that Henry was one of the foremost "fire-starters" of the American Revolution and one of the greatest Colonial champions of liberty. Though his orations were not paradigms of mastery of logic, they were stirring. It just might be the case that there would not have been a revolution without Patrick Henry.

Because Jefferson was not known for his oratorical skills, his medium was his pen, and so he had to make cogently his points with quill on paper. Because of the authorship of documents like Summary View of the Rights of British America and Declaration of Independence, he became, arguably, the most ardent global spokesman for liberty in his day. Even his zealous interest in science was for the sake of promotion of human liberty. "I endeavor to keep their attention fixed on the main objects of all science, the freedom and

---

[4] William Wirt, Sketches, 94–95.
[5] "Only say good things about the dead."

happiness of man"[6]—freedom ever conjoined with happiness, and liberty not autotelic, but ever in the service of human happiness, of human thriving.

Nevertheless, Jefferson was no cavalier spokesman for liberty. He was aware that liberty was not a plant that acclimates itself to any sort of climate. He writes to Marquis de Lafayette (2 Apr. 1790), "So far it seemed that your revolution had got along with a steady pace; meeting indeed occasional difficulties & dangers, but we are not to expect to be translated from despotism to liberty in a featherbed." Five years later, he says, "Being myself a warm zealot for the attainment & enjoyment by all mankind of as much liberty, as each may exercise without injury to the equal liberty of his fellow citizens, I have lamented that in France the endeavours to obtain this should have been attended with the effusion of so much blood."[7] To Dr. Benjamin Rush (22 Sept. 1809), Jefferson writes of the failure of the French Revolution.

> What is practicable must often control what is pure theory, and the habits of the governed determine in a great degree what is practicable. Hence the same original principles, modified in practice according to the different habits of different nations, present governments of very different aspects. The same principles reduced to forms of practice accommodated to our habits, and put into forms accommodated to the habits of the French nation would present governments very unlike each other. I have no doubt that a great man, thoroughly knowing the habits of France, might so accommodate to them the principles of free governments, as to enable them to live free. But in the hands of those who have not this *coup d'oeil* many unsuccessful experiments I fear are yet to be tried before they will settle down in freedom and tranquillity.

The key nodus is that liberty can only flourish in scientific soil, conditioned by a gentle climate where all are treated equally. Liberty, he tells Tench Coxe (1 June 1795), needs enlightened people, "for light & liberty go together." He adds that popular enlightenment is inevasible. Jefferson continues to Coxe, "This ball of liberty, once put into motion … will roll round the globe. It is our glory that we first put it into motion, & our happiness that being foremost we had no bad examples to follow." To Governor David Hall (6 July 1802), Jefferson notes that republican governors "have no interests nor passions different from those of our fellow citizens"—that is, governors are *primus inter pares* or stewards of their representatives. All wish for the success of

---

[6] TJ to Thaddeus Kosciusko, 26 Feb. 1810.
[7] TJ to Comte de Meusnier, 29 Apr. 1795.

representative government.[8] "Nor are we acting for ourselves alone, but for the whole human race."[9] Jefferson, thus, has the immodest goal of global revolution in the name of liberty. The essential event has been the American Revolution.

"Laws and institutions must go hand in hand…"
The Plaguy Problem of Political Relativism

What is "revolution" for Jefferson? The question is not idle, for being committed to human progress in morality and intelligence, no revolution, for Jefferson, ought to be undertaken without considerable thought about the defects of the government against which one is revolting and about the new government one wishes to implement. That leads to a singular issue, for though unbendingly committed to human progress, Jefferson often paints his prose in language consistent with political relativism—the notion that there is no one right political system, as systems need to accommodate regional differences, such as climate, land, and the customs and habits of people.[10]

Richard Matthews argues that the right to revolution, for Jefferson, guaranteed that each generation could draw up for itself its own constitution and its own form of government.[11] Being free, humans, it seems, are more desiderative than rational. Dumas Malone states that Jefferson shared the "thought habits of his age but tended and in fact had to be a relativist in practice,"[12] and adds in his last biographical volume, "There can be no doubt about [Jefferson's] adherence to [political relativism]." The context concerns the years of Jefferson's life after returning to the states from France.[13] Henry May says that Jefferson was a historical relativist when it came to all things other than humans' rights. "His belief in unalienable, natural rights may have sat a bit uneasily with his historical relativism: rights endure but everything else

---

[8] In the words of John Gordon, "*maior singulis, omnibus minor*," or "superior to each individual citizen, inferior to the whole."
[9] Cicero in *On Duties* writes, "We are born not for ourselves alone, but … as humans, we are born for humans." Cicero, *De Officiis* (Cambridge: Harvard University Press, 2001), I.22.
[10] My early thoughts on this topic can be found in the following. M. Andrew Holowchak, *Jefferson's Political Philosophy and the Metaphysics of Utopia* (London: Brill, 2017), 37–39.
[11] Richard K. Matthews, "The Radical Political Philosophy of Thomas Jefferson: An Essay in Retrieval," in *Midwest Studies in Philosophy*, Vol. 28, No. 1, 2004, 48.
[12] Dumas Malone, *Jefferson the President* (Boston: Little, Brown & Company, 1970), 31.
[13] Dumas Malone, *Jefferson & His Time, Volume 6: The Sage of Monticello* (Charlottesville, VA: University of Virginia Press, 1981), 138.

must change."[14] Political relativism too is the view of Gilbert Chinard[15] and Julian Boyd.[16] Finally, it is likely that Caleb Perry Patterson paints Jefferson in broad relativist brushstrokes when he says that "Jefferson is one of the few founding fathers on record with a theory of change as one of his constitutional principles."[17] For Patterson, political change is the political constant.

Political relativism fits with Jefferson's commitments to the right to revolution and periodic constitutional renewal. Jefferson is clear that the chief function of a federative government is to protect the rights of the citizens. Jefferson is clear that citizens have a right to choose their constitution. Jefferson is clear that a federative government that consistently does not protect the rights of its citizenry can rightfully be overthrown. Once overthrown, the citizens can craft a government of their choosing. Those principles are often taken as evidence of a commitment to political relativism in the manner of Montesquieu, where constitutions are fitted to particular peoples and there are no better or worse constitutions, or at least the best constitutions are they that best fit their citizenry.

In his widely read *Spirit of the Laws* (1748), Montesquieu lists three types of government—republican (best for small territories), monarchical (best for moderate territories), and tyrannical (needed for large territories)—but no best form of government. Governments are fitted to meet the needs of a people, and the needs of a people, due to differences in geography and climate and culture in each nation, are unique. Thus, it is pointless for one nation to critique the constitution of another, as each has often radically different needs, wants, and aims.

Montesquieu writes, "Different nations ought in time of peace to do one another all the good they can, and in time of war as little harm as possible." Those are two laws of nations. There is also "politic law," which controls the "particular forces of individuals," for each nation particularly considered. The political and civil laws of a nation "should be adapted in such a manner to the people for whom they are made, … should be relative to the nature and principle of the actual, or intended government, … [and] should be relative to the climate of each country, to the quality of the soil, to its situation and extent, to the manner of living of the natives, … should have a relation to the degree of liberty which the constitution will bear; to the religion of the inhabitants, to

---

[14] Henry F. May, "The Enlightenment," in *Thomas Jefferson: A Reference Biography*, ed. Merrill D. Peterson (New York: Charles Scribner's Sons, 1986), 52.
[15] Gilbert Chinard, *Thomas Jefferson: The Apostle of Americanism* (Ann Arbor, MI: The University of Michigan Press, [1929] 1962), 132–35.
[16] Julian P. Boyd, "Thomas Jefferson and the Police State," in *The North Carolina Historical Review*, No. 25, Vo. 2, 1948, 234.
[17] Caleb Perry Patterson, *The Constitutional Principles of Thomas Jefferson* (Gloucester, MA: Peter Smith, 1953), viii.

their inclinations, riches, number, commerce, manners, and customs." Thus, they will not be the same for any two nations.[18]

Republican government, Montesquieu asserts, can be democratic or aristocratic. Democratic republics are founded on virtue[19] and require "the whole power of education" to make the people recognize the subordination of private to public interest.[20] They are best only in small territories. In large expanses of land, they will not long survive, for in a large republic, there will be many men of large fortunes, each of whom might wish to use his wealth to oppress his fellow citizens to his own advantage. Moreover, the "public good is sacrificed to a thousand views. … In a small one, the interest of the public is easier perceived, better understood, and more within the reach of every citizen."[21]

If Jefferson was a political relativist, then revolution (as well as constitutional renewal) makes sense only when a constitution is alien to the needs of the citizens.

Ascription of political relativism to Jefferson fits him into a Montesquieuian frame, in which there are not better or worse constitutions, but where constitutions are fitted merely to particular peoples, like jackets to persons. There can be no one right sort of jacket for all persons.

There is an incommodious difficulty for depiction of Jefferson as a political relativist: Jefferson's dyed-in-the-wool commitment to human progress. Progress inescapably implies movement to some end, considered better than the current state of affairs. If humans are advancing in morality and intelligence, then constitutions must change, and advance, with them. As Jefferson states in a letter to Samuel Kercheval (12 July 1816): "Laws and institutions must go hand in hand with the progress of the human mind. As that becomes more developed, more enlightened, as new discoveries are made, new truths disclosed, and manners and opinions change with the change of circumstances, institutions must advance also, and keep pace with the times. We might as well require a man to wear still the coat which fitted him when a boy, as civilized society to remain ever under the regimen of their barbarous ancestors." Yet political relativism is inconsistent with human progress.

Another problem with painting Jefferson as a political relativist is popular consent. Jefferson did not believe that constitutions ought to be upheld with sanctimonious reverence. As people advanced in intelligence and moral sensibility, constitutions needed to be revised to accommodate those advances, hence there is political advance too. If we dismiss the notion of

---

[18] Montesquieu, *The Spirit of Laws*, 3rd ed., trans. Thomas Nugent (London, 1758), 8–9.
[19] Montesquieu, *The Spirit of Laws*, 28.
[20] Montesquieu, *The Spirit of Laws*, 48–49.
[21] Montesquieu, *The Spirit of Laws*, 175.

political progress, there is no reason to believe in intellectual or moral progress. We return to a Gordonian or Humean depiction of humans as wanting, not rational, beings, which political relativism best accommodates. If humans are driven by desires, not reason—in the words of Hume, if humans are the "slaves of passions"—then popular consent upon constitutional renewal would seem bootless, a matter of ceremony, not need.

Those problems are telling and argue against the sort of political relativism that Matthews and Malone maintain Jefferson advocated. Then again, there are in Jefferson's corpus numerous passages, like that of the 1809 letter to Rush of the prior section, that poignantly point in the direction of political relativism. How to we escape the quandary?

There are harmful and harmless forms of political relativism. Harmful relativism is subjective. *Subjective political relativism* implies that all constitutions are relative to geography, climate, and culture. Yet it also implies that there are no ideal (or nearly so) natural and cultural conditions suited to human thriving. Anything goes. Harmless relativism, *objective political relativism*, also implies that all constitutions are relative to geography, climate, and culture. Yet it concedes that there are natural and cultural conditions, ideal (or nearly so) for human thriving. Jefferson was of the latter sort, hence relativistic comments are reconcilable with progressivist claims. The axial principles of Jeffersonian republicanism—minified federal government, periodic constitutional renewal, participation of all citizens in governmental affairs, inasmuch as abilities and circumstances allow, *inter alia*—are articulated with an eye to actualizing the ideals, liberal, of human existence by putting into place a schema that allows all people everywhere to thrive to some extent, independent of circumstances. The difficulty is that most humans have been acclimated for centuries to anything but liberal ideals.

And so, when a people, clamoring for the ideals of liberalism, are forcibly kept from them by a government whose governors tend to their own interests, they have a right, even a civic duty, to revolt. Thus, disavowing harmful political relativism, revolution makes sense only when the governors of a people consistently violate the rights of all or some part of its citizenry. It follows that a revolution for Jefferson ought never to be arbitrary. It is the same with constitutional renewal. Both subserve the aims of an above-board Jefferson-liberal government.

"They are not qualified … to think and provide by themselves"
Outline of a Jeffersonian Revolution

"Revolution" is substantially different from "rebellion" for Jefferson. To William Stevens Smith (13 Nov. 1787), Jefferson writes concerning the worth of rebellions in a thriving republican government: "The tree of liberty must be refreshed from time to time with the blood of patriots and tyrants. It is it's natural manure." Manure is needed for healthy governing because those governing will tend to govern in their own interests if not carefully watched. Moreover, those governed will assume mistakenly that rights once granted will be rights always granted. Rebellion is the mechanism whereby those governing are periodically reminded that government in a Jeffersonian republic is of and for the people.[22] Revolution in contrast is an attempt to overthrow a government.[23]

Right to revolution is an important corollary of Jefferson's republican axioms. We saw earlier that in his Declaration of Independence, Jefferson begins with articulation of the rights of life, liberty, and pursuit of happiness and immediately adds, "Whenever any form of government becomes destructive of these ends, it is the right of the people to alter or abolish it, & to institute new government," forged to secure the happiness and safety of the citizenry. He continues by elaborating on two principles that justify revolution. "When a long train of abuses and usurpations, pursuing invariably the same Object evinces a design to reduce them [the people] under absolute Despotism, it is their right, it is their duty, to throw off such Government, and to provide new Guards for their future security."[24] That Jefferson couches the right to revolution in the consequent of a conditional (if-then) statement shows that it is a conditional, not an unconditional, right. There is no right to revolution unless there is governmental corruption. Moreover, the abuses and usurpations must be long and consistently symptomatic of despotic purpose. Thus, no revolution ought ever to be undertaken for slight reasons or because of singular cases of governmental abuse. Such are often the causes of rebellions, not revolutions.

---

[22] Mirkin does not distinguish between rebellion and revolution, but only between "two levels of revolt": populist rebellions and elitist threats of rebellion. The former, exemplified by Shays' and the Whiskey Rebellion, were local and presumably non-moral issues. The latter, exemplified by the Kentucky and Virginia Resolutions, were larger, morality-grounded issues. His distinction is, I believe, ungrounded. Shays' and the Whiskey Rebellion were morality-grounded as were the two resolutions. The difference is one of scope, size, and persistency. Rebellions are generally quick and often violent signals to government concerning abuses. Revolutions are long-term and usually violent attempts at overthrowing a government, deemed habitually abusive. Harris G. Mirkin, "Rebellion, Revolution, and the Constitution: Thomas Jefferson's Theory of Civil Disobedience," in *American Studies*, Vol. 13, No. 2, 1972: 64–65.
[23] Following my account in this essay. M. Andrew Holowchak, "Jefferson on Rebellion, Revolution, and Treason," *Journal of the American Revolution*, https://allthingsliberty.com/2022/05/acts-against-the-oppressions-of-the-government-jefferson-on-rebellion-revolution-and-treason/, accessed 20 Nov. 2023.
[24] Thomas Jefferson, Declaration of Independence, in *Thomas Jefferson: Writings*, ed. Merrill D. Peterson (New York: Library of America, 984), 19.

Revolution for Jefferson is a multipart phenomenon: There are generational responsibilities. To John Adams (4 Sept. 1823), Jefferson writes of the inchoation, sustainment, and resolution of revolutions. "The generation which commences a revolution can rarely compleat it. Habituated from their infancy to passive submission of body and mind to their kings and priests, they are not qualified, when called on, to think and provide for themselves, and their inexperience, their ignorance and bigotry make them instruments often, in the hands of the Bonapartes and Iturbides to defeat their own rights and purposes." So, no revolutions can be expected to establish with the first effort a sustainable, free government. Moreover, the revolutionary generation is generally suited to begin and sustain the revolution, but not to resolve it. It is, for Jefferson, incapable of fixing a viable republican constitution. Thus, the demolishers of the old constitution are not fit agents for crafting a new constitution.

Different generations involved in the revolution at different phases have different responsibilities for a Jeffersonian revolution to succeed. The role of the first generation is inchoation. Succeeding generations must sustain and complete the initial effort to usurp the coercive government. In the final phase, there is implementation of a constitution, reflective of the will of the people. Furthermore, it is incumbent on each successive generation, once an apposite constitution is in place, periodically to alter it in keeping with advances in knowledge and changes in the will of the majority.[25] Those changes, thinks Jefferson, will not be wholly discretionary, but in the main in pursuance of the advances of science and of the moral improvement over time of the citizenry.

Consequently, a Jeffersonian revolution is never rash. Generated by the indignancy of injustice, it is sustained by that indignancy, and it aims at the just implementation of a government reflective of the will of the people. Yet its success, like success at war, requires systemic planning. Precipitancy leads to failure.

A Jeffersonian revolution is always last resort. It is also well-planned and tardigrade. "Jefferson saw that when you have discounted the reaction which revolution always provokes," says T.V. Smith, "the long way of gradualism through compromise is ordinarily a shorter path to progress than any short cut of revolution." He sums, Jefferson's philosophy of means—gradualism by majority rule through the strategy of compromise—reduced 'the perfectibility of mankind' to a faith in the snail-like pace of evolution."[26]

---

[25] TJ to Marquis de Chastellux, 7 June 1785.
[26] T.V. Smith, "Thomas Jefferson and the Perfectibility of Mankind," in *Ethics*, Vol. 53, No. 4, 1943, 304.

When Jefferson defends the French Revolution in a letter to William Short (3 Jan. 1793), he writes of the dead—the guilty and the innocent—as ones who have "fallen in battle." He adds, "Time and truth will rescue & embalm their memories, while their posterity will be enjoying that very liberty for which they would never have hesitated to offer up their lives. The liberty of the whole earth was depending on the issue of the contest, and was ever such a prize won with so little innocent blood?" One can castigate Jefferson for indifference to the numerous thousands of lives lost in the struggle, but when one considers the rewards of liberty for the numerous millions of people in subsequent generations— e.g., real living through freedom from governmental encroachment, equality of opportunity, freedom of religion, free of speech and of presses, and general education for all—then the cost is insubstantial. The patriots lost in such a revolution will have given their life for human betterment.

Jefferson concedes that there are lumbering difficulties in start, sustenance, and success of a revolution. Yet he thinks that the reward of a successful revolution, if motivated by release from long abusive government, is ever worth the sanguinary effort. One may have some degree of security with coercive government, but a life without liberty is not worth having. Thus, a revolution is justifiable, when government has taken it upon itself to decide how the citizenry ought to live, and rebellions are necessary from time to time to remind governors that they are stewards of the people, not lords over them.

There is a sense of the sublime in Jefferson's account, but one might remonstrate that his theory of revolutions is misguided, even delusional, because it, focusing on the rational or theoretical aspects of a revolution, turns a blind eye to the role of human passions in a revolution. It effectively describes an ideal revolution, begun and sustained by real injustices, but not actual revolutions, in which passions overwhelm reason. Jefferson's many letters where he sweeps away the thousands killed in the French Revolution and his comments concerning Shays' Rebellion are evidence of that.

"The experiment has not yet had a long enough course"
Republicanism as an Experiment

Jefferson is clear in his Declaration of Independence that no revolution ought to occur for "light & transient causes."[27] Moreover, there must be beforehand an acknowledged goal of a revolution. Revolutions are sanguinary events and loss of life can only be warranted when the government which supplants the

---

[27] Thomas Jefferson, Declaration of Independence, in *The Scholars' Thomas Jefferson*, ed. M. Andrew Holowchak (Newcastle upon Tyne: Cambridge Scholars, 2021), 26.

prior government is a decided improvement upon the prior. As a dyed-in-the-wool empiricist, Jefferson was wont, like others of his day, to dub republicanism as an "experiment."[28] There was no guarantee that government of and for the people would work; Jefferson only knew that aristocracies—which ever tended to favor those "best," the wellborn and the wealthy—worked only for the sake of those best. That is why his reasoning was often eliminative:

1) There can be in place a republican government or an aristocracy.
2) Aristocracy typically exploits the many for the advantage of the "best."
3) Republicanism, though untried, promises to answer to the will of the majority of citizens, so long as that will is not exploitative and "reasonable."[29]
4) So, republicanism is the only viable alternative to aristocracy.

This argument, given skeletally, is no guarantee that republicanism will work—it might be that there are defects with both forms of government—but merely an invitation for it to be tried, hence Jefferson's frequent use of "experiment."[30] In the words of eminent historian Forest McDonald, "Republican theory was wondrous potent as an ideology of opposition. It remained to be seen whether it was a sound basis for administration."[31]

That argument comes out neatly in a letter, during Jefferson's presidency, to Abigail Adams (11 Sept. 1804). Republicans and Federalists aim at the public good, but they disagree about what that entails. "One fears most the ignorance of the people; the other, the selfishness of rulers independent of them. Which is right, time and experience will prove." Jefferson then adds: "One side of this experiment has been long enough tried, and proved not to promote the good of the many; & that the other has not been fairly and sufficiently tried."

For many of Jefferson's fellow revolutionists, the experiment merely involved doing what England was doing, but doing that without the corruption—*viz.*, with full respect for the rights of the citizenry and without a king.

---

[28] E.g., TJ to Abigail Adams, 11 Sept. 1804; TJ to Thomas Seymour, 11 Feb. 1807; and TJ to William Duane, 13 Nov. 1810.
[29] Thomas Jefferson, First Inaugural Address, in *The Scholars' Thomas Jefferson*, ed. M. Andrew Holowchak (Newcastle upon Tyne: Cambridge Scholars, 2021), 56.
[30] See M. Andrew Holowchak, *Dutiful Correspondent: Philosophical Essays on Thomas Jefferson* (Lanham, MD: Rowman & Littlefield, 213), chap. 1.
[31] Forest McDonald, *The Presidency of Thomas Jefferson* (Lawrence, KS: University of Kansas Press, 1976), 27.

For Jefferson, the experiment was moral and to a lesser extent rational. He ever thought that all people had full moral sensitivity and sufficient rationality to govern themselves through elected representatives, who, chosen for their virtue and genius, were to govern in pursuance of the will of their constituency. In 1788, Jefferson tells Angelica Schuyler Church (Feb. 17) that republicanism is "a new creation … because it is made on an improved plan." To George Mason (4 Feb. 1791), Jefferson states that "our experiment will still prove that men can be governed by reason," and by that he means the good judgment of the citizens, for the governors are mere stewards of the people. To John Adams (28 Feb. 1796), just prior to Adams assuming the first office of the U.S. government, Jefferson adds honesty to the mix and adds, "If ever the morals of a people could be made the basis of their own government, it is our case."[32] Honesty, of course, implies truth. "No experiment can be more interesting than that we are now trying, and which we trust will end in establishing the fact, that man may be governed by reason and truth. Our first object should therefore be, to leave open to him all the avenues to truth. The most effectual hitherto found, is the freedom of the press."[33] Free presses might be vehicles of misinformation and falsehoods, but no administration that conducts itself with integrity and common understanding" can be destroyed by a licentious press. "This experiment [will] demonstrate the falsehood of the pretext that freedom of the press is incompatible with orderly government."[34] Republicanism, consequently, for Jefferson is an experiment concerning the good moral judgment of the people and their possession of sufficiency of reason to conduct their own affairs and to oversee their governors.

In a letter to Joseph Priestley (19 June 1802), Jefferson speaks of republicanism as a system with machine-like consistency implicit in the passage.

> In the great work which has been effected in America, no individual has a right to take any great share to himself. Our people in a body are wise, because they are under the unrestrained and unperverted operation of their own understandings. Those whom they have assigned to the direction of their affairs, have stood with a pretty even front. If any one of them was withdrawn, many others entirely equal, have been ready to fill his place with as good abilities. A nation, composed of such materials, and free in all it's members from distressing wants, furnishes hopeful implements for the interesting experiment of self-government.

---

[32] See also TJ to Harry Innes, 23 Jan. 1800; TJ to A.L.C. Destutt de Tracy, 26 Jan. 1811; TJ to Isaac Tiffany, 26 Aug. 1816; and TJ to James Madison, 24 Dec. 1824.
[33] TJ to Judge John Tyler, 28 June 1804.
[34] TJ to Thomas Seymour, 11 Feb. 1807.

With mechanization occurring in many facets of human living, the metaphor of machine was commonly used. Thomas Hobbes' explanation of human behavior was wholly mechanistic. Here note how Jefferson speaks of able-bodied political representatives as if they were replaceable cogs in a machine.

There was for Jefferson the issue of government at the various levels: wards, counties, states, and the country. The largest problem concerned the federative and states' governments not overstepping by assuming powers that they ought not to assume. He writes to Archibald Stuart (23 Dec. 1791): "Tho' the experiment has not yet had a long enough course to shew us from which quarter encroachments are most to be feared, yet it is easy to foresee from the nature of things that the encroachments of the state governments will tend to an excess of liberty which will correct itself (as in the late instance) while those of the general government will tend to monarchy, which will fortify itself from day to day, instead of working its own cure, as all experience shews." Of the two evils—too much liberty and movement toward monocracy, the former is preferable. "I would rather be exposed to the inconveniences attending too much liberty than those attending too small a degree of it." And so, it is crucial to "strengthen the state governments" so that the federal government will not be tempted to assume powers not expressly delegated to it.

Jefferson proposes to Stuart the following federal changes: Lessen the number of representatives to 100 and lengthen their tenure; alter the method of appointing senators[35]; improve the desirability of the executive by making it "more independant of the legislature" by having him "be chosen by other electors, for a longer time, and ineligible for ever after"; and give the judiciary "firm tenure in office" and an equitable salary, while their number to ensure riddance of fecklessness. "This branch of the government will have the weight of the conflict on their hands, because they will be the last appeal of reason."

By his Second Inaugural Address, Jefferson claims brashly that the experiment of a government—"conducting itself in the true spirit of its constitution, with zeal and purity, and doing no act which it would be unwilling the whole world should witness, can be written down by falsehood and defamation"—has succeeded.

> The experiment has been tried; you have witnessed the scene; our fellow citizens have looked on, cool and collected; they saw the latent source from which these outrages proceeded; they gathered around their public functionaries, and when the constitution called them to the

---

[35] Article I, Section III, of the Constitution states: "The Senate of the United States shall be composed of two Senators from each state, chosen by the legislature thereof for six Years." That would be changed to direct election of senators by the people of each state in 1913 with the 17th Amendment.

decision by suffrage, they pronounced their verdict, honorable to those who had served them, and consolatory to the friend of man, who believes he may be intrusted with his own affairs.[36]

The success to which he refers concerns his easy reelection—a sign of the citizenry's confidence in Jeffersonian republicanism.

Jefferson's avowal of the success of the republican experiment, so boldly asserted in 1805, would later be rescinded. To Francis Adrian Van der Kemp (22 Mar. 1812), Jefferson writes that the object of good, healthy government is to secure the "greatest degree of happiness possible to the general mass of those associated under it." For that to happen, the people must have sufficient control over "those intrusted with the powers of their government," otherwise "these will be perverted to their own oppression, and to the perpetuation of wealth and power in the individuals and their families selected for the trust."[37] He sums, "Whether our Constitution has hit on the exact degree of control necessary, is yet under experiment." Jefferson here seems to have lost his faith in the goodness of the people, for it seems that just about anyone elected to an office of governance will shift from citizenry-interest to self-interest.

There is also Jefferson's atypical skepticism in Query XVII of *Notes on the State of Virginia*. He asks, "Is the spirit of the people an infallible, a permanent reliance? Is it government?" The spirit and the will may alter. The rulers, even the people, over time will become corrupt. "The time for fixing every essential right on a legal basis is while our rulers are honest, and ourselves united." With the Revolutionary War remote from the minds of the people, rights too will be remote from the minds of the people. "They will forget themselves, but in the sole faculty of making money, and will never think of uniting to effect a due respect for their rights."[38]

---

[36] Thomas Jefferson, Second Inaugural Address, in *The Scholars' Thomas Jefferson*, ed. M. Andrew Holowchak (Newcastle upon Tyne: Cambridge Scholars, 2021), 62.
[37] There is also the problem mentioned by John Gordon of public corruption through public emulation of corrupt, self-interested governors. "Public men are the patterns of private; and the virtues and vices of the governors become quickly the virtues and vices of the governed." John Trenchard and Thomas Gordon, *Cato's Letters*, ed. Ronald Hamowy (Indianapolis: Liberty Fund, 1995), 269.
[38] Thomas Jefferson, *Notes on the State of Virginia*, ed. William Peden (Chapel Hill: University of North Carolina Press, 1954), 161.

"Our fellow subjects in America…"

A Revolution for the Sake of Liberty

It is far too frequently presumed by Americans and scholars of American history that the Founding Fathers, in inciting their revolution with England, knew precisely what they were doing. We have only to consider their painstaking deliberations in the Continental Congress prior to deciding on war with England. Jefferson's Summary View of the Rights of British America proffers numerous reasons for revolution. So too does his Declaration of Independence. We find those, and other, reasons iterated in the writings, speeches, and even cabals of George Washington, Patrick Henry, Benjamin Franklin, John Hancock, George Wythe, Alexander Hamilton, George Mason, John Adams, Samuel Chase, William Floyd, Richard Henry Lee, Caesar Rodney, and even Thomas Paine.

Just what occurred in the initial sessions of the Continental Congress is unclear, but what is clear is that the representatives agreed that King George and England's Parliament were to be apprised of the Colonists' grievances. There was also discussion concerning how the individual colonies, which had hitherto functioned independently, could put up a united front against England to bargain—the problem of confederation. Yet those deliberations—we have no first-hand account of what went on in the Congress—eventually morphed into discussion about whether, or not, to begin a war with Britain, when fighting began early in 1775 with the Battles of Lexington and Concord.

Why was there a revolution?

One answer is that the constant stream of immigrants from Europe, England especially and just prior to the revolution, made inevitable, or at least probable, the revolution. Colonial America was early on a melting pot for the unwanted: as I have noted, prostitutes, urchins, prisoners, the penurious, Scots, Welsh, and Irish, *inter alii*. The danger of the trip itself was incentive for any of the daring to eschew the risks. Yet over time, the perception for many was that the possible rewards were worth any risks. Writes Sir Thomas Miller to Henry Howard Suffolk, "In this part of the Kingdom transportation to America begins to lose every characteristic of punishment." Persons with skills were beginning increasingly to begin life anew in the New World. England was beginning to lose some of "the most usefull of [its] people."[39]

---

[39] Miller to Suffolk, 25 Oct. 1773, in Bernard Bailyn, *Voyagers to the West: A Passage in the Peopling of America on the Eve of the Revolution* (New York: Alfred A. Knopf, 1986), 25.

With the throng of not merely desperate, but increasingly useful, people to the New World and with its relatively limitless resources, Colonial America would soon rival and then exceed the mother country. The *London Chronicle* reports in 1773: "Every sensible person must foresee that our fellow subjects in America will, in less than half a century, form a state much more numerous and powerful than their mother-country. At this time, were they inclined to throw off their dependency, it would be very difficult for this kingdom to keep them in subjection." The author imagines America in 50 years, when their number will have trebled from procreation without consideration of the increase from mass immigration.[40] The argument in gist is in this rhetorical question: Why would a satellite state, which has become much more powerful than its mother country and which is situated a good distance from it, not seek independence from it? Continued dependence would mean advantaging the mother country to the detriment of the much stronger satellite state.

Gordon Wood in *The Radicalism of the American Revolution* writes: "There was little evidence of those social distinctions we often associate with revolution. ... [There was] no mass poverty, no seething social discontent, no grinding oppression."[41] Americans were relatively prosperous and everyone was, in some sense, a commoner. Whatever distinctions that were between families and individuals were those of wealth, and though the wealthy in the 1700s were separating themselves from the non-wealthy, that was not a cause of anxiety. There was a general sense that any situation could be reversed: the wealthy could suffer a fall and the indigent could improve their situation through planning and toil.

There were no classes in Colonial America as there were in Europe. In Europe, because one was penurious, one worked; because one worked, one was penurious. Yet in Colonial America, there was belief that work could lead to prosperity and a change of circumstances.

Though there were no classes in Colonial America, there were two sorts of persons: dependents (servants or slaves) and independents. An independent was a person whose will and property were his own; a dependent, whose will and property were not his own. John Adams sums in an address to the colonists of Massachusetts-Bay. "There are but two sorts of men in the world, freemen and slaves. The very definition of a freeman, is one who is bound by no law to

---

[40] *London Chronicle*, 19 July 1773, in Bernard Bailyn, *Voyagers to the West*, 42
[41] Gordon Wood, *The Radicalism of the American Revolution* (New York: Vintage Books, 1991), 169.

which he has not consented." Should Americans be unable to give or withhold to the acts of the British parliament, they would be slaves, not freemen.[42]

The condition, adds Adams, is even worse. In England, both electors and elected have been softened by luxury, effeminacy, and venality. Both electors and elected are become "one mass of corruption." Debt and taxes are large due to "extravagance, and want of wisdom." To submit to subjection under such circumstances is not only submission to slavery, but also to "the most abject sort of slaves to the worst sort of masters."[43] The implication seems to be that it is the worst form of subjugation for thrifty, manly, and honest persons to submit to the extravagant, womanly, and dishonest.

Colonial Americans had, since colonizing the continent, been developing a strong sense of manly independence over the many decades. They had, of course, been first sent to North America without the patronage of the British government. They were "adventures"—in general, outcasts—sponsored by Virginia Company in 1607, with the goals of finding a route to the Orient, discovering gold, exporting raw goods, and even converting natives to Christianity.[44]

Except for the presence of Native Americans, the land was pure wilderness, and the experience of such a mass of wilderness would have been overwhelming to a European, situated lifelong, for instance, in or near a large city like London or Paris. It was a new world, the New World, and to one in possession of industry, patience, and imagination, there was no limit to the uses to which the land could be put.

Ownership of land was proprietary more than functional. It was not so much what one could do with a parcel of land to turn a profit—though owning land and failure to work it was pointless—but instead it was just that one owned land that *could* be put to use. One's identity was in large part determined by the land one owned, and that rang true especially throughout the South long after the American Revolution.

Colonial America, in short, was a place where a person without a name could make a name through industry and perseverance. Jefferson's father, Peter Jefferson (1707–1757), was just such a self-made man. From unassuming parentage, Peter was not formally educated—"my father's education had been quite neglected," says Thomas Jefferson in his *Autobiography*—but did much

---

[42] John Adams, "To the Inhabitants of the Colony of Massachusetts-Bay, 30 January 1775," *Founders Online*, National Archives, https://founders.archives.gov/documents/Adams/06-02-02-0072-00030, accessed 2 Jun 2022

[43] John Adams, "To the Inhabitants of the Colony of Massachusetts-Bay, 30 January 1775."

[44] William M. Kelso, *Jamestown: The Truth Revealed* (Charlottesville: University of Virginia Press, 2017), 1–2.

to improve himself. With strong mind, sound judgment and eager after information," Peter Jefferson read much and was chosen by Joshua Fry, professor of mathematics at College of William and Mary, to delineate with him the boundary between Virginia and North Carolina. With Fry, he made the first detailed map of Virginia.[45] Peter Jefferson would become a justice of the peace in Goochland County, sheriff, county surveyor, and member of House of Burgesses. He married Jane Randolph (1721–1776), daughter of neighbor Isham Randolph, a prominent Virginian and member of the Planter Aristocracy of Virginia. The Randolphs were of the gentry of Scotland and England. Peter would acquire some 7,200 acres of land over his life. His Piedmont property in Albemarle County would be called Shadwell.

The charter of Virginia Company would be revoked, "by a mixture of law and force," says Jefferson in Query XIII of *Notes on the State of Virginia*, and the land came under the yoke of King James in 1624, without Virginia Company receiving any recompense for their gross expenditure.[46] By March 1651, Commissioners Richard Bennett, William Claiborne, and Edmond Curtis signed 16 articles "agreed on & concluded at James Cittie in Virginia for the surrendering and settling of that plantation under the obedience & government of the common wealth of England." The first article stated that the people of Jamestown were declared subjects of the "Comon wealth of England," and that that subjection is acknowledged to be "a voluntary act not forced nor constrained by a conquest upon the country, and that they shall have & enjoy such freedoms and priviledges as belong to the free borne people of England." The Eighth Article states: "That Virginia shall be free from all taxes, customs & impositions whatsoever, & none to be imposed on them with out consent of the Grand assembly, And soe that neither ffortes nor castles bee erected or garrisons maintained without their consent."[47] As William Peden notes, the three commissioners were appointed by Cromwell for the sake of "reducing of Virginia and the inhabitants thereof to their due obedience to the commonwealth of England."[48]

Jefferson continues in Query XIII. Colonists assumed that they could participate in free trade, would be exempt from taxes not "of their own assembly," and would be excluded from British military force.[49]

---

[45] Thomas Jefferson, *Autobiography*, in *Thomas Jefferson: Writings*, ed. Merrill D. Peterson (New York: Library of America, 1984), 3–4.
[46] Thomas Jefferson, *Notes on the State of Virginia*, ed. William Peden (Chapel Hill: University of North Carolina Press, 1954), 113.
[47] Thomas Jefferson, *Notes on Virginia*, 114–16.
[48] Thomas Jefferson, *Notes on Virginia*, 283n4.
[49] Thomas Jefferson, *Notes on Virginia*, 116.

None of those promises were kept, however. Jefferson sums abuses in the first 15 years of the reign of George III.

> The colonies were taxed internally and externally; their essential interests sacrificed to individuals in Great-Britain; their legislatures suspended; charters annulled; trials by juries taken away; their persons subjected to transportation across the Atlantic, and to trial before foreign judicatories; their supplications for redress thought beneath answer; themselves published as cowards in the councils of their mother country and courts of Europe; armed troops sent among them to enforce submission to these violences; and actual hostilities commenced against them.[50]

The abuses were consistent and without remorse. Colonists were fronted with "unconditional submission" or "resistance," and they chose the latter.

The American Revolution was the revolution of the Enlightenment, which was a revolution against authority. The authorities targeted were chiefly Aristotle and the Church. There were new political, ethical/religious, and of course intellectual dimensions—the last of which I have covered fully in a prior chapter. Political ideals comprised governmental representatives by popular consent, human rights, institutionalization of liberty and equality, freedom of religion, and installation of governmental checks and balances, among other things. The most significant ethical/religious ideal was secularism. "Failure of religious doctrines concerning God and the afterlife to establish a stable foundation for ethics" turned many toward secular, naturalistic systems and deism. Along the same lines, many religions were naturalized insofar as enthusiasm, supernaturalism, and ecstasy were expunged.[51]

That is why Jefferson considered the American Revolution as a holy war. All Patriots in some sense grasped that the American Revolution was a holy war, as it was a revolution unlike any other in human history. It was a revolution about what Latin moralists called *honestum*—moral worth. Fought on behalf of human liberty, it was an expression that human "destiny" was not fatally determined by God, as the Calvinists asserted, or by the law-governed movement of bodies in the universe, as Pierre-Simon Laplace asserted in *Méchanique céleste*, but determined by the thoughts and actions of individual

---

[50] Thomas Jefferson, *Notes on Virginia*, 117–18.
[51] William Bristow, "Enlightenment," in *The Stanford Encyclopedia of Philosophy* (Fall 2017 Edition), ed. Edward N. Zalta, https://plato.stanford.edu/entries/enlightenment/, accessed 4 June 2022.

human beings. Humans were organisms unique and, in the words of Thomas Jefferson in his last letter, not "born with saddles on their backs."[52]

"De te fabula narratur"
Improvement on the British Model?

The Patriots seemed sure that their reasons for revolution were warranted, and beginning the revolution, because it required unanimity of all 13 colonies, was not easy. Yet sustaining the fever for revolution was also difficult. So, it was too with winning the war on its behalf.

Nonetheless, unanimity, though challenging, was had, and though soldierly men, munitions, and other supplies were scant, there was enough to sustain the fever for fighting, and the war, with the invaluable aid of the French, was won.

Yet perhaps the most difficult part of the process was construction of a new government, superior to the British government, which many Patriots—Hamilton, Adams, and even Jefferson among them—acknowledged was the best constitution in the world's history. With the war won, one can readily grasp that many Patriots sincerely asked: We have earned our freedom, but how do we write it into a constitution, much superior to that of England?

Here we return to Jefferson's 1823 letter to John Adams on the stages and generational responsibilities of a revolution. The generation that begins and sustains a revolution, he thinks, is not fit to conclude it: *viz.*, create a constitution reflecting the general will of the people. It is one thing to recognize and react to injustices by measuring the fast pulse of the angry people. Yet when the anger is abated and the pulse has returned to normalcy, there must be reflection on the causes of the injustices that feed the anger and the constitutional remedy for those injustices.

Here we return to Wood's concerns about the provenance of the American Revolution. Colonists were not kept from work, starved, or executed. They were merely governed by the British, but without the rights of British citizens—that is, treated as less than British. That is what in Wood's words made the revolution so radical.

Thus, the revolution of the Patriots was seen by many as the supreme act of hubris, and many Patriots, Washington and Adams among them, were unsure that there could be improvements on the British model. Their skepticism, over time, turned to pessimism.

---

[52] TJ to Roger Weightman, 24 June 1826.

Washington was no political philosopher, but he was committed to giving the sort of republicanism Jefferson and others envisaged a try. Jefferson writes to Dr. Walter Jones (2 Jan. 1814): "[Washington] has often declared to me that he considered our new constitution as an experiment on the practicability of republican government, and with what dose of liberty man could be trusted for his own good; that he was determined the experiment should have a fair trial, and would lose the last drop of his blood in support of it." Nonetheless, he was never certain of its success, even after victory in the war, and later in life, came to believe that political partisanship made impossible republicanism. He writes to John Trumbull (10 Aug. 1799): "Let [any] party set up a broomstick, and call it a true son of Liberty, a Democrat, or give it any other epithet that will suit their [the members'] purpose, and it will command their votes in toto! Will not the Federalists meet, or rather defend their cause, on the opposite ground? Surely they must, or they will discover a want of Policy, indicative of weakness, & pregnant of mischief; which cannot be admitted."

Adams, from the start, was skeptical of Jefferson-styled republicanism. He was, for instance, no champion of human reason. "Religion, superstition, oaths, education, laws, all give way before passions, interest, and power, which can be resisted only by passions, interest, and power." The "principles of authority—wisdom, prudence, courage, patience, temperance, and justice—for Adams, always are subservient to the principles of power"—riches, extraction, knowledge, birth, and reputation.[53] For Adams, there can be no republicanism founded on honesty and reason, but only on checks and balances. "There can be no government of laws without a balance, and that there can be no balance without the three orders"—the one, the few, and the many—each independent and acting as a check on the others.[54]

Finally, there is what might be fittingly described as the learned helplessness of Philadelphian Dr. Benjamin Rush, ardent revolutionist, representative of Pennsylvania in the Continental Congress, and signer of the Declaration of Independence. Rush was especially sanguine about the success of the United States after winning the Revolutionary War. His commitments to liberty and equality were reinforced after a visit in October 1768 to the House of Lords where he, through a cicerone, saw King George III's golden throne. Rush was mesmerized, and pleaded with the cicerone for the opportunity to sit on it. With a swirl of ideas speeding through his head, he thought: "This is the golden

---

[53] John Adams, *A Defense of the Constitutions of Government of the United States of America* (Philadelphia: Budd and Bartram, 1797), 324, 139, and 158.

[54] John Adams, *A Defense of the Constitutions of Government of the United States of America*, 99–100.

period of the worldly man's wishes. His passions conceive, his hopes aspire, after nothing beyond this Throne."[55]

Sanguineness eventually turned toward disaffection. Rush tells Adams in an 1805 letter of a certain dream he had that has disinclined him from political activity of any sort (Mar. 23).

> About the year 1790 I imagined I was going up second Street, in our city, and was much stuck by observing a great number of people assembled near Christ Church, gazing at a man who was seated on the ball just below the vane of the Steeple of the Church. I asked what was the matter;—One of my fellow citizens came up to me, and said, the man whom you see yonder, has discovered a method of regulating the weather, & that he could produce rain, & sun shine, & cause the wind to blow from any quarter he pleased. I now joined the crowd in gazing at him. He had a trident in his hand which he waved in the air, and called at the same time to the wind which then blew from the north East, to blow from the north West. I observed the Vane of the Steeple while he was speaking, but perceived no motion in it. He then called for rain, but the Clouds passed over the city without dropping a particle of water. He now became agitated & dejected, and complained of the refractory elements in the most affecting terms. Struck with the issue of his conduct—I said to my friend who stood near to me, "The man is certainly mad." Instantly a figure dressed like a flying mercury descended rapidly from him, with a Streamer in his hand, and holding it before my eyes bid me read the inscription on it. It was "De te fabula narratur."[56] The impression of these words was so forcible upon my mind, that I instantly awoke, and from that time I determined never again to attempt to influence the opinions & passions of my fellow Citizens upon political Subjects.[57]

Rush would become so disaffected by political matters that he, early in the nineteenth century, cast all his acquired data for his memoir on the American Revolution into a fire,[58] and he chose to spend the remainder of his life attending to medical and religious matters.

---

[55] Richard R. Beeman, *Our Fortunes & Our Sacred Honor: The Forging of American Independence, 1774–1776* (New York: Basic Books, 2013), 4.
[56] "The story is about you."
[57] Adams cleverly replies (Apr. 11) that it is beyond question that men such as Andrew Brown, Peter Markoe Bache, Ben Austin, and Tom Paine have certainly influenced the affairs of men and so inactivity is morally opprobrious.
[58] Gordon Wood, *The Radicalism of the American Revolution*, 366.

Crises like Shays' Rebellion were reasons for panic. That rebellion, which occurred only a few years after the surcease of the American Revolution, began at the lead of Daniel Shays, a captain in the Continental Army, who had yet to be paid for his services in the war and whose land was about to be seized by the government for non-payment of debts and local taxes. Shays and numerous other angry farmers of Massachusetts, gathered an army of some 1,200 men and aimed to storm the Springfield magazine.[59] The rebellion, though subdued in its varied stages during the winter of 1786–1787 by local and state militia, was contagious, and so sympathy for the rebellion quickly spread to states outside Massachusetts: e.g., Connecticut, Pennsylvania, and New York.[60]

Shays' Rebellion, covered more fully in chapter 10, was a wake-up call for many Americans. First, it was a microcosm of the recently finished American Revolution, but here played out in and around Massachusetts. Second, it was a sign of the volatility of the fledgling confederation of states—the instability of government by the people. Third, it was a sign of the impuissance of the federal government, which, under the Articles of Confederation, lacked the authority to raise money for opposition to the rebellion. To the rebels, however, it signaled the abuses of heavy-handed government—the reason why the Revolutionary War was begun.

The contagion of Shays' Rebellion was especially worrisome. Would it lead to numerous other rebellions—perhaps even another wholesale revolution? "What a triumph for the advocates of despotism," said Washington to John Jay (15 Aug. 1786), "to find that we are incapable of governing ourselves, and that systems founded on the basis of equal liberty are merely ideal & falacious!"

On account of Shays' Rebellion, it was clear that a strong federal government was needed for political stability. The Articles of Confederation were impuissant. The Congress lacked power of taxation, it could not establish consistency in foreign policy or consistency in interstate commerce, both of which were in the power of the individual states, and it even lacked power to demand attendance of its members at Congressional assemblies. While Jefferson was attending to his duties as minister plenipotentiary in France, Washington and James Madison called for a constitution to replace the Articles of Confederation.

Upshot

The focus in this chapter has been "revolution" and attendant problems. I aim to show, the American Revolution notwithstanding, separation from the

---

[59] Lenard Richards, *Shays's Rebellion: The American Revolution's Final Battle* (Philadelphia: University of Pennsylvania Press, 2003), 27–28.

[60] Lenard Richards, *Shays's Rebellion*, 84–88.

mother country was inevitable. The revolution was merely a matter of Colonists expediting what was eventually, as it were, in the cards.

Yet there were other botherations. For Jefferson, revolutions were complex matters, not to be decided by dint of human passions. Inchoation needed to be begun on account of long and clear abuses, and if successful, there needed to be some grasp of how the new constitution would be a decided improvement on the past model—*viz.*, how it would fully, or better, serve to preserve human liberties.

Chapter VIII

The Revolution of 1800

Political liberty, for Jefferson, is derivative of personal liberty. Jefferson writes at the start of Bill for Establishing Religious Freedom, "Almighty God hath created the mind free, and manifested his supreme will that free it shall remain by making it altogether insusceptible of restraint."[1] He writes in 1774, "The God who gave us life gave us liberty at the same time; the hand of force may destroy, but cannot disjoin them."[2] Each person's will is his own and though acts of coercion might force behavioral conformity, such behaviors without sanction of will are not one's own.[3]

Given Jefferson's view of freedom of the human mind, it follows ineluctably that the most natural political state for humans collectively is one that allows each person utmost expression to his freedom of mind and to actions consistent with them in any social setting. Thus, despite Jefferson's avowed aversion to metaphysics, his political views are fundamentally metaphysical: Liberty presupposes human will, which Jefferson very probably considered to be free in some unspecified sense. The difference between personal and civil liberty Jefferson sums thus to Isaac Tiffany (4 Apr. 1819): "Of liberty then I would say, that, in the whole plenitude of its extent, it is unobstructed action according to our will. But rightful liberty is unobstructed action according to our will within limits drawn around us by the equal rights of others. I do not add 'within the limits of the law,' because law is often the tyrant's will, and is always so when it violates the right of an individual."

Jefferson's ascendancy to the American presidency in 1800 (literally early 1801) occurred because of his perception that the country was sliding away from the pure liberal principles that fomented and sustained the American Revolution. His election he considered to be the Second American Revolution—"the revolution of 1800," as he says in the 1819 letter to Spencer Roane, and one founded by the "suffrage of the people." His Inaugural Address articulated the principles behind this second revolution, and he lauded the

---

[1] Thomas Jefferson, Bill for Establishing Religious Freedom, in *The Scholars' Thomas Jefferson* (Newcastle upon Tyne: Cambridge Scholars, 2021), 153.
[2] Thomas Jefferson, Summary View of the Rights of British America, in *The Scholars' Thomas Jefferson* (Newcastle upon Tyne: Cambridge Scholars, 2021), 16.
[3] My early thoughts on the subjects in this chapter are in chapter 5 of my book *Jefferson's Political Philosophy and the Metaphysics of Utopia* (London: Brill, 2017).

American people for recognition that there needed to be a return to those principles.

"You was fast asleep in philosophical Tranquility"
The Slide toward Monocracy

We have already noted that George Washington was unsure if the sort of republicanism Jefferson championed would work, yet he was willing to give it a fair try. His presidency, it cannot be said, was a period in which he aimed to give it that try. There was no precedent for being the first president of the United States—"as the first of everything in our situation will serve to establish a precedent," writes Washington to James Madison (5 May 1789), "it is devoutly wished on my part that these precedents be fixed on true principles." And so he surrounded himself with an intelligent and diverse cabinet—John Adams (vice president), Thomas Jefferson (secretary of state), Alexander Hamilton (secretary of treasury), Henry Knox (secretary of war) and Edmund Randolph (attorney general)—and he enlisted their opinions before coming to decisions on weighty matters.

Though the Federalism of Hamilton and the Republicanism of Jefferson were birthed in his presidency, it is best to describe Washington as nonpartisan, although he leaned toward strong government with all its trappings. Jefferson himself endorses a nonpartisan verdict of Washington. He writes in a letter to John Melish (13 Jan. 1813):

> General Washington did not harbor one principle of federalism. He was neither an Angloman, a monarchist, nor a separatist. He sincerely wished the people to have as much self-government as they were competent to exercise themselves. The only point on which he and I ever differed in opinion, was, that I had more confidence than he had in the natural integrity and discretion of the people, and in the safety and extent to which they might trust themselves with a control over their government. He has asseverated to me a thousand times his determination that the existing government should have a fair trial, and that in support of it he would spend the last drop of his blood. He did this the more repeatedly, because he knew General Hamilton's political bias, and my apprehensions from it. It is a mere calumny, therefore, in the monarchists, to associate General Washington with their principles.

The presidency of John Adams, however, was a decided slide toward monocracy. The war between England and France led to that slide. Tensions between France and the United States brought the two into what is today called the Quasi-War (1798–1800). Involvement necessitated enlargement of both the U.S. navy and the U.S. army, so Adams pushed through the Direct Tax of 1798, which angered the general citizenry. Rebellions broke out. To quiet the unrest, congress passed the Alien and Sedition Acts (1798)—four bills which passed into law restrictions on U.S. citizenship for immigrants (an immigrant would have to wait 14, not five, years before becoming a citizen) and punishments in the form of imprisonment of miscreants or dangerous persons and deportation of non-citizens, adjudged threatening. Anyone making malicious or false statements about the federal government could be imprisoned, and of course, Jeffersonian Republicans were victims. David Brown, who led a demonstration against the acts, was arrested in Andover, Massachusetts, fined 480 dollars, and sentenced to 18 months in prison.[4] James Thomson Callender—who spewed vitriol against Adams and who was "a repulsive pedant, a gross hypocrite, and an unprincipled oppressor"—too was fined (200 dollars) and imprisoned (nine months). So too were Republicans Matthew Lyon of Vermont and Benjamin Franklin Bache of Philadelphia, who accused the "blind, bald, crippled, toothless" Adams of nepotism.[5]

As vice president, Jefferson responded with his Kentucky Resolutions, while James Madison penned, though more mildly, his Virginia Resolutions. In his fair copy of Kentucky Resolutions, Jefferson writes, "The powers not delegated to the United States by the Constitution, nor prohibited by it to the States, are reserved to the States respectively, or to the people." He continues, "Where powers are assumed which have not been delegated, a nullification of the act is the rightful remedy: that every State has a natural right in cases not within the compact, (*casus non fœderis,*) to nullify of their own authority all assumptions of power by others within their limit."[6] Jefferson is arguing that in matters not explicitly limned as within the province of the federal government, the individual states are sovereign. When the federal government passes into law an act that exceeds the authority of the enumerated powers of the federal government, the individual states have the right to nullify that act.

In defense of his actions decades thereafter, Adams writes castigatorily to Jefferson (30 June 1813) of the "terrorism" of "Chaise's [Shays'] Rebellion" in Massachusetts, Gallatin's Insurrection in Pennsylvania, Fries' Rebellion in Pennsylvania, and Genet's Insurrection in Philadelphia, "when ten thousand

---

[4] Geoffrey R. Stone, *Perilous Times: Free Speech in Wartime from the Sedition Act of 1798 to the War on Terrorism* (New York: W.W. Norton & Company, 2004), 63–64.
[5] John Chester Miller, *Crisis in Freedom: The Alien and Sedition Acts* (New York: Little, Brown and Company, 1951), 211–20.
[6] Thomas Jefferson, Kentucky Resolutions (fair copy), in *The Scholars' Thomas Jefferson,* ed. M. Andrew Holowchak (Newcastle upon Tyne: Cambridge Scholars Press, 2021), 50–55.

People in the Streets of Philadelphia, day after day, threatened to drag Washington out of his House, and effect a Revolution in the Government, or compel it to declare War in favour of the French Revolution." Adams adds: "Nothing but the Yellow Fever … could have Saved the United States from a total Revolution of Government. I have no doubt you was fast asleep in philosophical Tranquility."

There is meat to Adams' argument. This was genuinely a frightening time for Americans—"perhaps the most frightening moment in all of American history," says on scholar.[7] The reasons were that the country was immature and militarily vulnerable, France had the largest army in the world at the time, and the possibility of a French invasion was no Fata Morgana, but very real.

And so, while Jefferson, through his Kentucky Resolutions, was accusing Adams of a willowy interpretation of the Constitution, neglect of citizens' rights, and of being a dictator instead of the nation's first citizen, Adams was accusing Jefferson of having no grasp of the fragility of the new government, of not seeing the danger that France posed to it, and of harboring "eleutherophilia," or love of freedom, more than patriotism.

Tensions between Jefferson and Adams were decupled when Jefferson, not Adams, was elected to the presidency in 1800. So irked was Adams upon losing that he left Philadelphia before Jefferson took the oath of office. Yet before leaving the presidency, the bitter and vindictive Adams, knowing that Jeffersonians would occupy the presidency and dominate the Congress, made one desperate attempt to hold on to power. Adams' administration enacted the Judiciary Act of 1801. That act added six circuit courts and 16 Federalist judges, appointed for life, as well as many Federalist marshals, district attorneys, and justices of the peace in Washington, and thereby stacked the judiciary with Federalists. Adams also culled John Marshall to be chief justice of the country.[8] Those last-minute actions have come to be dubbed "Midnight Appointments." While there was no Constitutional warrant for the appointments, there was no Constitutional warrant for their removal, and Jefferson, who was ever a strict constructionist, was handcuffed by the appointments.

Of Adams' discretionary and opprobrious move, Jefferson, as president, writes to John Dickinson (19 Dec. 1801): "on their part they have retired into the Judiciary as a strong hold. there the remains of federalism are to be preserved & fed from the treasury, and from that battery all the works of republicanism are to be beaten down & erased. by a fraudulent use of the constitution which

---

[7] Gordon Wood, *Friends Divided: John Adams and Thomas Jefferson* (New York: Penguin, 2017), 305–6.
[8] Gordon Wood, *Friends Divided*, 323 and 336.

has made judges irremoveable, they have multiplied useless judges merely to strengthen their phalanx." Jefferson would a few years later (13 June 1804) write Abigail Adams about his rocky relationship with her husband, in reply to a kindly letter from Adams (20 May 1804) concerning the death of Jefferson's daughter Maria:

> I can say with truth, that one act of Mr. Adams's life, and one only, ever gave me a moment's personal displeasure. I did consider his last appointments to office as personally unkind. They were from among my most ardent political enemies, from whom no faithful co-operation could ever be expected; and laid me under the embarrassment of acting thro' men whose views were to defeat mine, or to encounter the odium of putting others in their places. It seemed but common justice to leave a successor free to act by instruments of his own choice.

Abigail's response (1 July 1804) would not be conciliatory, but vitriolic. Jefferson would never forget Abigail's vitriol. Even though Jefferson would reconcile fully with Adams, his relationship with Adams' wife would never be the same.

"A rising spread over a wide and fruitful land…"
The Election of 1800

Jefferson always considered Adams to be a monocrat. He writes to William Wirt (8 Jan. 1825): "Can any one read Mr. Adams' defence of the American constitutions [his book of the same name] without seeing that he was a monarchist? And J.Q. Adams, the son, was more explicit than the father, in his answer to Paine's *rights of man*. So much for leaders. Their followers were divided. Some went the same lengths, others, and I believe the greater part, only wished a stronger Executive."

Despite his lifelong expression of execration of politics—an execration which many scholars find hypocritical or fake—Jefferson agreed to be Washington's secretary of state (1790–1793), a tenureship that got the better of Jefferson before the surcease of Washington's second term. The political climate of the jejune nation seemed to him to have changed since his time as minister plenipotentiary in France (1784–1789). "When I arrived at New York in 1790, to take a part in the administration," he continues in the 1801 letter to Dickinson, "being fresh from the French revolution, while in its first and pure stage, and consequently somewhat whetted up in my own republican principles, I found a state of things, in the general society of the place, which I could not have supposed possible." Jefferson was feted at large dinner parties, but the conversation, about the revolution, was conducted in "monarchical sentiments." There was little discussion of republicanism. "The furthest that any one would go, in support of the republican features of our new government, would be to say, 'the present constitution is well as a beginning, and may be allowed a fair trial; but it is, in fact, only a stepping stone to something better.'" Thus, it is fair to say that the perceived decay of republican sentiments and an upsurge of monocracy alarmed Jefferson and were the main causes of his grudging willingness, at the behest of Madison and others, to run for the presidency in 1796, though he would lose in a close race to John Adams.[9]

Though he disliked the storm of politics, Jefferson disliked even more non-involvement in human affairs. When, for illustration, he as president became apprised of daughter Maria's social withdrawal, he scolded her. He informed Maria that his longed-for retirement to his plantation in 1793 and his withdrawal from social and political events after his painful tenure as secretary of state was not a blissful time. "I am convinced that our own happiness requires that we should continue to mix with the world, and to keep pace with it as it goes." Those willfully withdrawing from it are "severely punished by the state of mind into which they get." They become misanthropes, "unfit for society."[10] As painful as was Jefferson's time as secretary of state, retirement to direct his plantation as overseer was more painful. Jefferson was a man of Brobdingnagian abilities, uncommon focus, and great energy for tackling large projects, and so the sort of life that preoccupied his brother, Randolph—that of a lifelong planter—could never have satisfied him. As Aristotle noted, great men are best occupied with great affairs. Moreover, Jefferson was too much under the spell of "liberty" not to involve himself in the unfolding of it in America and in global affairs.

Consequently, in 1800, Jefferson again ran for the presidency. Unlike his run in 1796, his reticence to run for the nation's highest office was gone. The monocratic tendencies of Adams' tenure convinced him that it was his civic duty to reverse the process of slide toward British monarchism, otherwise there would have been little point to the American Revolution. "I feel no impulse from personal ambition to the office now proposed to me," he writes to daughter Maria Eppes (15 Feb. 1801), "but on account of yourself and your sister and those dear to you. I feel a sincere wish, indeed, to see our Government brought back to its republican principles, to see what kind of government firmly fixed to which my whole life has been devoted."

---

[9] By only three electoral votes, and each state had its own method of choosing electors.
[10] TJ to Maria Eppes, 3 Mar. 1802.

Having earned the same number of votes as his eventual vice-president, Aaron Burr, Jefferson eventually won the presidency after 36 ballots of the House of Representatives.[11]

On the day of his inauguration, Jefferson played the part, consistent with his political philosophy, of man of the people. He was ushered in no stately carriage, but merely walked causally down Pennsylvania Avenue. Moreover, his inaugural speech showed him to be no political partisan. The room in which he spoke was crammed with curious people, and all would be astonished at what they were soon to hear.

Jefferson's Inaugural Address, comprising 1,730 words, I consider to be his singular writerly achievement. What is so singular about the speech, and this typifies his Declaration of Independence as well, is Jefferson's uncanny capacity to write both a timely and timeless document. The speech shows an acute awareness of just what he has inherited from Washington and Adams, of the uncertain times, and of the pulse of the citizenry. The speech also shows profound awareness that the young country can be a pathbreaker for Jeffersonian republicanism—an amalgam of Lockean liberalism and Greek and Roman communitarianism, or what I call Jefferson's liberal eudaimonism.

Jefferson begins with due humility: The task of first citizen "is above my talents." Yet there is immediate movement to a foreseeable future, intentionally couched in foggy, dreamlike terms: "a rising spread over a wide and fruitful land, traversing all the seas with the rich productions of their industry, engaged in commerce with nations who feel power and forget right, advancing rapidly to destinies beyond the reach of mortal eye." The fogginess is intentional, for those are "transcendent objects"—things filmy, but highly desirable. There follows "the honour, the happiness, and the hopes of this beloved country committed to the issue and the auspices of this day." The alliteration is doubtless too intentional. Yet it is not within the powers of one man to bring about this utopia of industrious Americans. There are many Americans—and many are in the room as legislators and their associates in which Jefferson speaks—with wisdom, virtue, and zeal to assist in the worthwhile project and "to steer with safety the vessel in which we are all embarked, amidst the conflicting elements of a troubled world."

The second paragraph begins with an oblique reference to the suffocation of free expression—"the contest of opinion"—in the prior administration. Yet this contest has been decided by "the voice of the nation" and pursuant to "the rules of the constitution." The nation, through the will of the majority, has freely

---

[11] For more on the ravelment of the election, see Dumas Malone, *Jefferson the President* (Boston: Little, Brown & Company, 1970), 3–16.

spoken, with Jefferson's election, on behalf of free expression. Yet Jefferson sagaciously cautions, "All too will bear in mind this sacred principle, that though the will of the majority is in all cases to prevail, that will, to be rightful, must be reasonable; that the minority possess their equal rights, which equal laws must protect, and to violate would be oppression." The "reasonable" of which Jefferson speaks is chiefly a declaration that the majority's will, when fully expressed through action, must never burke the rights and liberties of the minority.

That cautionary qualification leads in a sequacious manner to a plea for unity of heart and mind through harmonious and affective social intercourse. That is an appeal that reason ought to be obedient to moral duty. Without such a harmony of interests, liberty, even life, "are but dreary things." To affect such a harmony, there must be banishment of religious intolerance.

Noting that "every difference of opinion is not a difference of principle," Jefferson calls for Federalists and Republicans to come together under the banner of liberty. What characterizes champions of liberty is adherence to the principle that differences of opinion need not to be a reason for "luxation" or dissolution. "We have called by different names brethren of the same principle. We are all republicans: we are all federalists. If there be any among us who would wish to dissolve this Union, or to change its republican form, let them stand undisturbed as monuments of the safety with which error of opinion may be tolerated, where reason is left free to combat it."

Nonetheless, can a government whose strength is its liberal animus be strong? Is not freedom chaotic? Where is the unifying energy of republicanism? Asseverates Jefferson: "This government, the world's best hope, ... [will prove to be] the strongest government on earth," for "every man, at the call of the law, would fly to the standard of the law, and would meet invasions of the public order as his own personal concern." The sentiment is that the citizens will give much to a government which gives all—which lets its citizens decide for themselves their manner of living.

What of the remonstrance that "man cannot be trusted with the government of himself"?

Jefferson to that offers this counter-remonstrance through a rhetorical question: "Can he then be trusted with the government of others?" The notion, cunning, is that if men cannot be trusted to manage their own affairs, then it is worse to appoint some other, equally untrustworthy in his own affairs, to manage their affairs. In sum, if persons are inept in managing their own affairs, is there any reason to think that they are ept in managing the affairs of others? "Have we found angels, in the form of kings, to govern him?" The implicit sentiment in that second rhetorical question is that monarchism has been tried over millennia and it has failed.

Americans are fortunate to find themselves an ocean's distance from the "exterminating havoc" of Europe and "possessing a chosen country, with room enough for our descendants to the thousandth and thousandth generation." Americans have the "equal right" to express themselves as they deem fit. Americans have the right to acquire from their own industry. Americans judge others not by birth or wealth, but by their actions. Americans are "enlightened by a benign religion" that is professed and practiced multifariously, but each "inculcating honesty, truth, temperance, gratitude and the love of man, acknowledging and adoring an overruling providence." And so, can anything be wanting for their happiness—be wanting "to close the circle of our felicities"?

One thing is still sorely needed: "a wise and frugal government, which shall restrain men from injuring one another, shall leave them otherwise free to regulate their own pursuits of industry and improvement, and shall not take from the mouth of labor the bread it has earned."

Just what does that wise and frugal government comprise?

Jefferson then limns the "essential principles of our government." I use his words.

> 1. "Equal and exact justice to all men, of whatever state or persuasion, religious or political";
> 2. "peace, commerce, and honest friendship with all nations, entangling alliances with none";
> 3. "the support of the state governments in all their rights, as the most competent administrations for our domestic concerns, and the surest bulwarks against anti-republican tendencies";
> 4. "the preservation of the General government in its whole constitutional vigor, as the sheet anchor of our peace at home, and safety abroad";
> 5. "a jealous care of the right of election by the people, a mild and safe corrective of abuses which are lopped by the sword of revolution where peaceable remedies are unprovided";
> 6. "absolute acquiescence in the decisions of the majority, the vital principle of republics, from which is no appeal but to force, the vital principle and immediate parent of the despotism";
> 7. "a well disciplined militia, our best reliance in peace, and for the first moments of war, till regulars may relieve them";
> 8. "the supremacy of the civil over the military authority";
> 9. "economy in the public expence, that labor may be lightly burthened";
> 10. "the honest payment of our debts and sacred preservation of the public faith";
> 11. "encouragement of agriculture, and of commerce as its handmaid";
> 12." the diffusion of information, and arraignment of all abuses at the bar of the public reason";

13. "freedom of religion; freedom of the press; and freedom of person, under the protection of the Habeas Corpus"; and
14. "trial by juries impartially selected."

Some comments are in order. Principle one asserts that justice is unqualified. Political or religious differences between men are irrelevant. The second principle implies no favored-nation status in commerce with other nations. Principles three and four imply a strict constructionist interpretation and allowance for states to handle their own affairs, without the intrusions of the federal government. Subservience of the military to the civil authority, the asserting of principle eight, rules out autocracy. Principle nine implies light taxation. Use of "handmaid" in principle 11 implies the primacy of husbandry and the subservientness of commerce. Principle 12 is vague. "Diffusion of information" is unclear. Is Jefferson talking generically about freedom of expression, about which he is clearer in principle 13? Principle 12 mandates that any abuses of freedom of expression will be handled in a court of law and settled by reason. The thirteenth principle, which is really three principles, is given as one conjunctive claim, hence my preference for taking it as illustrative of the prior principle. The last principle is a preference for trials by a jury of one's peers, not a judge. Jefferson consistently adhered to a preference for the judgment by a jury of one's peers, as it is easier to corrupt the judgment of one man than of many.[12]

Those principles have guided both the sages and the bloodied patriots of the revolution and the reformation. "They should be the creed of our political faith; the text of civic instruction, the touchstone by which to try the services of those we trust." When Americans find that they have strayed from them, it is merely for them to recapitulate their steps "to regain the road which alone leads to peace, liberty and safety."

"The more knowledge is diffused…"

The Second American Revolution

The perlocutionary effects of the address, uttered by President Jefferson, could not be felt, because Jefferson was in possession of a voice neither loud nor

---

[12] To Abbé Arnoux (19 July 1789), Jefferson writes: "We all know, that permanent judges acquire an Esprit de corps, that being known they are liable to be tempted by bribery, that they are misled by favor, by relationship, by a spirit of party, by a devotion to the Executive or Legislative; that it is better to leave a cause to the decision of cross & pile, than to that of a judge biased to one side; and that the opinion of 12. honest jurymen gives still a better hope of right, than cross & pile does."

booming. Jefferson, anticipating that, had numerous copies of the address printed out in advance for public consumption.

Yet, as I mention above, the speech was both timely and timeless. It was timely in that it addressed one enormous nodus of the day—the fractionization of the country. Adams did his part to aggravate Jefferson and his fellow Republicans with his divisive actions as president. Jefferson responded, to the astonishment of most, with conciliation, not vengefulness. No one anticipated that. It was timeless for the same reason as it was timely. Jefferson responded to Adams' divisiveness with conciliation, which was a magnanimous illustration of the strength of republican government. A government, grounded on liberty, gave allowance to voices of all pitches and with variegated messages to be heard.

The greatness of Jefferson's inaugural speech was that it captured completely the inscape, the essence, of Thomas Jefferson. He bared his soul in the address, which was in essence a paean to liberty and Jefferson's wholesale purchase of it.

The potency of the speech was the paradoxical claim that a country with an inflexible commitment to lean federal government—a federal government that attends chiefly to foreign diplomacy and preservation of its citizens' rights and stays away from matters that are best left to individual citizens and the individual states—will prove to be the strongest government on earth. Strength, paradoxically, will be demonstrated by inactivity. The strength of the United States, with its commitment to federative principles of governing, will be its unyielding commitment to the liberty, and happiness, of its citizens—with liberty not as an end, but in the service of happiness. The U.S., with its stunning victory in its war for independence with Britain and with the election of Jefferson and fellow Jeffersonian republicans in the congress in 1801, was acting on behalf of all persons everywhere. To Joseph Priestley (19 June 1802), Jefferson writes, "It is impossible not to be sensible that we are acting for all mankind; that circumstances denied to others, but indulged to us, have imposed on us the duty of proving what is the degree of freedom and self-government in which a society may venture to leave it's individual members." Jefferson writes weeks later to Gov. David Hall (6 July 1802): "We [are not] acting for ourselves alone, but for the whole human race. The event of our experiment is to shew whether man can be trusted with self-government. The eyes of suffering humanity are fixed on us with anxiety as their only hope, and on such a theatre for such a cause we must suppress all smaller passions and local considerations."[13]

---

[13] See also John Adams, 28 Feb. 1796; "Second Inaugural Address," 1805; TJ to Thomas Seymour, 11 Feb. 1807; TJ to A.L.C. Destutt de Tracy, 26 Jan. 1811; TJ to James Madison, 24 Dec. 1824; and "Draft Declaration and Protest of the Commonwealth of Virginia," 1825.

Jefferson firmly maintained that if the people were left to themselves and if the federal government tended to those few things for which it was best suited, all would be for the best. The key, however, was that the people would voluntarily agree to participate in governmental affairs inasmuch as time and talent allowed. Says Jefferson to Abbé Arnoux (19 July 1789): "We think in America that it is necessary to introduce the people into every department of government as far as they are capable of exercising it; and that this is the only way to ensure a long continued & honest administration of it's powers."

Jefferson expatiates in the letter on that involvement. The people are unqualified to exercise the first office, but they are qualified to choose the executive. The people are unqualified to legislate, but they are qualified to choose their legislators. Finally, the people are unqualified to adjudicate questions of law, but they are qualified to judge questions of fact. Thus, the people in the form of juries are to decide all matters concerning contravention of laws, but not matters concerning the constitutionality, polysemy, and vagueness of laws.

One of the key theses of this book is that liberty for Jefferson is a concept readily grasped, but one, he learns throughout the decades, of great difficulty in application. It is easy to understand what it means for government to be only minimally involved in the affairs of its citizens—to be involved in directing its foreign affairs and in protecting citizens' liberties—but difficult to put into praxis such thin government. Opportunities for thickness ever get in the way. Jefferson would learn that in his two terms as president.

Jeffersonian government, with its paired axioms of equality and liberty, places large volitional demands on its citizens. For republicanism to work, citizens must be utmostly involved in governmental affairs, insofar as their affairs allow for involvement. They are expected to participate in such affairs, for instance, through jury duty, voting, overseeing the actions of elected governors, and even participation in governing, if only in local wards. Knowing of the corruptive enticement of power through governing, they are asked to oversee their governors.[14]

Here volition is critical. Citizens liberated from the yoke of suffocative government, for Jefferson, will recognize that a government protective of their rights, can only thrive when all citizens take active interest in it. They, however, are not mandated to do so, and there will be no need of any sort of trickery to entice them. They will, thinks Jefferson, merely choose to do so from

---

[14] See M. Andrew Holowchak, "The Moral Underpinning of Jeffersonian Republicanism" at Abbeville Institute, 26 Apr. 2023, https://www.abbevilleinstitute.org/the-moral-underpinning-of-jeffersonian-republicanism/, accessed 20 Nov. 2023.

recognition that republicanism cannot work unless they sacrifice some of their time and that that is the right thing to do.

In short, Jeffersonian republicanism is not without its flaws. It perhaps presents itself as one horn of a dilemma.

> 1. Citizens can choose (or have imposed on them) an aristocratic form of government (e.g., monarchy of some sort) or they can govern themselves in some manner.
> 2. All aristocratic forms of government have proven themselves to be abusive to the interests of the general citizenry.
> 3. Pure self-government (as Plato has shown[15]) is anarchy.
> 4. So, citizens can choose between coercion and anarchy.

This is clearly the sort of argument that John Adams might endorse. Yet Adams merely thinks that any form of government other than aristocracy is impossible: Any form of democracy will naturally slip into an aristocracy. He argues thus in a letter to Jefferson (15 Nov. 1813). Let any 100 men choose to form of government and give to each one vote. In a short manner of time, 25 of those men will have gained, willy-nilly, the vote of 25 others, and those select 25 will be men of wealth, birth, and even beauty, not virtue and genius. "Nobility in Men is worth as much as it is in Horses Asses or Rams."[16] Of those, men of wealth will hold the first place of power in a civilized society.

Why is that the case?

Adams continues. "Religion, superstition, oaths, education, laws, all give way before passions, interest, and power, which can be resisted by passions, interest, and power."[17] What of Jefferson's remedy: the diffusion of knowledge? Adams asserts, "The more knowledge is diffused, the more the passions are extended, and the more furious they grow."[18] In short, the passions are fueled and thus decupled by the addition of knowledge.

Jefferson agrees with Adams. Yet the argument for him can be salvaged by adding an addition al premise. While pure self-government is anarchical, self-government through elected representatives might not be so. And so, Jefferson would thus, and in its baldest sense, recast the argument:

---

[15] *Republic*, Books VIII and IX.
[16] John Adams to TJ, 9 July 1813.
[17] John Adams, *A Defense of the Constitutions of the Government of the United States of America* (Philadelphia: Budd and Bartram, 1797), 158 and 324.
[18] John Adams, *Discourses on Davila* (Boston: Russell and Cutler, 1805), 85.

1. Citizens can choose an aristocratic form of government (e.g., monarchy of some sort) or they can govern themselves in some manner.
2. All aristocratic forms of government have proven themselves to be abusive to the interests of the general citizenry.
3. Pure self-government (as Plato has shown) is anarchy.
4. Yet self-government through elected representatives, republicanism, has not been tried.
5. So, citizens can choose between coercion and an untried form of self-governing: republicanism.

As we have seen in his First Inaugural Address, Jeffersonian republicanism is much more than government by the people through elected representatives. I descant.

A Jeffersonian republic is a system of government that is grounded on robust individualism. There are individuals and their families; families are parts of small, self-sufficient governmental entities, called wards (or hundreds); wards are parts of self-sufficient counties; counties are parts of self-sufficient states; and states are parts the nation, whose function is to ensure, *inter alia*, that individuals thrive by protection of their rights. The key to success of this system is civic liberty, and civic liberty entails that individuals of families are freed to do as they please within wards; wards, within counties; counties, within states; and states, within the nation. Moreover, as we saw in Jefferson's fair copy of his Kentucky Resolutions, the powers granted political entities are (roughly) increased as we work downward—an indication of their philosophical worth, Jefferson's axiology. Families, as it were, are the axial "political" entities, while individuals are the axial agentive entities of the political system, graspable as Jefferson's political philosophy.

What makes the system work, at least on paper for Jefferson, is liberty—the freedom for every person to have a self-determined life. Yet it was well-known from at least Plato's day—premise 3 in the first articulated dilemma—that a governmental "system" in which each citizen merely did as he pleased to do would be bedlam, hence political philosophers' revulsion of democracy over the millennia and even in Jefferson's day.

If the freedom for self-determination—to do as one wishes to do so long as one's actions do not impede others' self-determined actions—is essentially what makes human life worth living, why then will citizens compromise self-interest for the sake of other-interest, that is, accept limits on what they wish to do? If we grant that a Jeffersonian republic cannot work unless all participate in some significant measure in the tasks of governing as their time and talents allow, then what guarantee can we have that all, or at least most, citizens will do that? For Jones, as a blacksmith, to take time away from his craft to attend to political duties will entail that he spends less time at blacksmithing, and that comes at the expense of his personal well-being.

Jefferson's plantation, it is commonly known, ever suffered from mismanagement, when he was away from Monticello as governor of Virginia, minister to France, secretary of state, vice president, and president. Upon retirement as secretary of state, Jefferson writes of the sad state of his fields and his plan to rejuvenate them through rotation of his crops to George Washington (14 May 1794): "But it will take me from 3. to. 6. years to get this plan underway. I am not yet satisfied that my acquisition of overseers from the head of Elk has been a happy one, or that much will be done this year towards rescuing my plantation from their wretched condition. Time, patience & perseverance must be the remedy; and the maxim of your letter, 'slow & sure,' is not less a good one in agriculture than in politics."[19] Great-granddaughter Sarah Randolph sums the scenario prior to and during his presidency: "His private affairs were in sad need of his constant presence at home after such long absences in the public service. He now owned in his native State over ten thousand acres of land, which for ten long years had been subject to the bad cultivation, mismanagement, and ravages of hired overseers."[20]

In sum, almost any form of political participation will come at the detriment of one's personal affairs, with little remuneration to compensate for that participation; substantial participation, substantial detriment. Thus, if not much motivated by desire for notoriety, there is, it seems, little personal motivation for political participation.

Here we fall back on the empiricist's metempiricism—Jefferson's metaphysics. Each person, except few defective sorts like Napoleon, is born with a faculty that naturally senses right from wrong action: the moral sense. When the sense is properly cultivated through maturation—encouraging morally correct action and discouraging morally opprobrious action—there is no need of deliberating on proper courses of moral action: One merely feels the right thing to do, and if schooled on acting on those feelings, one does the right thing to do. He writes to John Adams (14 Oct. 1816). "I believe that it is instinct, and innate, that the moral sense is as much a part of our constitution as that of feeling, seeing, or hearing; as a wise creator must have seen to be necessary in an animal destined to live in society: that every human mind feels pleasure in doing good to another." Jefferson, in a letter to Peter Carr (19 Aug. 1785), compares the moral sense to a limb, whose functionality is perfected with proper use or is

---

[19] See also TJ to James Madison, 27 Apr. 1795.
[20] Sarah N. Randolph, *The Domestic Life of Thomas Jefferson* (Cambridge: University Press, 1939), 191.

debilitated through overuse or underuse. The notion of proper use, for the sake of moral accountability, is critical, and here the analogies with a sensory organ or a limb invite different ways of cashing out proper use.

For Jefferson, benefaction is an instrumental part of moral sensing. We simply feel that other-concern is right, and so we tend to act on other-interest. That is, as we might say today, just how humans are wired. In sum, if humans are freed to do as they please and there are no rational impediments to what they sense as morally right, they will merely tend to act in socially and politically beneficial ways.

Plato encountered the same nodus in *Republic* when Socrates expiscated what an ideal republic would be like. For Plato, there were two basic sort of persons: the courageous and the appetitive. The appetitive, dominated by passions, would comprise the largest group: the laborers. The courageous, dominated by spirit, would comprise the protectors: the police-force to secure the polis and the army in times of war. The best of the courageous, those showing a capacity for intellect, would, after a lengthy education, become the rules of the polis, and Plato included women among the protectors and rulers: elite protectors. To parry the protest that many would object to being cast as laborer or protector, Plato devised a "great lie": a story told at the incunabula of the ideal polis—its first stage—that some men were made from bronze, some from silver, and some from gold. When one of Socrates' interlocutors objects that no one will believe that fabrication, Socrates counters that few in the first generation will believe the story, but it will take root in subsequent generations.[21]

Jefferson proffers no great lie to get citizens to participate as fully as they can in any Jeffersonian republic. Yet he does posit the existence of a moral sense in all humans. That is not a tendentious maneuver by Jefferson. It is part of what he inherited from the moral sentimentalists and moral-sense theorists of his day, such as Early of Shaftesbury, David Hume, Lord Kames, Francis Hutcheson, and Adam Smith.[22] Still, it may be that Jefferson's solution to Plato's problem is no better than Plato's. While Plato's republic suffers because it is founded on a great lie, it might be that Jefferson's suffers from great metaphysical callowness: the metempirical posit that all humans are equally moral and that they will, with gentle prodding, act on what they sense to be morally right, when governmental constraints are absent. Jefferson would surely counter that existence of a moral sense is not a metaphysical posit, but

---

[21] Plato, *Republic*, trans. G.MA. Grube (Indianapolis: Hackett, 1992)414b–415d and 42b–423c.

[22] For more, see Antti Kauppinen, "Moral Sentimentalism," in *The Stanford Encyclopedia of Philosophy*, ed. Edward N. Zalta, https://plato.stanford.edu/archives/win2018/entries/moral-sentimentalism/

it is shown true by appeal to human experience. Against that remonstrance, one might object that no one has had "experience" of a moral sense till Enlightenment times. So, why then did it take so long to observe something so obvious—something that is merely part of humans' constitution?

"I consider 4. of these bills…"
Implementing Jeffersonian Reforms

Implementation of republican government, for Jefferson, was not merely fixing into place a system—at the levels of wards, counties, states, and the federal government—of representatives of the people. Many other political reforms were needed in the direction of popular governing and from aristocratic governing. There needed to be fundamental changes at all levels of American society for Jeffersonian republicanism to take root, to effloresce, and to thrive. Four essential reforms, in the form of four bills introduced by Jefferson, were riddance of entails, abolition of primogeniture, freedom of religion, and systemic educational reform. Much of the reformation was to occur through reviewing and rewriting the complete code of Virginia's laws, outdated because they were not written "for the good of those for whose government it was framed." The laborers of that behemothic task, begun in 1776, were Jefferson, George Wythe, Edmund Pendleton, George Mason, and Thomas L. Lee. Mason and Lee were excused, as each, without the needed training in law, believed himself inferior to the task, and so Jefferson, Wythe, and Pendleton were the agents of reform.[23]

Abolition of entails was begun by Jefferson on January 12, 1776. It allowed for transmission of property from generation to generation in the same family, and that led to "a Patrician order" or "a distinct set of families … privileged by law in perpetuation of their wealth." From that Patrician order, from that "aristocracy of wealth," the king of England customarily chose his counselors with the expectation that they, in turn, would align their interests with that of the crown. Abolition of each would allow for "the aristocracy of virtue and talent, … essential to a well ordered republic." Abrogation of entails was essential to allow for "the aristocracy of virtue and talent."[24] In the words of Adam Smith: "Upon the whole nothing can be more absurd than perpetual entails. In them the principle of testamentary succession can by no means take place. Piety to the dead can only take place when their memory is fresh in the minds of men: a power to dispose of estates for ever is manifestly absurd. The

---

[23] Thomas Jefferson, *Autobiography*, in *Thomas Jefferson: Writings*, ed. Merrill D. Peterson (New York: Library of America, 1984), 37–38.
[24] Thomas Jefferson, *Autobiography*, 32.

earth and the fullness of it belongs to every generation, and the preceding one can have no right to bind it up from posterity; such extension of property is quite unnatural."[25] Smith's utterance is, of course, what Jefferson would later commonly state: the principle of generational sovereignty, or the notion that each generation is sovereign in its own time.

Abolition of primogeniture, which also led to an uneven distribution of wealth in familial inheritance and the aristocracy of wealth, was also needed for Jeffersonian republicanism. Primogeniture granted the first-born son the privilege of the entirety of an inheritance. Jefferson in his *Autobiography* notes that Pendleton, a mawkish conservative, wished to preserve this law, but seeing that Jefferson and Wythe opposed him, settled for the Jewish custom of a double portion for the oldest son. Jefferson with callidity countered that that might be justifiable, if the eldest son did twice the work of the others or ate twice as much.[26] Order of birth was no right measure of desert.

Third, Jefferson recognized the need of freedom of religion. In *Notes on the State of Virginia*, Jefferson notes that rulers can control the natural rights of the citizenry only if the people grant such submission and they could never grant any government the authority to dictate rights of conscience, for which each is answerable to his deity. "The legitimate powers of government extend to such acts only as are injurious to others. But it does me no injury for my neighbor to say there are twenty gods, or no god. It neither picks my pocket nor breaks my leg." Partnership of government with any particular religion, Anglicanism in the case of England, meant formal recognition of the illegitimacy of all religions, not sanctioned, and that individuals not of the sanctioned religion would themselves be politically illegitimate and pay "taxation for the support of a religion not theirs."[27] That bill was passed, much at the urging of James Madison, while Jefferson was tenured as minister in France.

Finally, Jefferson apprehended the need of educational reforms for republicanism to work. Government of and for the people required that all citizens could be given an education, suited to their needs. That meant that each citizen would be generally educated to be capable of conducting his personal matters, of governmental participation since his circumstances would allow, and of understanding, maintaining, and exercising his rights. Hence, that was the motivation for Bill 79 in 1779, Bill for the More General Diffusion of

---

[25] Adam Smith's "Lectures on Jurisprudence," in *Adams Smith Works*, https://www.adamsmithworks.org/documents/digital-jurisprudence, accessed 3 Mar. 2023.
[26] Thomas Jefferson, *Autobiography*, 38–39.
[27] Thomas Jefferson, *Notes on the State of Virginia*, ed. William Peden (Chapel Hill: University of North Carolina Press, 1954), 159–61.

Knowledge, and his later bill some 40 years later, Bill for Establishing a System of Public Education (1817).

In both bills, Jefferson proposed systemic reforms, with emphasis on public schools to educate generally the citizenry. He had ever considered introduction of general education more important than higher education, for without general education for all, there would merely be continuancy of the sort of political dominance by the wealthy and wellborn, whose children were privately educated and had access to higher education. As he writes in *Notes on Virginia:* "Every government degenerates when trusted to the rulers of the people alone. The people themselves, therefore, are its only safe depositories. And to render even them safe, their minds must be improved to a certain degree. This indeed is not all that is necessary, though it be essentially necessary."[28] Again, years later (13 Jan. 1823), he adds to Joseph C. Cabell: "Were it necessary to give up either the Primaries or the University, I would rather abandon the last, because it is safer to have a whole people respectably enlightened, than a few in a high state of science, and the many in ignorance. The last is the most dangerous state in which a nation can be. The nations and governments of Europe are so many proofs of it." The sentiment is that a government by and for the people, with an ignorant citizenry, is not a government by and for the people, but a coercive aristocracy that feeds off the people.

Jefferson writes of his four bills: "I considered 4. of these bills, passed or reported, as forming a system by which every fibre would be eradicated of antient or future aristocracy; and a foundation laid for a government truly republican."[29]

Upshot

Jefferson was successful in riddance of entails and primogeniture, and in securing freedom for all Virginians to worship as they best saw fit to worship. He was, however, unsuccessful in his attempts to implement a system of education in Virginia, though he did in the last two decades of his life found University of Virginia. The system he ever proposed was, as the letter to Tyler indicates, a matter of roughly parsing out Virginian land into wards or "hundreds"—at times defined as 10-by-10-mile plots—having a ward school centrally located in each ward, having a college or grammar school in each county, and having a large high-level institution like University of Virginia, roughly in the center of the state.[30]

---

[28] Thomas Jefferson, *Notes on Virginia*, 148.
[29] Thomas Jefferson, *Autobiography*, 44.
[30] He toyed also with the notion of a federal institution of learning to teach republican values. TJ to Gov. Wilson Cary Nicholas, 22 Nov. 1794, and TJ to M. D'Ivernois, 6 Feb. 1795.

That system was never adopted in Virginia during Jefferson's life largely because it was opposed by the Virginian gentry. Their problem was the perceived prodigious cost of implementation. Jefferson knew otherwise, as he claimed the Virginians were now paying more for a part of a system than for the whole, if implemented as Jefferson outlined.[31] The nodus was that the Virginian gentry were nowise inclined to send their children to public-funded ward schools—that was beneath them—and they resented any bill that would force them to pay for the education of the *hoi polloi*—that is, to pay twice for their children's education. Consequently, Jefferson directed his efforts, once retired, to birthing an establishing the University of Virginia.

Yet these early efforts to reform politically the Virginia of his time, prior to his presidency, show his work toward implementation of Jeffersonian republicanism from the ground up, as it were.[32] His tenure as secretary of state under George Washington and as vice president under John Adams convinced him that all might be lost—that the American Revolution might have been for naught, for the country was headed toward monarchism. With his election to the presidency in 1801—a decided victory for Republicans—his faith in the goodness, intelligence, and moral sensibility of the citizenry was restored. Hence, he regarded his election as the Second American Revolution, or "the revolution of 1800."

---

[31] TJ to Joseph Cabell, 14 Jan. 1818.
[32] Thomas Jefferson Foundation scholar at UVa, Alan Taylor, incorrectly and astonishingly notes that Jefferson's approach to education was top down—that is, Jefferson's interest was principally in high-level education. Such an oversight is colossal for one who is the Thomas Jefferson Foundation Scholar at University of Virginia. Alan Taylor, *Thomas Jefferson's Education* (New York: W.W. Norton, 2019), 222.

Chapter IX

The Spread of Liberty in the Americas

The significancy of the American Revolution cannot be understated. While scholars today focus all too much on what it did not, at least forthwith, bring about—the end of slavery and the social equality of women, and the Founders today are typically inculpated for those "failures"—it led to a social milieu, grounded on the wholesale purchase of equalitarianism and liberty, that made inevitable the abolition of slavery and the equality of women. It also led, for better or worse, to American political and economic climates that catered to and were grounded on the wants of the *hoi polloi*.

In this chapter, I begin with the uniqueness of the American Revolution and then turn to Jefferson's discussion in several letters of the contagion of liberty throughout much, or all, of North America and even throughout South America. I follow in gist and expand on the account I give in another book.[1]

"The God who gave us life gave us liberty at the same time"

American Revolution, Redux

Following the thesis of Gordon Wood, the American Revolution was an unusual revolution. There were few of the components that typify a revolution: an economic crisis, a push for nationalism by some ethnic group, or exposure of citizens to insufferable despotism. The Colonists were relatively well-to-do fiscally, there was no push for nationalism by Colonists or by any group of Colonists, and King George III cannot be said to have been as despotic vis-à-vis the Colonists as earlier kings: e.g., Charles II and James II. Writes Wood of Colonists of the social condition of Colonial America:

> The social conditions that generically are supposed to lie behind all revolutions—poverty and economic deprivation—were not present in colonial America. ... The white America colonists were not an oppressed people; they had no crushing imperial chains to throw off. In fact, the colonists knew they were freer, more equal, more prosperous, and less

---

[1] M. Andrew Holowchak, *Jefferson's Political Philosophy and the Metaphysics of Utopia* (London: Brill, 2017), chap. 6.

burdened with cumbersome feudal and monarchical restraints than any other part of mankind in the eighteenth century.[2]

What Wood means by "any other part of mankind in the eighteenth century" is unclear, but what he says in the main is compelling.

Nonetheless, some historians downplay the significancy of the American Revolution as an event that shaped the course of American culture. They note that the unique social conditions of Colonial America would have led sooner or later to separation from the mother country.[3] The social conditions were just too different from that of England. That is likely the case. Moreover, it seems only natural that a group of colonies in North America, far exceeding the size of their mother country and rich in untapped natural resources, would at some point seek its independency if only because being governed from afar by an invisible king and parliament is grossly inefficient and because there was much to be gained economically by a separation.

Yet that presumption leaves unexplained how the Colonists, without the occurrence of the revolution, would have come together so seamlessly—unanimity was adjudged to be essential—to be able to have the power needed to separate from the mother country, which of course had a formidable army and the world's most powerful navy. And so, to say that Colonial independence was, so to speak, in the cards is etiologically aidless. It does not explain why the American Revolution—a distinct event in a relatively fixed period—occurred. Thus, even if independence was at some point inevitable, we still have need to ask why the American Revolution happened just when and as it happened. As I have noted in earlier chapters, it is the job of historians to answer plausibly questions like that.

The war had roots in the practice of British mercantilism, which was put into practice in the British colonies to keep fat the mother country at the expense of its leaner North American colonies. Colonial merchants were greatly restricted in what they could sell and to whom they could sell it. Tobacco farmers, for instance, were confined to selling their product to England and British-owned territories. Thus, they received a fixed price for tobacco when trading on a free market would have given them access to competitive bidding and higher prices, though confinement led to a consistent demand for their tobacco. It was

---

[2] Gordon Wood, *The Radicalism of the American Revolution* (New York: Alfred A. Knopf, 1991), 4.
[3] E.g., Jack P. Greene, "The Social Origins of the American Revolution: An Evaluation and an Interpretation," in *Political Science Quarterly*, LXXXVIII, 1973: 21.

the same with other raw goods.[4] Colonial merchants, of course, objected to lack of a free market.

Numerous other events led to the separation of Colonial England and England and to development of a separate colonial identity. After the death of Cromwell in 1658, Charles II's return to the British throne in 1661 led to increased tension between the New England colonies and Britain. New Englanders tended to support Cromwellians who sent Charles I to the guillotine. When Cromwell was overthrown, Charles II became king and promoted actions that led to tighter control of New England colonists. James II thereafter continued those efforts.

The crucial period was from 1763, marking the end of the French and Indian War (aka, the Seven Years War), to 1776.

With surcease of the war with the Treaty of Paris, England was awarded a large swath of the North American continental land: from the land surrounding Hudson Bay and all the land of the Eastern North American coast to all the land east of the Mississippi River. Yet acquisition was not without weighty problems. There was foremost the nodus of policing and overseeing the territory, which would require a large investment of British soldiers. Again, there were still numerous French settlers, unwilling to cede what they had claimed at theirs to Britain. Moreover, how were the exasperated Native Americans, who fought with the French, be assuaged? Also, what was to prevent Colonists from moving West and claiming and settling on unpoliced land?

To address those weighty difficulties, King George III, who gained the throne in 1760, issued his Royal Proclamation of October 7, 1763. That proclamation detailed the newly acquired lands to England's "loving subjects" under England's "Paternal care" and "immediate Government." It went forth to warn those "loving subjects" of settling into the new lands:

> And We do hereby strictly forbid, on Pain of our Displeasure, all our loving Subjects from making any Purchases or Settlements whatever, or taking Possession of any of the Lands above reserved, without our especial leave and Licence for that Purpose first obtained.
>
> And We do further strictly enjoin and require all Persons whatever who have either wilfully or inadvertently seated themselves upon any Lands within the Countries above described or upon any other Lands which,

---

[4] Robert P. Thomas, "A Quantitative Approach to the Study of the Effects of British Imperial Policy of Colonial Welfare: Some Preliminary Findings," in *Journal of Economic History*, Vol. 25, No. 4, 1964: 615–638.

not having been ceded to or purchased by Us, are still reserved to the said Indians as aforesaid, forthwith to remove themselves from such Settlements.[5]

The Colonists were, by fiat and "on Pain of [Royal] Displeasure," bound to the Appalachian lands, but not beyond them.

Colonists were incensed. Many had fought with the British against the French and Native Americans and they were thus being strictly forbidden and strictly enjoined not to settle Western lands. Yet many Colonists recognized that the proclamation was issued precisely because England could not enforce it. Thus, they merely ignored it, and removed to the forbidden Western lands.

The Proclamation of 1763 marked the provenance of George III's attempts to exercise tight control of the colonies, which had been relatively independent since the first settlers came to North America. The Colonists were then taxed. There were the Sugar Act (1764), the Currency Act[6] (1764), the Stamp Act (1765), and the Quartering Act[7] (1765), *inter alia*. The Stamp Act was especially opprobrious, for it was the most visible tax. It mandated that all legal documents needed to be stamped paper as proof of payment of tax. Non-legal items, like playing cards and newspapers, too were stamped, otherwise illegal. Consequently, Colonists saw the effects of the Stamp Act in many facets of everyday life.

From the British point of view, the taxes were reasonable. The Seven Years' War had drained the British system and England needed some revenue for the high cost of maintaining a British military presence in North America. Moreover, the taxes were not crippling, and Colonists were taxed less than British citizens. The king, thus, merely wanted the Colonists not to eschew their obligations to their mother country.

The Colonists reasoned otherwise. As they would charge in a congressional writ from New York in 1765, the Colonists were deserving of "all the inherent rights and liberties of his natural born subjects within the kingdom of Great-Britain." They added that "no taxes be imposed on them, but with their own consent, given personally, or by their representatives."[8] And so, taxation, in

---

[5] "The Royal Proclamation of 1763," at *U.S. History*, https://www.ushistory.org/us/9a.asp, accessed 7 Mar. 2023.

[6] To stabilize and gain control over the Colonists' economy. With want of British currency, colonies began to issue their own bills, without the backing of silver or gold, hence, a fluctuant system.

[7] Mandating that colonists provide food and shelter for British troops.

[8] "Resolutions of the Stamp Act, 1765" and "The Stamp Act Controversy," at *U.S. History*, https://www.ushistory.org/us/9b.asp, accessed 8 Mar. 2023.

itself, they did not find objectionable, but objectionable was taxation without consent. Furthermore, with the Seven Years' War ended, what was the purpose of a military presence in the colonies? The British soldiers in North America, they thought, were there only to police the Colonists, which they deemed offensively paternalistic.

The issue for Colonists was British conceit and hypocrisy. The colonies were founded by private investors (e.g., Virginia Company) and the crown took an interest in them only after the colonies began to prove profitable. Furthermore, while the taxes to them were not disabling, they were imposed without Colonists' consent, and so, gratuitous. Moreover, Colonists' grievances were mostly ignored, and when they were addressed, the responses were much delayed on account of the ocean between America and England. Additionally, as the proclamation of 1763 shows, the British crown spoke paternalistically to the Colonists, their "loving subjects," who were strictly forbidden and strictly enjoined upon the "Pain of [England's] Displeasure" to do as they were told to do. As I have noted earlier, the first settlers were a mélange of prostitutes, urchins, prisoners, the penurious, Scots, Welsch, and Irish, as well as some adventurous aristocrats. Mongers such as Samuel Adams, John Hancock, and John Adams—all Bostonians—did much to stir up anti-British sentiments and even the prospect of a call to arms.

When the highly unpopular Stamp Act was repealed a year after it was made law, Parliament responded with the Declaratory Act (1766), which asserted that the "King's majesty" along with parliament "ought to have, full power and authority to make laws and statutes of sufficient force and validity to bind the colonies and people of *America*, subjects of the crown of *Great Britain*, in all cases whatsoever"[9]—another act made law because it was unenforceable.

For Jefferson, the issue was ever liberty. As Jefferson notes vociferously in his 1774 wide-read publication, Summary View of the Rights of British America, the forebears of the colonists were "free inhabitants" of England, in which "chance, not choice, has placed them." Expatriation is a right, sanctioned by nature, and when people establish a new society, they have the right to establish "such laws and regulations as to them shall seem most likely to promote public happiness." The laws established by the crown are without warrant—the decrees of British legislators who take it on themselves to "give law to four millions in the states of America," where every individual is the equal of any British individual. The laws have been many, each unjust. "Single acts of tyranny may be ascribed to the accidental opinion of the day; but a series

---

[9] "The Declaratory Act," at *U.S. History*, https://www.ushistory.org/declaration/related/declaratory.html, accessed 8 Mar. 2023.

of oppressions, begun at a distinguished period, and pursued unalterably through every change of ministers too plainly proves a deliberate, systematic plan of reducing us to slavery." Jefferson closes famously, "The God who gave us life gave us liberty at the same time; the hand of force may destroy, but cannot disjoin them."[10]

"It is by division and subdivision of duties..."
Three Letters in 1816

Jefferson was only 31 when he penned his Summary View of the Rights of British America. The work contains an enumeration of the rights of free people and offers the British king a schoolmasterly lecture on the duties of a sovereign. He begins by reminding George III that he is merely *primus inter pares*, "the chief officer of the people, appointed by the laws, and circumscribed with definite powers, to assist in working the great machine of government." Jefferson ends by asserting the same sentiment: "Kings are the servant, not the proprietors of the people." Any tax proposed on a colony will be proposed by legislators of that colony. He then thus snootily enjoins George: "Do your duty."[11]

Jefferson's Summary View is a sketch of a political philosophy, fully developed by the time of his presidency (chapter 8) and fleshed out in several letters in 1816.[12] The fundamental axiom of Jeffersonian republicanism, those letters show, the topic of this section, is embrace and execution of the will of the people, generally enlightened. I examine the philosophical content of those three letters.

On April 24, Jefferson writes to Pierre Samuel Dupont de Nemours (1739–1817), a French economist, politician, and political reformist who moved to American during the French Revolution. Dupont has sent to Jefferson a little "gospel" on Spanish republics (31 Mar. 1816), and he asks Jefferson for his approbation and blessing.

Jefferson begins with a lesson, learned by experience, apropos of social wellbeing. Any society is best administered when the people are left to themselves both to conduct those affairs of which they are capable of

---

[10] Thomas Jefferson, Summary View of the Right of British America, in *The Scholars' Thomas Jefferson*, ed. M. Andrew Holowchak (Newcastle upon Tyne: Cambridge Scholars, 2021), 3–16.
[11] Thomas Jefferson, Summary View of the Right of British America, 3 and 15.
[12] For the significancy of the year 1816, see M. Andrew Holowchak, "On Weather and History: Thomas Jefferson's Climate-Induced 'Philosophical Hangover' Explained," in *Thirty-Six More Short Essays, Plus Another, on the Probing Mind of Thomas Jefferson* (Newcastle upon Tyne: Cambridge Scholars, 2020), 150–53.

conducting and to delegate to representatives, "removable for unfaithful conduct," the conduct of those affairs of which they are incapable.

Jefferson next turns to "the moral principles on which the government is to be administered." That is a singular claim, for as I note throughout this book, politics for Jefferson is answerable to morality: that is, the notion of a good society is to be determined by the notion of what it means for individuals to thrive. I quote in full (numbers mine):

> I believe with you (1) that morality, compassion generosity are innate elements of the human construction; (2) that there exists a right independant of force; (3) that a right to property is founded in our natural wants, in the means with which we are endowed to satisfy these wants, and the right to what we acquire by those means without violating the similar rights of other sensible beings; (4) that no one has a right to obstruct another, exercising his faculties innocently for the relief of sensibilities made a part of his nature; (5) that justice is the fundamental law of society; (6) that the majority, oppressing an individual is guilty of a crime, abuses it's strength, and by acting on the law of the strongest breaks up the foundations of society; (7) that action by the citizens in person, in affairs within their reach and competence, and in all others by representatives, chosen immediately, & removable, by themselves, constitutes the essence of a republic; (8) that all governments are more or less republican in proportion as this principle enters more or less into their composition; and (9) that a government by representation is capable of extension over a greater surface of country than one of any other form.

As I have elaborated on the principles limned in Jefferson's First Inaugural Address—many are identical—I opt not to say anything here. It is noteworthy, however, that Jefferson begins with a statement of the axiality of morality and ends with a statement about the great extensibility of republican government.

Jefferson adds before closing a statement on the necessity of ward-school education. With the citizenry generally enlightened, "tyranny and oppressions of body and mind will vanish like evil spirits at the dawn of day."

On May 28, Jefferson writes John Taylor, who has piqued Jefferson's interest in political philosophy by sending Jefferson his "Enquiry into the Principles of Our Government," in which there is "much matter for profound reflection."

Jefferson reflects and notes that when one examines the sorts of republics that exist, "republic" is "of very vague application." His objective is to disambiguate the term. "were I to assign to this term a precise and definite idea, I would say that, purely and simply, it means a government, by it's citizens, in mass, acting directly and personally, according to rules established by the majority: and that every other government is more or less republican in proportion as it has in it's composition more or less of this ingredient of the direct action of the citizens."

Yet such direct action of a citizenry is possible only in "very narrow limits of space and population"—e.g., a New England township. Hence, he iterates principle 7 in his letter to Dupont de Nemours: need of elected and recallable representatives for larger application.

Jefferson then reiterates the fundamental principle of the true measure of republicanism: "the control of the people over the organs of their government." He sums with a rough definition, "Governments are more or less republican as they have more or less of the element of popular election and controul in their composition [and] the mass of the citizens is the safest depository of their own rights, & especially that the evils flowing from the duperies of the people are less injurious than those from the egoism of their agents."[13]

Last, there is a letter to Samuel Kercheval (July 12). The spirit of republican government is in the spirit of its people. "Governments are republican only in proportion as they embody the will of their people, and execute it." In a government, republican, each citizen "has his equal voice in the direction of its concerns ... by representatives chosen by himself, and responsible to him at short periods." Addition of "short intervals" implies fixed terms for representatives—a deterrent to corruption.

The enormousness of the United States—the Louisiana Territory was then incorporated and there were 19 states in 1816—added to the complexity of representative government. Jefferson's solution, expressed in this letter but first stated many decades earlier, is "by division and subdivision of duties"—to create four republics, by division of the federal government into component states, each state government into component counties, and each county government into component wards. Jefferson writes:

> We should thus marshal our government into 1. the General federal republic, for all concerns foreign & federal; 2. that of the State for what relates to our own citizens exclusively. 3. the County republics for the duties & concerns of the county, and 4. the Ward-republics, for the small, and yet numerous & interesting concerns of the neighborhood: and in government, as well as in every other business of life, it is by division and subdivision of duties alone, that all matters, great & small, can be

---

[13] The Judiciary, he notes, is anti-republican, in that judges are elected for life, and thus, are immune to any verdict of the people.

managed to perfection. and the whole is cemented by giving to every citizen personally a part in the administration of the public affairs.

Several scholars have argued that Jefferson never had a well-thought-out political philosophy.[14] Perusal of his writings from his Summary View to the three letters in 1816 shows that that thesis is untenable. The most significant factors in the development of that philosophy over the decades were his involvement in the struggle for American independence, his tenure in France and his interaction there with *philosophes* and French political agitators and mongers, his feuds with Alexander Hamilton when the two were part of Washington's cabinet, and the heavy-handed presidency of John Adams and his High Federalist cabinet.

"The moral duties which exist…"
Grounding Jeffersonian Republicanism

What made the people so capable of Jefferson-styled self-government? I here return to expiscation of Jefferson's moral sense and the debate in chapter 6 between those who take Jefferson to be a Lockean liberal and those who take Jefferson to be a Classical Republican.

That politics is answerable to morality is a large claim, which favors a philosophical interpretation of Jefferson as a liberal atomist or Lockean liberal, and philosophically speaking, that view is, I believe, philosophically correct, or at least part of the overall philosophical picture.

Government for Jefferson was for the sake of the wellbeing of all citizens, each considered the political equal of all others and deserving of the same rights. That noted, for Jefferson, humans—like herds of elephants, prides of lions, pandemonia of parrots, packs of wolves, puffinries of puffins, and rafts of penguins—are fundamentally social creatures.

Jefferson's most comprehensive explication of humans' social instinct occurs in his "Opinion on the French Treaties" (1793), written while Jefferson was George Washington's secretary of state. Jefferson begins with a statement, smacking of liberal atomism. "I consider the people who constitute a society or nation as the source of all authority in that nation." He continues:

> The Moral duties which exist between individual and individual in a state of nature, accompany them into a state of society & the aggregate of the

---

[14] E.g., Ari Helo and Peter Onuf, "Jefferson, Morality, and the Problem of Slavery," in *William and Mary Quarterly*, Vol. LX, No. 3, 2003, 584.

duties of all the individuals composing the society constitutes the duties of that society towards any other; so that between society & society the same moral duties exist as did between the individuals composing them while in an unassociated state, their maker not having released them from those duties on their forming themselves into a nation. Compacts then between nation & nation are obligatory on them by the same moral law which obliges individuals to observe their compacts.[15]

There is no cleaner statement by Jefferson that political right and wrong are merely answerable to each individual's sense of right and wrong, taken in the aggregate—Jefferson's liberal atomism. Hence, we can now grasp Jefferson's statement concerning the rarity of public sentiment adjudging "immorally or unwisely,"[16] We can also now grasp Jefferson's preference to a trial by jury in preference to a verdict by a single judge and why Jefferson champions government by the people, and not any group of "aristoi."

Just how does the moral sense work?

I described what it is, not how it works, in chapter 5. Whenever we are about to speak or act wrongly, he tells daughter Martha (11 Dec. 1783), we shall feel something within that is prohibitive of what we are about to say or do. Whenever we speak or act against this feeling, we are generally driven to do so by skewed reasoning or the pressure of others. Jefferson says unequivocally that rationality is a separate faculty from moral sensing and that the intrusions of reason pertaining to moral "judgments" are almost always faulty.[17]

Yet the moral sense is a faculty, unlike seeing or hearing, that binds all humans to each other through affectionate bonds—benevolence being foremost. Consequently, the state of nature, as we see in the 1824 letter to Ludlow (chapter 1), cannot be an asocial state, though it is an apolitical state. It is the state of Native Americans, who form not societies, but small tribes, and thus, are in no need of laws, but are guided solely by their moral-sense faculty. And so, humans, for Jefferson, like for Aristotle, are essentially "social animals," not atoms. Therefore, there is also an inevasible communitarian strain in Jefferson's thinking—called Classical republicanism in today's secondary literature on Jefferson.

---

[15] Thomas Jefferson, "Opinion on the French Treaties," in *The Scholars' Thomas Jefferson*, ed. M. Andrew Holowchak (Newcastle upon Tyne: Cambridge Scholars, 2020), 41.
[16] TJ to William Findley, 24 Mar. 1801.
[17] E.g., TJ to Maria Cosway, 12 Oct. 1786; TJ to Peter Carr, 10 Aug. 1787; and TJ to James Fishback, 27 Sept. 1809; and TJ to Thomas Law, 13 June 1814. For more, see M. Andrew Holowchak, *Thomas Jefferson, Moralist* (Jefferson, NC: McFarland, 2017), chap. 3.

We are, it seems, pulled in antipodal directions. Was Jefferson fundamentally an atomist or a Classical republican?

The Lockean liberal interpretation is championed by scholars such as Joyce Appleby[18] and Luigi Marco Bassani.[19] The Classical republican interpretation is championed by scholars such as J.G.A. Pocock,[20] Lance Banning,[21] and Garry Wills.[22] That discussion occurs only on account of entertaining a false dichotomy: Jefferson was either committed to liberal individualism (primacy of the individual) or to republican communitarianism (primacy of the state), grounded in Greco-Roman thinking. Neither side seems to think that the two views are reconcilable. They are. The influence of both traditions on Jefferson's political philosophy is profound, and his political philosophy is fundamentally a reconciliation of the two: His political thinking privileges individuals, but his commitment to a moral sense makes humans axially social creatures with social duties. In consequence, I have, from the start of my scholarship on Jefferson, dubbed him a liberal eudaimonist.[23]

We are now in the right position to grasp the need of freedom of religion in a Jeffersonian republic. Freedom of religion, he argues persuasively in Query XVII of *Notes on the State of Virginia* and as we have already noted, is a fundamental right of citizens in any civilized nation and one of Jefferson's four fundamental liberal reforms, mentioned in his *Autobiography*. "The legitimate powers of government extend to such acts only as are injurious to others."[24]

Yet there is now more to say. Jefferson is clear that once one divests most sectarian religious of their metaphysical trappings, one is left with the core principles of naturalized religion, dictated by duties to and love of God and duties to and love of other men. Those core principles are also identical to the

---

[18] Joyce Appleby, *Liberalism and Republicanism in the Historical Imagination* (Cambridge, Massachusetts: Harvard University Press, 1992).
[19] Luigi Marco Bassani, "Jefferson on Property Rights," in *Journal of Libertarian Studies*, Vol. 18, No. 1, 2004: 31–57.
[20] J.G.A. Pocock, *The Machiavellian Moment: Florentine Political Thought and the Atlantic Republican Tradition* (Princeton: Princeton University Press, 1975).
[21] Lance Banning, *The Jeffersonian Persuasion: Evolution of a Party Ideology* (Ithaca: SUNY Press, 1978).
[22] Gary Wills, *Inventing America: Jefferson's Declaration of Independence* (New York: Doubleday, 1978).
[23] *Eudaimonia* being the Greek word for "happiness" or "human thriving." M. Andrew Holowchak, *Dutiful Correspondent: Philosophical Essays on Thomas Jefferson* (Lanham, MD: Rowman & Littlefield, 2013), chap. 1.
[24] Thomas Jefferson, *Notes on the State of Virginia*, ed. William Peden (Chapel Hill: University of North Carolina Press, 1954), 159.

core principles of morality.²⁵ And so, Jeffersonian republicanism is grounded on naturalized religion, the subject of the next section.

"We will agree, to disagree"
Jefferson's "Political" Ambassador, Jesus

Enlightenment times were characterized by reluctance to trust traditional authorities, like the Catholic Church and Aristotle, and by appeal to experience to settle unsettled matters such as the motions of the planets, exploding stars, the existence of fossils, the similarities and differences between varieties of plants and of animals, the racial differences between types of humans, the mystery of projectile motion, and the strange phenomenon of tides. Almost all branches of learning during the Enlightenment, religious learning especially, were called into question.

The Bible itself, with numerous passages inexplicable to a mind of rational bent (e.g., Old Testament: Cain somewhere finding a wife after killing brother, Abel [Genesis 4:17], and Moses fasting for 40 days without food and water [Exodus 34:28]; New Testament: Jesus feeding 5,000 with five fishes and two loaves of bread [Mark 9:41]; and Jesus walking on the sea [Matthew 14:25]), became a subject of weighty criticism.

Jefferson, especially early in life, was no stranger to biblical criticism. I have elsewhere argued that Jefferson went through in his life two phases vis-à-vis the Bible.²⁶ There was the *literary-criticism phase* of his salad years and the *naturalized-religion phase* of his later, more mature years. In the former, Jefferson, a disciple of Lord Bolingbroke, uses the Bible to hone his developing critical faculties. There is little concern for salvaging anything from it. In the latter, Jefferson has come to recognize the gems—often dubbed "diamonds from dunghills"²⁷—in the New Testament. He has come to recognize the philosophical significance of Jesus—he will often refer to Jesus as the world's foremost moralist—and that leads him to expurgation of the four Gospels, or a sort of cleaning the Augean Gospels.

---

[25] M. Andrew Holowchak, *American Messiah: The Surprisingly Simple Religious Views of Thomas Jefferson* (Abilene: Abilene Christian University Press, 2020), 47–78.
[26] For a full exposition, see M. Andrew Holowchak, *American Messiah*, 79–108, and M. Andrew Holowchak, *Thomas Jefferson's Bible: Text with Introduction and Critical Commentary* (Berlin: De Gruyter, 2018).
[27] TJ to John Adams, 12 Oct. 1813 and 24 Jan. 1814; TJ to F.A. Van der Kemp, 25 Apr. 1816; and TJ to William Short, 31 Oct. 1819.

As part of the purgative process, Jefferson begins his own bible, *The Philosophy of Jesus*, in 1804—a "harmony" of the New Testament called *Philosophy of Jesus*. (*PJ*) The book aims merely to disclose the true moral teachings of Jesus. There is, thus, no need of concern for chronology. No known copy exists. Dissatisfied with the outcome, he will undertake the project more extensively in 1819 and include what can be salvaged concerning the life of Jesus. In this project titled *The Life and Morals of Jesus of Nazareth* (*LMJ*), finished in 1820, he does what he can to weave a narrative of the life of Jesus, while preserving his sagacity through his teachings. He will create Greek, Latin, French, and English texts, suggestive of a wish that the book reach a larger audience than its creator.[28]

It is noteworthy that Jefferson begins his first harmony during the final year of his first term as president. That is a strange time to begin such a project, for as president, he is daily bogged down with a multiplicity of important affairs—the most pressing being the newly purchased Louisiana Territories (Dec. 1803). That cannot be overpassed. There must be a certain urgency to the project, if it is to be undertaken in the most significant portion of his decades-long political life and just after the most significant event in his two-term presidency. The project is not merely personal—an 1813 letter to John Adams (Oct. 13) indicates that it is "for my own use"—it is also moral and political—at least, that much can be said for *PJ*.

There are two significant questions. How were the harmonies crafted? Why has Jesus become so important to Jefferson in his mature years? The two questions are related.

Scholars who write of the harmonies—the focus is almost always *LMJ*, as it is the only book that survives—typically proceed by analysis of relevant letters and of the finished product. For a thorough grasp of Jefferson's intendment, that is necessary but not sufficient. Study of what Jefferson excises is also critical.

Jefferson practices both deselection and selection. He certainly begins with the former, as it is the easiest way to proceed. Deselection is guided by two theses: unnaturalness and inconsistency. The *unnaturalness thesis* says that all passages at variance with the laws of physical nature are to be stripped. The *inconsistency thesis* says that all passages inconsistent with Jesus' character, based on satisfactory testimony, are to be stripped. Finally, there are Jefferson's principles of selection, advanced in a letter to William Short (4 Aug. 1820)—sublimity, purity, and guilelessness. *Selection by sublimity* entails culling all verses expressing notions of "the Supreme Being." *Selection by purity* entails

---

[28] See M. Andrew Holowchak, *American Messiah*, 79–108.

culling all "aphorisms and precepts of the purest morality and benevolence." *Selection by guilelessness* entails culling all verses that show Jesus to have lived "a life of humility, innocence and simplicity of manners, neglect of riches, absence of worldly ambition and honors, with an eloquence and persuasiveness which have not been surpassed."

Once Jefferson has plucked all the diamonds from the dungheaps—a metaphor that is axiologically rich and revelatory—what have we left?

We are then left with a peerless philosopher—a man, not a deity or demigod—who is in possession of no superman powers, but who preaches and practices the simplest and purest principles of morality: love of and duties to God and love of and duties to one's fellow man, *without* concern for reward or punition—a selfish motive at odds with human benevolence.

Jefferson continues in the 1820 letter to Short, "It is the innocence of [Jesus'] character, the purity & sublimity of his moral precepts, the eloquence of his inculcations, the beauty of the apologues in which he conveys them, that I so much admire." Jesus, thus, is the paradigm Jeffersonian republican, the model citizen of Jefferson's ideal political system, and his "principles" of morality, love of others and of God, are the fundamental moral principles of Jeffersonian republicanism—principles to which his political principles are answerable. That is something that he perhaps learned from Dr. Benjamin Rush, who was ever a devoted republican, in Jefferson's sense, and who ever championed the marriage of Christianity and republicanism. He writes to Jefferson (22 Aug. 1800): "I have always considered Christianity as the *strong ground* of Republicanism. Its Spirit is opposed, not only to the Splendor, but even to the very *forms* of monarchy, and many of its precepts have for their Objects, republican liberty & equality, as well as simplicity, integrity & Oconomy in government. It is only necessary for Republicanism to ally itself to the christian Religion, to overturn all the corrupted political and religious institutions in the World."

Jefferson, whose fascination with Jesus was at its zenith at the time of Rush's letter, agrees. Yet his Christianity—the adoption of two of Jesus' three axiomata, as he rejects Jesus' assertion of an afterlife—is not Rush's. Rush was ever committed to the divinity of Jesus. When Jefferson finally sends to Rush a précis of his views of Christianity—"ascribing to himself every *human* excellence; & believing he never claimed any other" (21 Apr. 1803)—Rush merely coolly replies (5 May 1803), "we will agree, to disagree."

Jefferson does not agree philosophically with Jesus on all moral matters. He writes to William Short (13 Apr. 1820): "It is not to be understood that I am with him in all his doctrines. I am a Materialist; he takes the side of spiritualism: he preaches the efficacy of repentance towards forgiveness [of sin], I require a counterpoise of good works to redeem it &c, &c"—" &c, &c," indicative of more areas of disagreement, e.g., Jefferson's disavowal of an afterlife.

That noted, Jefferson, like Rush, is committed to the paring of republicanism and Christianity, in Jefferson's detoxified sense, inasmuch as politics for Jefferson is answerable to and grounded in morality and as detoxified Christianity is equivalent to morality. Thus, though freedom of religion is needed for Jeffersonian republicanism, Jefferson is not championing all types of Christianity, but merely depolluted, naturalized Christianity: the core principles of all reasonable sectarian religions that acknowledge the twin towers of duties to God and man, founded in each person's moral sense and preached especially eloquently by Jesus the Nazarian.

"Thereby converting dangerous Enemies into valuable friends"
"Liberty" and "Empire"

The American Revolution, those who were the major movers in it recognized, was an event singular in the history of the world. That the colonies could have both come together in unanimity to uprise against England and win its independence from their mother country through a sanguinary war were sufficiently singular happenings. After winning the war, the problem the Colonists faced was the problem that all revolutionary leaders face when their actions are successful: What now are we to do?

Most politically savvy Colonists conceded that the British manner of government, howsoever defective, was the best manner of government on the globe. Yet even the best government on the globe had its problems. The king and the parliament had passed numerous acts pertaining to the colonies without Colonists having any say in those matters. Jefferson limns, in his *Summary View of the Rights of British American* and *Declaration of Independence* the king's "long train of abuses & usurpations pursuing invariably the same object": despotism or treating the Colonists as slaves, not citizens. The American Revolution, thus, was for the sake of human rights, grounded on liberty and equality. Jefferson writes noteworthily in *Notes on the State of Virginia:* "Every species of government has its specific principles. Ours perhaps are more peculiar than those of any other in the universe. It is a composition of the freest principles of the English constitution, with others derived from natural right and natural reason."[29]

To Jefferson, the American Revolution was an experiment concerning that "boisterous sea of liberty." For republicanism to work, there needed to be many

---

[29] Thomas Jefferson, *Notes on Virginia*, 84.

significant reforms so that all vestiges of artificial aristocracy needed to be removed for there to be government for and of the people. Their elected representatives would be culled on behalf of their genius and their virtue. To guard against corruption due to the bait of power, Jefferson mandated that the citizenry needed to be watchful of their representatives, each of whom were to govern for fixed terms. Again, there would be periodic constitutional renewal to be brought about by suitable delegates, not by those governing. The citizenry could be the chief governing body, because Jefferson assumed that all persons, born with a moral sense, were possessed both of an equal capacity for virtue and of adequate rationality to conduct their own affairs without governmental intervention. He was mating a Christianized ancient virtue ethics with the liberalism of his day, hence liberal eudaimonism and not just Classical republicanism or Lockean liberalism.

Republicanism was an experiment for Jefferson because it was not known if the people could, as it were, self-govern. "Experience has proved it safer, for the mass of individuals composing the society, to reserve to themselves personally the exercise of all rightful powers to which they are competent," says Jefferson to Dupont de Nemours (24 Apr. 1816), "and to delegate those to which they are not competent to deputies named, and removable for unfaithful conduct, by themselves immediately." The "experience" to which Jefferson refers is not that of the mass of individuals exercising all the powers of which they are capable. That has never yet been tried. It instead concerns what happens when the people do not govern themselves. Anyone in a position of power uses the masses to his advantage.

John Adams, Alexander Hamilton, and High Federalists insisted that they the *hoi polloi* could not self-govern. We return to Adams' celebrated thought experiment. Let any 100 people begin a society and give each an equal vote/role. In due time, 25 of those persons will have handed over their vote to 25 others, whom Adams calls the natural *aristoi*. Jefferson makes it clear to Adams (28 Oct. 1813) that the real natural *aristoi* is of genius and virtue, not of wealth and blood. Jefferson adds that "that form of government is the best which provides the most effectually for a pure selection of these natural aristoi into the offices of government." Wise and virtuous federal governors will govern with utmost disinterest and attend only to such matters to which the Constitution mandated that they attend: chiefly matters related to securing citizens' rights and conducting foreign affairs.

So committed was Jefferson to a weak federal government that he sometimes cared little about its necessity. He writes in 1783 to Barbé-Marbois (Dec. 5): "The constant session of Congress can not be necessary in time of peace, and their separation will destroy the strange idea of their being a permanent body, which has unaccountably taken possession of the heads of their constituents, and occasions jealousies injurious to the public good." The sentiment seems to be that the need of the federal government was merely to conduct war with England. With the surcease of the war, it will be best for surcease of the federal government. There needs to remain only such a bond between the states to rally them to unity in the event of another major war.

Yet the Congress did not surcease, and while Jefferson was in France from 1784 to 1789, there was in America discussion of a constitution to supplant the Articles of Confederation. Jefferson's two concerns, when given a draft of the proposed constitution, were no limit to the tenure of the executive and lack of any explicit expression of the rights of American citizens.[30]

The key to implementation of government of and for the people was thin, ramified government: a Constitution-bound federal government comprising states, state governments comprising counties, counties comprising wards which are self-governed. Citizens' thirst for liberty was the trunk of ramified government.

"Liberty" in the civic sense, even if a derivative concept, occupied the most privileged place in Jefferson's political philosophy, though it was ever heterotelic—that is, for the sake of human thriving or happiness, not for its own sake. Moreover, as we have seen, liberty in America was uniquely linked with land, hence Jefferson's link of "liberty" and "empire" in certain letters apropos of America.

Jefferson first links "empire" with "liberty" in a letter to George Rogers Clark (25 Dec. 1780). The backdrop is Clark's valiant efforts as leader of American troops in the Illinois Campaign (1778–1779) of the Revolutionary War, and his battles at and around Detroit thereafter.

> If that Post [i.e., the fighting in the territory to the northwest of the colonies] be reduced we shall be quiet in future on our frontiers, and thereby immense Treasures of blood and Money be saved; we shall be at leizure to turn our whole force to the rescue of our eastern Country from subjugation, we shall divert through our own Country a branch of commerce which the European States have thought worthy of the most important struggles and sacrifices, and in the event of peace on terms which have been contemplated by some powers we shall form to the American union a barrier against the dangerous extension of the British Province of Canada and add to the Empire of liberty an extensive and fertile Country thereby converting dangerous Enemies into valuable friends.

---

[30] E.g., TJ to James Madison, 31 July 1788, and TJ to William Short, 20 Sept. 1788.

Clark's efforts in the Northwest Territory led the way for the Treaty of Paris (1783), which formally marked the end of the American Revolution, and a large parcel of land ceded to the United States by Britain. Jefferson writes Clark concerning future quiet on western frontiers. In the event of peace with garrulous European nations, the American union of states will become a "barrier against the dangerous extension" of British Canada, "intended ... as a bulwark against republicanism."[31] It is here not so much what the fledgling "Empire of liberty" is, it is rather what it is not: an imperial power like England, which employs economic and naval coercion to sustain and distend its empire.

Jefferson's next links "empire" and "liberty" vis-à-vis the United States in a letter, during term two of his presidency to Benjamin Chambers (28 Dec. 1805). The reference concerns acquisition of the Louisiana territories. He states:

> The addition of a country so extensive, so fertile, as Louisiana, to the great republican family of this hemisphere, while it substitutes, for our neighbors, brethren & children in the place of strangers, has secured the blessings of civil & religious freedom to millions yet unborn. by enlarging the empire of liberty, we multiply it's auxiliaries, & provide new sources of renovation, should it's principles at any time, degenerate; in those portions of our country which gave them birth. the securing for you the peace & friendship of the various Indian tribes is among the highly valued advantages of this acquisition.

Last, Jefferson conjoins the two terms in a letter, just after his presidency, to President James Madison (27 Apr. 1809). Jefferson discusses acquisition of the Florida lands and Cuba.

> That he [Bonaparte] would give us the Floridas to withold intercourse with the residue of those colonies cannot be doubted. But that is no price, because they are ours in the first moment of the first war, & until a war they are of no particular necessity to us. But, altho' with difficulty, he will consent to our recieving Cuba into our union to prevent our aid to Mexico & the other provinces. That would be a price, & I would immediately erect a column on the Southernmost limit of Cuba & inscribe on it a Ne plus ultra as to us in that direction. We should then

---

[31] To instantiate British extension, John Graves Simco allowed the acquisition of land at six cents per acre to western settlers, loyal to the crown. Lawrence B.A. Hatter, "The Narcissism of Petty Differences? Thomas Jefferson, John Graves Simcoe and the Reformation of empire in the Early United States and British-Canada," in *American Review of Canadian Studies*, Vol. 42, No. 2, 2012, 130--41.

have only to include the North in our confederacy, which would be of course in the first war, and we should have such an empire for liberty as she has never surveyed since the creation: & I am persuaded no constitution was ever before so well calculated as ours for extensive empire & self government.

There are 17 states at the time—Vermont, Ohio, Kentucky, and Tennessee have been added to the original 13 states. Jefferson imagines here acquisition of Cuba and the Florida lands to the south and then the lands to the north, and bounded by the eastern part of the Mississippi River, in possession of the U.S. since the war: what are now Michigan, Indiana, Illinois, Wisconsin, and the northeastern part of Minnesota.

What of the objection that acquisition of Cuba will whet the hungriness for future acquisitions? "Cuba can be defended by us without a navy. & this developes the principle which ought to limit our views. Nothing should ever be accepted which would require a navy to defend it." The sentiment is that need of a navy will necessarily fatten government by increase in federal expenditures, which is at odds with Jeffersonian republicanism, and also involve the country in the broils of Europe.

How would the new territories, ultramontane (and the mountains here are the Allegheny Mountains), best be zonated?

Jefferson addresses that question in an earlier letter to James Monroe (9 July 1786). He phrases the nodus in the form of this question: "How may the ultramontane territory be disposed of so as to produce the greatest & most immediate benefit to the inhabitants of the maritime states of the union?" That question is reduceable to another: "How may the territories of the Union be disposed of so as to produce the greatest degree of happiness to their inhabitants?"

Would it be best to limit them to some 30,000 square miles, roughly the size of Pennsylvania, or allow them to be as large as 160,000 square miles, which is larger than today's Texas?

Jefferson, upon considering the American people generally and circumstantially, asserts that such a large state would soon "crumble into little ones," as is the case with small Native American societies. "They will not only be happier in states of a moderate size, but it is the only way in which they can exist as a regular society." They certainly will not be happy that way, and so such enormous states, each sovereign, will tend to divide themselves. Thus, "they will end by separating from our confederacy & becoming it's enemies."

Why is that the case, for it is certainly unclear how such enmity will follow from size and the need to divide?

If the Congress lays off them into small or moderate states, "they will acquiesce, and we shall have the advantage of arranging them so as to produce the best combinations of interest." The intimation here is that such divisions will be according to local interests, whereas in large states, various sectors will have different interests and that will force tensions and divisions. He continues, "Upon this plan, we treat them as fellow citizens, they will have a just share in their own government, they will love us, & pride themselves in an union with us."

"Upon the other [plan of allowing for large states,] we treat them as subjects, we govern them, & not they themselves, they will abhor us as masters, & break off from us in defiance."

Why must the federal government dictate over large states?

Jefferson does not fully explain, but the suggestion is that large states will be difficult to manage, because they will be riven by the tensions of the local passions of its various "districts," here not used in a formal sense. That is the argument given in his Second Inaugural Address.[32]

Upshot

The aim of this lengthy chapter has been to show how, for Jefferson, liberty could enroot and spread in America, even in the American hemisphere. In doing so, I have returned to certain issues covered in prior chapters—the American Revolution, the nature of Jeffersonian republicanism, and its grounding, essentially "religious"—in my effort to make sense of Jefferson's pairing of "liberty" and "empire." Again, Jefferson's notion of "empire of liberty" betrays his belief in liberty as a force that drives human affairs and presses them forward to a human "Promised Land" where liberty and equality find such full social expression that the concepts are in some sense vacuous, because they are fully actuated.

---

[32] Thomas Jefferson, Second Inaugural Address, in *The Scholars' Thomas Jefferson*, ed. M. Andrew Holowchak (Newcastle upon Tyne: Cambridge Scholars, 2021), 60.

Chapter X

The Spread of Liberty across the Globe

The spread of liberty in North America, even the American hemisphere, was the subject of the previous chapter. In this final chapter, I examine Jefferson's expectations, or at least hopes, for the enrooting and spread of liberty in Europe—the French Revolution was to him critical—and the possibility of a global empire of liberty.

"Watching always the favorable moment…"
The Failed French Revolution

As the 1820 letter to Marquis de Lafayette in the preface shows, Jefferson believed that humans were naturally liberty-embracing creatures and that in the course of earthly, if not universal events, there was a slow unfolding of liberty—*viz.*, humans were, through a sluggish course of development, coming to actualize themselves. That sluggish process was outlined in his letter to Ludlow about four stages of human development. With the success of the American Revolution, Jefferson expected that the "disease of Liberty" would spread throughout North America, South America, and Europe. That spread, because of peoples' access to news through pamphlets, newspapers, and books would be expedited.

We saw, in the 1809 letter to Madison in the last chapter, that Jefferson envisaged the spread of liberty through Jeffersonian republicanism throughout a large part of North America. Other earlier letters show interest in the land west of the Mississippi River.[1] To Alexander von Humboldt (6 Dec. 1813), Jefferson envisages a time, 50 years hence, where the two Americas are republicanized, where "America has a hemisphere to itself."

Not all American politicians shared Jefferson's enthusiasm about Westward migration. Many, like George Washington, preferred a gradualist approach. Haste might eventuate in pandemonium. Ultraist Federalists worried that the Western push would eventually result in creation of republican states—republican because agrarian—and result in the loss of Federalists' congressional power. Yet Jefferson feared that undue caution would open the door to the possibility of Spanish expansion in North America or renewed interest by

---

[1] TJ to George Rogers Clark, 4 Dec. 1783, and TJ to John Jay, 14 Aug. 1785.

England or France in the continent. He was adamant that if North America was not wholly in possession of the United States, then states or nations, independent of the U.S., needed to be wedded to republican governing.²

Success of republican governing in America would (hopefully quickly) incentivize European nations to republicanize. During his tenure in Paris as minister plenipotentiary (1784–1789), he was privy to the ferment of French revolutionary febrility, and even hosted a dinner engagement to key political figures, interested in the discussion of democratizing the nation. His early assessment of the numerous local unrests is cheery. "The revolution of France has gone on with the most unexampled success, hitherto," he tells James Madison (11 May 1789). The shedding of blood in those unrests he explains by the extremely cold winter and want of food. "There have been some mobs, occasioned by the want of bread, in different parts of the kingdom, in which there may have been some lives lost; perhaps a dozen or twenty. These had no professed connection, *generally*, with the constitutional revolution."³ It is a developing situation on which he shall keep a close eye until he returns to Virginia later in 1789. When he does return—and the French Revolution blocks any attempt at a return to Paris—he does what he can to keep up with events through newspapers and correspondence with French connections.

Jefferson was, at least from a theoretical angle, heavily invested in the French Revolution. He writes to Marquis de Condorcet (30 Aug. 1791): "I am looking ardently to the completion of the glorious work in which your country is engaged [the French Revolution]. I view the general condition of Europe as hanging on the success or failure of France. Having set such an example of philosophical arrangement within, I hope it will be extended without your limits also, to your dependents and to your friends in every part of the earth."

Soon the French king is beheaded, Napoleon Bonaparte affects a successful coup, and in time the push for something like a Jeffersonian republic in France is supplanted by a government by a ruthless dictator, with ambitions to capture as much of the civilized world as is possible.

Nonetheless, Jefferson's hopes for the contagion of liberty are never dashed. He even at first has a positive spin on Napoleon's dictatorship. He states to John Breckinridge (29 Jan. 1800) of his fear of a permanent dictatorship and "of the influence of the example on our countrymen." Yet he adds, "Perhaps it is now

---

² For more, see M. Andrew Holowchak, *Thomas Jefferson's Political Philosophy and the Metaphysics of Utopia* (London: Brill, 2017), chap. 6.

³ See also TJ to William Carmichael, 4 Mar. 1789, and TJ to David Humphreys, 18 Mar. 1789. For more on the revolution, see M. Andrew Holowchak, *Thomas Jefferson in Paris: The Ministry of a Virginian "Looker on"* (Wilmington, DE: Vernon Press, 2023), chap. 22.

to be wished that Buonaparte may be spared, as, according to his protestations, he is for liberty, equality & representative government, and he is more able to keep the nation together, & to ride out the storm than any other." The qualification shows that Napoleon might be nothing more than a large wave on the "boisterous sea of Liberty." To Samuel Adams (16 Feb. 1800), Jefferson says that Napoleon's rise to power is a lesson for true republicans. "Whatever his views may be, he has at least transferred the destinies of the republic from the civil to the military arm. Some will use this as a lesson against the practicability of republican government. I read it as a lesson against the danger of standing armies." Jefferson comes only in a tardigrade manner to recognize—so bewitched is he by the notion of the inevitable contagion of the "disease of liberty"—that Napoleon is "a cold-blooded, calculating, unprincipled usurper, without a virtue"[4] and that there is no chance of a viable French republic with him as autocrat.

Failure of the French Revolution could only have been devastating to Jefferson. France was pivotally involved in the success of the American Revolution, and Jefferson formed many close friends among the French in his stint as governor of Virginia and minister to France. It was natural for him to consider France as the nation most suited to republicanize—to contract the disease of liberty and to spread it, via contagion, to other European nations.

It is meet here to mention several obstacles to the spread of Jeffersonian republicanism. I follow here and in gist the thread of my lengthy argument in *Thomas Jefferson's Political Philosophy and the Metaphysics of Utopia*.

First, there is the nodus of blueprint. There is no blueprint, as it were, for a Jeffersonian republic, because there is no precedent. The political philosophy that Jefferson sketches in his First Inaugural Address and several letters offers the nuts and bolts of a thriving republic. It tells us what is needed for a thriving republic, not what is sufficient for one in a certain set of circumstances. In short, there can be constitutional principles shared by, because they are needed for, all thriving republics, but no one constitution is sufficient for a prosperous republic. The French nation, for illustration, has been for centuries echeloned axiologically—that is, separated into wealthy aristocrats and penurious peasants—and it would not have been easy either for aristocrats to find liberation in having a status the equal of any peasant and "donating" their abundancy of goods (e.g., their abundancy of lands) for *saluti populi* (the overall good of the people/nation). It would not have been easy for peasants to express their newly found liberty without substantial governmental reforms (e.g., seizure and equitable distribution of goods). Even with such reforms,

---

[4] TJ to John Adams, 5 July 1814.

peasants would not readily have taken to equality and liberty—concepts just too foreign to them.

Second, there is the nodus of timeliness. There is a kairotic moment, a right time, for any republican revolution. Jeffersonian republicanism, as I show in the prior paragraph, cannot be exported before a people are ready for it. The French Revolution was abortive because "liberty" and "equality" were notions too difficult to grasp for a people nurtured for centuries in a culture of oppression of the masses and inequality. Novelty was clashing with tradition, and the novelty was merely too novel and the tradition was too deep-rooted for a republican revolution to have resulted in a republican constitution.[5] As was the case with France, it was the case with numerous other non-republican nations.[6]

Those nodi return us to the problem of political relativism. Yet once again, we must resist the temptation to reduce this relativism to the subjective, arbitrary sort. The nodi of blueprint and timeliness are driven by objective circumstances and dictate merely that the nuts and bolts of Jeffersonian republicanism be used uniquely for every state or nation. That is the ponderous task of application—a separate nodus. Each state or nation, aiming at republicanizing, must advance at its own pace. Jefferson writes to Dr. Thomas Cooper (7 Oct. 1814): "We cannot always do what is absolutely best [i.e., morally right]. Those with whom we act, entertaining different views, have the power and the right of carrying them into practice. Truth advances, and error recedes step by step only; and to do to our fellow men the most good in our power we must lead where we can, follow where we cannot and still go with them, watching always the favorable moment for helping them to another step."

"I like a little rebellion now and then"

Shays' Rebellion

Jefferson's love of and commitment to liberty can be measured by his response to Shays' Rebellion—an uprising, begun in Massachusetts and led by Daniel

---

[5] Philipp Ziesche, "Exporting American Revolutions: Gouverneur Morris, Thomas Jefferson, and the National Struggle for Universal Rights in Revolutionary France," in *Journal of the Early Republic*, Vol. 26, 2006, 447.

[6] See also TJ to Abigail Adams, 22 Feb. 1787; TJ to Madame de Tessé, 20 Mar. 1787; TJ to Thomas Paine, 23 Dec. 1788; TJ to Nicholas Lewis, 9 Feb. 1791; TJ to Walter Jones, 31 Mar. 1801; TJ Dr. Joseph Priestley, 29 Nov. 1802; TJ to Barnabas Bidwell, 5 July 1806; TJ to Joel Barlow, 10 Dec. 1807; TJ to Gov. John Tyler, 26 May 1810; TJ to Marquis de Lafayette, 14 Feb. 1815; TJ to David Barrow, 1 May 1815; TJ to P.S. Dupont de Nemours, 24 Apr. 1816; TJ to Joseph C. Cabell, 16 Feb. 1818; and TJ to James Pleasants, 26 Dec. 1821.

Shays in 1786 by former soldiers of the Revolutionary War and farmers. The concern here is that the spread of liberty throughout the country might have disastrous consequences: It might enflame anarchists.

The protestors objected to taxes larger than what they paid before they were "freed" of British yoke, lack of payment for service as soldiers in the cause of the American Revolution, and intolerance of deferment of debts, for many, incurred while they were in the service of the Continental Army. In protest, they seized governmental buildings like courthouses and rallied, though unsuccessfully, to seize the Springfield Armory. The uprising spread to neighboring states and that eventuated in large-scale panic. To many in Massachusetts, it seemed as if the uprising might result in another large-scale revolution.[7] We recall John Adams' barb in 1813 that Jefferson, when that event and other threatening events occurred, was "fast asleep in philosophical Tranquility."

Jefferson, still in France, wrote several revelatory letters on the event and the prize of liberty. Those letters have prompted one scholar to claim that Jefferson, at least from the years 1787 to 1793, had a sort of sickly attachment to "liberty," which he considered to be autotelic[8]—a topic to which I later return. And so, attention to a representative selection of Jefferson's writings on the rebellion is worth fulsome analysis. My preference is for representation of Jefferson's mindset through his words, not paraphrase.

On January 30, 1787, Jefferson writes alludes to the rebellion to his close friend James Madison. He writes of the benefits and ills of representative government:

> The mass of mankind under that enjoys a precious degree of liberty & happiness. It has it's evils too: the principal of which is the turbulence to which it is subject. But weigh this against the oppressions of monarchy, and it becomes nothing. *Malo periculosam libertatem quam quietam servitutem.*[9] Even this evil is productive of good. It prevents the degeneracy of government, and nourishes a general attention to the public affairs. I hold it that a little rebellion now and then is a good thing, & as necessary in the political world as storms in the physical. Unsuccessful rebellions indeed generally establish the encroachments on the rights of the people which have produced them. An observation of this truth should render honest republican governors so mild in their

---

[7] History.com Editors, "Shays' Rebellion," https://www.history.com/topics/early-us/shays-rebellion, accessed 18 Mar. 2023.
[8] Conor Cruise O'Brien, *The Long Affair: Thomas Jefferson and the French Revolution, 1785–1800* (Chicago: University of Chicago Press, 1996).
[9] "I prefer boisterous liberty to quiet slavery."

punishment of rebellions, as not to discourage them too much. It is a medicine necessary for the sound health of government.

The argument here is that when weighed on an axiological scale, the benefits/banes of liberty are preferable to the benefits/banes of monarchy. Even what seems to be a bane, turbulence, is really a benefit. Turbulence through periodic uprisings turns the eyes of governors toward public affairs and that keeps them honest. It is thus a needed panpharmacon—a consequence of representative government.

To Abigail Adams (22 Feb. 1787), Jefferson writes: "The spirit of resistance to government is so valuable on certain occasions, that I wish it to be always kept alive. It will often be exercised when wrong, but better so than not to be exercised at all. I like a little rebellion now and then. It is like a storm in the Atmosphere."

This letter to Adams acknowledges that an uprising may at times be wrongheaded. Even so, the profits gleaned from just uprisings more than compensate for the harms of ones wrongheaded.

Last, there is one of Jefferson's strangest letters, which occurs later in 1787. Jefferson says to William Stevens Smith (Nov. 13):

> Can history produce an instance of rebellion [Shays'] so honorably conducted? I say nothing of its motives. They were founded in ignorance, not wickedness. God forbid we should ever be twenty years without such a rebellion. The people cannot be all, and always, well informed. The part which is wrong will be discontented in proportion to the importance of the facts they misconceive. If they remain quiet under such misconceptions, it is a lethargy, the forerunner of death to the public liberty. We have had 13. states independent 11. years. There has been one rebellion. That comes to one rebellion in a century & a half for each state. What country before ever existed a century & half without a rebellion?[10] & what country can preserve it's liberties if their rulers are not warned from time to time that their people preserve the spirit of resistance? Let them take arms. The remedy is to set them right as to the facts, pardon & pacify them. What signify a few lives lost in a century or two? The tree of liberty must be refreshed from time to time with the blood of patriots & tyrants. It is it's natural manure.

There is much here to unpack. First, why was the rebellion so "honorably conducted"? The answer is likely because only four lives were lost. Second, why

---

[10] An argument first articulated in a letter to David Hartley, 23 Apr. 1787.

were the motives "founded in ignorance"? The uprisers, unremunerated soldiers especially, were objecting loudly to perceived injustices, which analysis shows to be actual injustices. Nonetheless, Jefferson seems to be warranting rebellious activity *in ignorantiam* and that is atypical of him. It is certainly at odds with his notions on revolutions in his Declaration of Independence. It is better to rise up for a cause even if you have not all the facts, because quietness while misconstruing something is lethargy and that is death to liberty. That is a very strange argument—atypically paralogistic, for Jefferson. Third, Jefferson argues that periodic rebellions serve as a check to the ambitions of guileful politicians. If uprisers misconstrue the facts, it is the role of elected officials to "set them right," and the suggestion here is by argument, not by force. Finally, Jefferson argues that the several lives lost in protest against perceived injustices are counterpoised by the salutary effect of rebellions on self-leaning governors.

Last, to William Short (3 Jan. 1793), Jefferson castigates his young friend for his misconstrual of the French Revolution. Jefferson grants that many lives have been lost in the failed revolution. He asserts: "The liberty of the whole earth was depending on the issue of the contest, and was ever such a prize won with so little innocent blood? My own affections have been deeply wounded by some of the martyrs to this cause, but rather than it should have failed, I would have seen half the earth desolated. Were there but an Adam and Eve left in every country, and left free, it would be better than as it now is."

The secondary literature has typically been cruel to Jefferson for his pro-rebellion sentiments, especially in the letter to Short. William Howard Adams writes disparagingly of Jefferson's "virtual sermon on republican theology" in his 1787 letters on the rebellion.[11] Thomas Fleming speaks of Jefferson's hypocrisy. Such bold utterances on the importance of rebellion are strange given Jefferson's own cowardice when governor of Virginia.[12] Joe Ellis writes of the "extremely radical statements" that "placed Jefferson far to the left of any responsible political leader of the revolutionary generation." He adds, "His deepest allegiances were not to the preservation of political stability but to its direct opposite."[13] Michael Hardt states, "Celebration of rebellion and his apology for political violence can only be seen as a recipe for anarchy."[14] Finally, ultraist Conor Cruise O'Brien argues that at least from the years 1787 to 1793,

---

[11] William Howard Adams, *The Paris Years of Thomas Jefferson* (New Haven: CT, Yale University Press, 1997), 257.

[12] Thomas Fleming, *The Great Divide; The Conflict Between Washington and Jefferson that Defined a Nation* (Boston: De Capo Press, 2015), 34.

[13] Joseph Ellis, *American Sphinx: The Character of Thomas Jefferson* (New York: Alfred A. Knopf, 1997), 100.

[14] Michael Hardt, "Jefferson and Democracy," in *American Quarterly,* Vol. 59, No. 1, 58-65.

Jefferson espoused an anything-goes liberalism. During that time, he was "in the grip of a fanatical cult of liberty," to which "it would be blasphemous to assign limits." He adds, "The liberty that Jefferson adored is … a wild liberty, absolute, untrammeled, universal, the liberty of a great revolutionary manifesto: the Declaration of Independence."[15]

In what follows, my concern is with the tendency of scholars to disparage Jefferson for insensitivity to human wellbeing (Adams) and for espousal of liberal anarchism (Ellis, Hardt, and O'Brien). Flemings' charge of cravenness, itself a craven potshot, can be overpassed, as it is unsupported by facts.

The thesis that Jefferson was espousing a sort of radical liberalism can be readily dismissed. Jefferson, as I have elsewhere shown, never at any time viewed liberty as an end, but only as a means to, or a needed condition of, human flourishing.[16]

The most substantive objection is that Jefferson's comments betray insensitivity to human wellbeing. That warrants fuller treatment.

First, as I have already noted, we must not confuse "rebellion," the subject of his 1787 letters, and "revolution," the subject of his 1793 letter to Short.

Rebellions, Jefferson thinks, are relatively infrequent phenomena. Though turbulent, they tend not toward much violence. A few lives might be lost over the course of some 150 years, but the purgative effect, a stark warning from time to time to elected officials, is worth the cost.

Revolutions are concerted attempts to overthrow a government, deemed corrupt, and replace it with one better or less corrupt. They are even more infrequent than rebellions. Over 20,000 soldiers lost their lives in battle in the American Revolution. Many thousands more succumbed fatally to disease. We have seen above that Colonists were not revolting against a government that they adjudged to be corrupt from soup and nuts. They were instead fighting for an ideal: liberty. The French, however, were revolting against a sort of aristocratic corruption much worse than that of England. To castigate Jefferson for his verbal succor of the French Revolution but not object to his role in the sanguinary American Revolution seems scholarly hypocritical.

Yet there is Jefferson's puzzling claim, "Were there but an Adam and Eve left in every country, and left free, it would be better than as it now is." Scholars

---

[15] Conor Cruise O'Brien, *The Long Affair: Thomas Jefferson and the French Revolution, 1785–1800* (Chicago: University of Chicago Press, 1996). See also Conor Cruise O'Brien, "Thomas Jefferson: Radical and Racist," in *Atlantic Monthly,* October 1996, 53–74.

[16] M. Andrew Holowchak, *Thomas Jefferson: Uncovering his Unique Philosophy and Vision* (Amherst, NY: Prometheus, 2014), 108–18.

amazingly fail to construe that this is merely hyperbole, which Jefferson uses very sparingly in his writings. Note also that that use of hyperbole is in a letter to an intimate friend, who likely would have recognized hyperbole as hyperbole. Reference to Adam and Eve, however, is not happenstance. The sentiment is that it is preferable to repopulate the globe by a potent first man and fecund first woman in every country—and potency and fecundity are here guaranteed by their Jeffersonian love of liberty—than to keep things as they are, where most of the people of the globe suffer the indignity of non-autarchy or incapacity to live as one chooses to live. In that regard, Adam and Eve—having eaten of the forbidden Tree of Knowledge—were certainly for Jefferson heroic mythical figures.

"The question of '85"

A Biggish Fly in the Ointment

As we have seen in the 1824 letter to William Ludlow (chapter 1), Jefferson is committed to four stages of progressive human historical development: pastoral living (hunters and gatherers), sedentary living (frontiersmen), cultivation of the land (husbandmen), and (small townsmen). It is almost certain that Jefferson does not consider unqualifiedly the "movement" from agrarianism to life in small seaport towns to be an advance, despite him calling the latter "the most improved state." Like other utopists of his day—e.g., More, Condorcet, and Mercier—agriculture was the most important economic activity. Yet not only did the labor of husbandmen feed the body, if fed the soul. "Those who labour in the earth are the chosen people of God, if ever he had a chosen people, whose breasts he has made his peculiar deposit for substantial and genuine virtue," say Jefferson in Query XIX of *Notes on the State of Virginia*. There is no instance throughout recorded history of the praxis of farming corrupting farmers. Again, husbandmen do not depend for subsistence on "casualties and caprice of customers"—that is, they do not have artificially to create a demand for their produce. Such artifice tends to "subservience and venality" and "prepares fit tools for the designs of ambition." Jefferson says algorithmically that any state can be adjudged sound and moral by proportioning "its unsound to its healthy parts"—the number of its husbandmen to its non-husbandmen. The danger of much manufacture is the growth of cities and its obliquitous mobs, which are as "sores … to the strength of the human body."[17]

---

[17] Thomas Jefferson, *Notes on the State of Virginia*, ed. William Peden (Chapel Hill: University of North Carolina Press, 1954), 164–65.

Jefferson never disavowed his views on the preeminence of farming for a thriving state. With a focus on farming, much of the manufacture needed by husbandmen could be produced by each at his own estate, given sufficient size. He did, however, grudgingly concede as early as 1784 that Americans cannot do without British manufactured goods, even if they were fripperies. He writes on March 15 to George Washington: "Was [sic] it practicable to keep our new empire separated from them we might indulge ourselves in speculating whether commerce contributes to the happiness of mankind. But we cannot separate ourselves from them. Our citizens have had too full a taste of the comforts furnished by the arts and manufactures to be debarred the use of them." That sentiment is ensconced in his mind later in life. He states to Gen. Thaddeus Kosciusko (28 June 1812), "Manufactures are now as necessary to our independence as to our comfort." The American demand for British manufactured goods over the decades beyond independence showed him the only way to break the bond of dependency on such goods, most unneeded, was for Americans to turn to manufacture as well as agriculture. That was a matter of acknowledging citizens' demand for more unsound parts.

There is a presentiment of that view at the end of Query XVII, "Religion," of *Notes on the State of Virginia*. There, for some reason, Jefferson atypically waxes melancholy. He enjoins Americans to fix their essential rights, while the time is kairotic, for "from the conclusion of this [Revolutionary] war we shall be going down hill." The people will forget about all things except making money, and "will never think of uniting to effect a due respect for their rights." The shackles that Colonists wore have not been removed with the cessation of the war. They, instead, will become "heavier and heavier" until such time that "our rights shall revive or expire in a convulsion."[18]

To what precisely is Jefferson here referring?

There was debate concerning the U.S. Constitution while Jefferson was in France and haggling to publish his various versions of *Notes on Virginia*.[19] Letters to friends back in the states show Jefferson's large concern for lack of a bill of rights as part of the proposed constitution.[20] Is a bill that legally guarantees citizens' right such a thing that revives the citizenry by reviving their rights? That seems unlikely, as embrace of rights is a way of life, devoted to love of liberty. What Jefferson is advocating is republicanism as a way of life.

---

[18] Thomas Jefferson, *Notes on Virginia*, 161.
[19] For more, see M. Andrew Holowchak, *Thomas Jefferson's* Notes on the State of Virginia: *A Prolegomena* (Vernon Press, 2023), chap. 2.
[20] E.g., TJ to Edward Carrington, 27 May 1788, and TJ to James Madison, 31 July 1788.

For Jefferson, liberty, in its civic sense, is like air or water. It is not much appreciated until it is severely wanting or absent. Moreover, its relative lack can be suffered so long as there are diversions—e.g., opportunities for making money, feeding human covetousness and selfishness, being the most notorious diversion. Yet when it is severely wanting or absent, for Jefferson, it is recognized as the most precious of human goods, *sine qua non* for human happiness.

In most liberal societies today, there are degrees of freedom insofar as there are degrees to which governments intervene unjustly in the affairs of their citizens. Moreover, the mostly agrarian lifestyle of a Jeffersonian republic is not blissfully embraced by most Americans. That Jefferson comes to recognize later in life. Americans, like all other people, covet things other than things needed for a modest, unpretentious agrarian life.

In that sense, Jefferson *qua* political philosopher faces the same problem as did Plato *qua* political philosopher over two millennia before him. So, I begin with Plato.

In Book II of *Republic*,[21] Plato (427–347 B.C.), through a conversation between Socrates and Glaucon, discusses an ideal or just polis (*kallipolis*). The people come together because of need: No one is wholly self-sufficient. Things needed, in order of priority or worth, are food, shelter, and clothes. Thus, the *kallipolis* will need farmers, builders, weavers, toolmakers, and cobblers, *inter alii*. Each citizen will specialize in that craft for which he is most suited. Craftspersons will make bread, wine, cakes, clothes, shoes, and houses. In such a way, the people will feast and sing hymns to the gods.

Glaucon objects stentorianly that there are no delicacies.

Socrates, pausing and acknowledging the objection, adds that there will be salt, olives, cheese, roots, vegetables, figs, chickpeas, and beans for the people, while they moderately consume wine mixed with water. "And so they will live in peace and good health, and when they die at a ripe old age, they will bequeath a similar life to their children."

Socrates, much contented that he has delineated an ideal human life, is taken aback when Glaucon rejoins that Socrates is "founding a city for pigs," where there are few delicacies and pleasures, not a city for humans.

Socrates concedes that he must delineate a febrile or feverish city (*phlegmainousan polin*), which includes servants, hunters, artists, poets, actors, dancers, prostitutes, inventors of gadgets, more servants, tutors, wet nurses, nannies, beauticians, barbers, chefs, cooks, and swineherds as well as many more cattle, if people are to eat meat. All such things will lead to a much greater

---

[21] Plato, *Republic,* trans. G.M.A. Grube (Indianapolis: Hackett, 1992), 369a–373d.

need for physicians. To procure all such things beyond the limit of things needed, citizens will have to steal from each other, and from those in neighboring poleis. Socrates, with reflective sadness, concedes that there will then inevitably be wars.

Returning to Query XIX of *Notes on Virginia,* Jefferson appeals to the European principle of self-sufficiency: "Every state should endeavour to manufacture for itself." Yet espousal of that principle is because all their land is cultivated or "locked up against the cultivator." Hence, they must resort to manufacture "to support the surplus of their people." In America, it is otherwise. There is surfeit of uncultivated, arable land. So, Americans have the choice of turning wholly to husbandry or of having half of the population turn to husbandry and half, to manufacture. Given what he thinks of the haleness of agriculture and the sterility and degeneracy of manufacture, and of the accumulation of vices that occur in large cities, Jefferson's preference, at the time, is wholesale commitment to husbandry.[22]

While the book is published in many forms during his tenure in France in the 1780s, he over time, perhaps as early as his presidency, becomes convinced that a thriving U.S. economy requires an equal share, or nearly so, of manufacture. "Experience has taught me that manufactures are now as necessary to our independence as to our comfort," says Jefferson to Benjamin Austin (9 Jan. 1816). Jefferson refers to "the question of '85"—a clean reference to Query XIX of *Notes on Virginia*. His wholesale commitment to agrarianism has evanesced. Theory must yield to experience. "In so complicated a science as political economy, no one axiom can be laid down as wise and expedient for all times and circumstances, and for their contraries."

What here is the issue?

Jefferson has learned from experience that export of farmed goods to other nations and import of manufactured goods will lead America into the broils of Europe or exclude them from trans-Atlantic commerce. He refers implicitly to the war between France and England from 1793 to 1802 in which America was "completely excluded from the ocean." He sums: "There exists both profligacy and power enough to exclude us from the field of interchange with other nations: that to be independent for the comforts of life we must fabricate them ourselves."

We have here another significant Jeffersonian compromise. His on-paper purchase of a country wholly, or even chiefly, devoted to farming is gone. The issue is independence. Wholesale devotion to agriculture makes Americans

---

[22] Thomas Jefferson, *Notes on Virginia,* 165.

dependent on imported, mostly British, manufactured goods, and experience has shown that that dependency could have a ponderous price.

Dependency on manufactured British goods also makes Americans dependent on the fluctuant British markets for the sort of unneeded manufactured goods that Americans covet, with markets being so unstable because many of the goods are unneeded. And so, engagement in the virtuous profession of farming American soils is trumped by an economic concern: American consumers being dependent on foreign markets for coveted, but unneeded goods. Economic dependency, it seems, can only be eschewed by a robust American commitment to manufacture of the sort of goods, gewgaws included, that Americans desire. That leads Jefferson, like Plato, to recognition that the best to which Americans can aspire is a feverish nation of some sort—a compromise to his '85 ideal, inspired by the utopists he read and admired, of a healthy agrarian nation.

Upshot

I end this final chapter with some elaboration of Jefferson's dream of the spread of liberty, at some point in time, across the globe. I discuss two large albatrosses: the link of liberty with anarchy and the problem of human acquisitiveness. I address each problem in turn.

First, the significance of Shays' Rebellion cannot be sufficiently underscored. It occurred not long after the surcease of the Revolutionary War and it led many Americans to wonder whether they, in fighting for liberty, had opened Pandora's Box. Was liberty really such a prize? Was Plato, over two millennia ago, right to equate liberty and anarchy?[23] That conceded in general in Jefferson's day. Montesquieu in *The Spirit of Laws*, merely followed Aristotle in noting that democracies could exist only in small states. Jefferson thought otherwise. The spirit of democracy, government of and for the people, could be captured by compromise: representative government and the dividing and subdividing of the federal government. Yet he acknowledged that Jeffersonian republicanism was an experiment and that implies possibility of failure. Shays' Rebellion intimated to many that the experiment was doomed to fail.

Second, there is the "question of '85" in Jefferson's 1816 letter to Austin. Jefferson gives up on his dream of seeing America as predominantly an agrarian nation, devoted only to such manufacture to complement an agrarian lifestyle. Experience has shown that America in extreme times could be barred from European markets, and so focus on farming would lead in such times to economic hardship to be alleviated only by Americans either engaging in

---

[23] Plato, *Republic*, Books VIII and IX.

manufacture of their own needed and coveted goods or involving themselves in the broils of Europe. There also seems to be, at least implicitly, the concern that Americans have a desire for the things, unneeded for human thriving, that money can buy, and that that desire is as large as Europeans.' That is his concern at the end of Query XVII, when Jefferson worries about Americans concerning themselves more about making money than about having their rights preserved.

Epilog

The typical scholarly response, for those who focus on Jefferson the politician, is to ask what went wrong. That question is pertinent today, as we are embarrassingly very distant from Jeffersonian principles of governing, but also was pertinent in his day.

Jefferson in the 1780s envisaged a country that was essentially agrarian and relatively self-sufficient. Americans would use their abundancy of land to engage in the honest and virtue-enhancing discipline of husbandry. Americans would feed themselves and export their surplus of farmed goods to nations that needed those goods in exchange for needed manufactured products. In such a manner, America could escape the problems of urbanization—e.g., drinking, crime, gambling, and prostitution—due to overcrowding and restiveness. Ruralism, in contrast, would not only promote virtue, it would also remove persons from the temptations of vice. Furthermore, intimate attachment to the land would promote readiness to defend one's country during war. A farmer who has worked his plot of land for many years will willfully fight to preserve it as a member of its militia during time of war. Americans would engage in such manufacture as was needed to promote its agriculture and self-sufficiency: e.g., tools for farming and machines for clothing. Jefferson ever held up Monticello as a model of American self-sufficiency. It was for America as a nation to mimic what Jefferson had done at Monticello—minus the heavy debt.

There was quickly the realization that Jefferson's agrarian ideal would never be realized. First, Jefferson, as the 1816 letter to Benjamin Austin shows, recognized at some point that the export of farmed goods and import of manufactured goods would at some point embroil the United States in the problems of Europe. Economic ravelment entailed political ravelment. Americans needed to engage in the manufacture of the goods they desired, he realized, if self-sufficiency was indeed to be achieved. Second, the desire by Americans for unneeded goods, most British, was large. Americans wanted much more than they needed. Thus, they were not so different from Europeans, though Jefferson customarily said that they were. Jefferson, while in France, implores James Monroe (17 June 1785) to visit Paris so he can see just how lucky he is to be a Virginian. "The pleasure of the trip … will make you adore your own country, it's soil, it's climate, it's equality, liberty, laws, people & manners. My God! how little do my country men know what precious blessings they are in possession of, and which no other people on earth enjoy."[1] Yet the agrarian ideal of America, comprising yeomen farmers, overall appealed to too few Americans.

We have also seen that the principles Jeffersonian republicanism, articulated in his First Inaugural Address (chapter 8), are predicated on two fundamental assumptions, which Jefferson would say are principles, experience-generated: the existence of a moral sense in all humans and sufficient rationality in all humans, exceptions here being material freaks.[2] The first entails that humans are materially constructed so that they are inclined, unless they are obstructed (say, by faulty reasoning or coercion), to do what is right. It is not clear that that is apparent by appeal to experience. The second entails enough rationality for each human to conduct his own affairs without the intervention of others. It is also not clear that that is apparent by appeal to experience.

Failure of the system Jefferson had put into place in the earliest years of University of Virginia is some evidence that Jefferson's two assumptions are false. Jefferson wanted to make his institution the model of liberal instruction. There was to be elective education, the interaction of students with faculty outside of time in the classroom, a large library with liberty-inspiring literature, no partnership of the university with any one religion and no religious instruction, no president, and a panel of students to decide the fate of their fellow students, deemed miscreants. This experiment in large-scale liberal education, it is well-known, was in some measure disastrous. Students gambled, drank, and even accosted professors. Shortly after Jefferson's death, Professor of Law, John Anthony Gardner Davis, was shot by a student-miscreant and died on November 14, 1840—so much for moral sensitivity and rationality.[3]

The problem for University of Virginia was that Jefferson assumed that all students had his love of learning and concern for virtuous behavior. His appetence for learning is evident from letters—especially one to John Minor.[4] We note that while at William and Mary, Jefferson befriended his professor, William Small, lawyer George Wythe, and Governor Francis Fauquier, each of whom was a pivotal figure in his life. He certainly did not typify the average student of the institution, or the average student of any institution of higher learning. Thus, the system of education could work only on assumption that all students matriculating at University of Virginia were Jeffersonian, lifelong learners.

---

[1] See also TJ to Charles Bellini, 30 Sept. 1785, and TJ to Anne Willing Bingham, 7 Feb. 1787.
[2] Jefferson was a complete materialist.
[3] See Rex Bowman and Carlos Santos, *Rot, Riot, and Rebellion* (Charlottesville: University of Virginia Press, 2013), chap. 13.
[4] TJ to John Minor, 30 Aug. 1814.

That leads to some observations by the great American historian Forrest McDonald. McDonald notes that Jefferson's political vision was beautiful in its simplicity and consistency, but oversimple. Jefferson championed thin government and states' rights, nearly non-existent taxation, elimination of public debt, no standing army (or navy), and noninvolvement in the broils of belligerent European nations. Yet the government, for instance, was involved in certain very heavy-handed activities (Louisiana Purchase and the embargo), could not balance its aim of elimination of federal debt with actions such as war with the Barbary Pirates, and was almost wholly run by duties on imported goods and that involved the federal government in the intrigues of Britain and France. Still, Jefferson had a remarkably cooperative cabinet and large success in moving the Congress to act in a Jeffersonian-republican manner, and he did so without use of bribery, patronage, corruption, and coercion. Yet the fatal flaw of the system, evident after his second term, was that it could be run successfully "only with a Thomas Jefferson at the helm." Thus, his legacy to Madison proved to be a "can of serpents," no mere can of worms. McDonald continues: "When Jefferson left the office, all the shortcomings of his method of administration became manifest. The cabinet became a center of petty bickering and continuous cabalizing, and Congress split into irreconcilable factions and repeatedly asserted its will against the president."[5]

Jefferson's biggest flaw, according to McDonald—and this is the reason for McDonald's often harsh treatment of Jefferson—is failure to see that history was not unfolding in a Jeffersonian, but in a Hamiltonian, manner. And so, in setting out to "deflect the course of History," "History ended up devouring them and turning even their memory to its own purposes."[6]

Are such objections categorically damning? Is there too little worth salvaging?

What Jefferson did get right is the marriage of "liberty" and "knowledge." The two were mutually entailing—that is, materially equivalent. That means that the material conditions in which liberty thrives are identical to the material conditions in which knowledge thrives. He states that in a 1795 letter to Tench Coxe (June 1). "This ball of liberty, I believe most piously, is now so well in motion that it will roll round the globe. At least the enlightened part of it, for light and liberty go together. It is our glory that we first put it into motion, and our happiness that being foremost we had no bad examples to follow." To John Adams, Jefferson writes later in life (12 Sept. 1821), "I shall not die without a hope that light and liberty are on steady advance. we have seen indeed once

---

[5] Forrest McDonald, *The Presidency of Thomas Jefferson* (University of Kansas Press, 1976), 163–69.
[6] Forrest McDonald, *The Presidency of Thomas Jefferson*, 169.

within the records of history a compleat eclipse of the human mind continuing for centuries."

Light (enlightenment) and liberty do go together. No government that does not prioritize education of a liberal sort can be great, just. The "liberalism" practiced by today's Progressive democrats is paternalistic and autocratic—not far from the step to dictatorial rule. Radically conservative republicans proffer in response their own paternalism and autocracy: the hand of a strong executive to right the ship, as it were, and Jefferson detested strong executives. Light and liberty cannot flourish where there is amaranthine partisan bickering.

It is here that we might benefit wholesomely by returning to Jefferson's First Inaugural Address. "We are all Republicans, we are all Federalists." We are "brethren of the same principle": liberty. Our failing today is failure to grasp that liberty cannot flourish without knowledge. We grasp "liberty" to entail "diversity," "inclusion," and "equity" (the DIE creed)—this is perhaps better understood to be a definition—and that leads to the slide to the sort of mobocracy that Plato describes with derogation in Books VIII and IX of *Republic:* each person strutting about the market and boasting that he is best suited to rule his polis. That is the message of Beckerian Progressivism: "Everyman [is] his own historian."[7] Beckerian Progressivism is Plato's ochlocracy—rule of the mob.

Jefferson's last known letter is to Governor Roger C. Weightman, governor of the city of Washington. Jefferson and John Adams have been sent formal letters of invitation (June 14) to attend a celebration of the fiftieth anniversary of the Declaration of Independence. Adams declines in a short letter on June 22. Jefferson, though in ill health, pens a lengthier letter of declination on June 24, and that is typical of Jefferson, perhaps in recognition that the letter will be his epistolary swan's song.

Were his health better, Jefferson writes, he would "with peculiar delight, have met and exchanged there, congratulations personally, with the small band, the remnant of that host of worthies, who joined with us, on that day, in the bold and doubtful election we were to make, for our country, between submission, or the sword." He hopes that the celebration will be "to the world … (to some parts sooner, to others later, but finally to all) the Signal of arousing men to burst the chains, under which Monkish ignorance and superstition had persuaded them to bind themselves, and to assume the blessings & security of self government." American self-government is liberty-loving, as it champions "the unbounded exercise of reason and freedom of opinion." He adds:

---

[7] Carl Becker, "Everyman His Own Historian," in *The American Historical Review,* Vol. XXXVII, No. 2, 1932, 221–36.

all eyes are opened, or opening to the rights of man. the general spread of the light of science has already laid open to every view the palpable truth that the mass of mankind has not been born, with saddles on their backs, nor a favored few booted and spurred, ready to ride them legitimately, by the grace of god. these are grounds of hope for others. For ourselves let the annual return of this day, for ever refresh our recollections of these rights and an undiminished devotion to them.

If we take Jefferson's words here sincerely and explicitly, it is his final expression of his perhaps Micawberish belief that liberty is on the move because of the "general spread of the light of science." Yet even if the sentiment is Micawberish, it inspires, because it makes much, even if too much, of the human organism. At the base of Jefferson's conception of civic liberty, there is Jefferson's man, who is respectful of his creator, awed by God's creation, and looks with hope toward a future where the ideals of Jesus qua philosopher, not deity, are universally championed and where humans and countries interact with each other with amicableness and dignity because the ideal of civic liberty is doled out equally to each citizen of the globe.

The alternative is radical equalitarianism described by Plato in *Republic* and championed by American Progressive liberals like Becker: each person doing whatever he wishes to do at any time and each person deemed justly fit to rule all others. It is noteworthy that Platonic democracy, Plato believed, slips neatly and inevitably into dictatorship. The complete chaos of radical equalitarianism sets the stage for restoration of "order" of the worst sort: order at the injunctions of a strong tyrant, ruled wholly by his strong appetites. That today seems to be the ideal of the American radical conservatives' antidote to the chaos of Progressivism.

Jefferson does have much to teach us today. It is time to return to reconsideration of the political medialism Jefferson expresses in his First Inaugural Address and in other philosophical writings. We can do so only if we recognize that liberty without light is an obliquitous ideal and that only liberty with light can lead to some degree of human flourishing. It may be, however, that despite the moral and aesthetic attractions of that pairing, humans are just too developmentally immature to put into praxis such attractive philosophical ideals. That, however, might change over time, and there are no good reasons not to aim to live up to, to approximate, such ideals.

Index

A

Abbé Arnoux: 154n12, 156.
Adams, Abigail: 94, 130, 149, 190.
Adams, John: ix, 16n38, 27, 30–31, 33, 42, 72, 73, 74, 77, 85, 86, 87, 94, 96, 97, 103, 128, 131, 134, 135–36, 139, 140, 141, 141n57, 146–49, 150, 151, 155, 157, 159, 169, 173, 177, 180, 189, 190, 201, 202.
   on *aristoi*:156–57.
   midnight appointments of: 148.
Adams, John Quincy: 149.
Adams, Samuel: 169, 187.
Adams, William Howard: 191–92.
Alien and Sedition Acts: 147.
Anglicanism: ix, 52n4, 162.
Appleby, Joyce: 21.
Aristotle: viii, viiin2, ix, x, xi, xin4, 3–4, 4–6, 38, 53, 58, 61–62, 72, 100, 105, 108, 150, 174, 176, 197.
   cosmos of: 61–62.
Austin, Benjamin: 141n57, 196, 97, 99.

B

Bache, Benjamin Franklin: 147.
Bacon, Edmund: 94.
Bacon, Francis: 3, 6, 52, 72, 87, 94.
Bailyn, Bernard: 109.
Barlow, Joel: 28.
Baxter, John: 40–41, 41n13.
Becker, Carl: 20, 54, 59n14, 202, 203.
Bolingbroke, Lord: 26–31.
Bolingbroke's conditions for history: 26–31
Bonaparte, Napoleon: 51, 187.
Boyd, Julian: 124.
Boyle, Robert: 63, 64, 72, 87.
Brahe, Tycho: 5, 62.
Breckinridge, John: 186.
Brown, David: 147.
Buffon, Comte de: 6, 7, 66.

C

Cabanis, Pierre: 74.
Cabell, Joseph: 163.
Callender, James: 147.
Carr, Peter: 84, 159.
Carrington, Edward: 14.
Catholic Church: ix, 5, 58, 176.
Chambers, Benjamin: 182.
Chastellux, Marquis de: 31.
Chinard, Gilbert: 124.
Chrysippus: 88.
Church, Angelica: 131.
Cicero: 23, 126n9.
Clark, George Rogers: 181–82.
Clay, Rev. Charles: 17.
Colonies/Colonial America: ix, 57, 59, 74, 75, 76, 80, 103, 134–36, 165–66.
Condorcet, Marquis: 16, 38, 39, 53, 186, 193.
conjectural history: 13.
constitution(s): 5, 10, 29, 40, 41, 42, 43. 68, 104, 139, 179, 187, 188.
constitution, renewal of: 113, 123–26, 128, 180.

Constitution, U.S.: viii, 27, 132, 132n35, 133, 139, 140, 142, 143, 147, 148, 149–50, 151, 180, 181, 183, 194.
Constitution, Virginian: 85n4, 114.
Cooke, J.W.: 109–10.
Copernicus, Nicholas: 5, 62.
Cosway, Maria: 112.
Coxe, Tench: 122.
Cromwell, Oliver: 168.
Cuvier, Georges: 6, 7–8.

D

Declaration of Independence: 30, 39, 42, 44, 46, 74, 76, 77–80, 81, 82, 111, 121, 127, 129, 134, 140, 151, 179, 191, 192.
Dickinson, John: 30, 30n24, 148, 149.
Duane, William: 37.

E

Ebeling, Christoph Daniel: 28.
Election of 1800: 149–54.
Ellis, Joseph: 55–56, 58, 191, 192.
Enlightenment: 3, 4, 5, 9, 12, 36–38, 53, 58–60, 64, 77, 83, 87, 100, 109, 114, 122, 138, 161, 176.
entails and primogeniture: ix, 161, 163.
Eppes, John Wayles: 111, 119.
Eppes, Maria (Jefferson): 149.

F

Faulkner, Robert: 65, 110.
Federalism: vii, 28, 32, 32n27, 42, 44, 130, 140, 146, 148, 152, 173, 185 202.
Flemings, Thomas: 191.

Flourens, Jean Pierre: 74.
Foucault, Michel: 59–60.
Franklin, Benjamin: 29n21, 59, 64 69, 77, 134.
freeman defined: 135.
French and Indian War: 167.

G

Galileo: 5–6, 38, 62–63, 64, 71, 72, 87.
Gallatin, Albert: 147.
Gay, Peter: 59.
Gilmer, Francis: 93.
Goldsmith, Oliver: 6–7.
Gordon, Thomas: 102–4, 133n37.
Grigorenko, Petro: xii.

H

Habermas, Jürgen: 59–60.
Hall, David: 122, 155.
Hamilton, Alexander: 30–31, 43, 134, 139, 146, 173, 180, 201.
Hardt, Michael: 191.
Hargraves, Neil: 10n18.
Helvétius, Claude–Adrien: 10.
Henry, Patrick: 29, 31, 120–22, 123, 134.
Herodotus: 5, 23–25, 33.
Hesiod: 16.
Hippocratic physicians: 5, 7.
History, republican: 37–39.
history from above and below: 55.
historiography, definition of: 23.
historiography, isms of: 53–55.
Hobbes, Thomas: 25, 38, 76, 79, 88–89, 93, 97, 100, 101, 104, 106, 107, 108, 111, 132.
Horace: 32n26.
Hume, David: 8, 10, 27, 28–29, 40, 41–43, 87, 100, 104–6, 126, 160.

Index 207

Hutcheson, Francis: 160.

I

Inaugural Address, First: 65, 145, 151, 155, 158, 171, 200, 202, 203.
Inaugural Address, Second. 85n24, 132, 184, 187.

J

James, William: 53.
Jefferson, Peter: 136–37.
Jefferson, Thomas
  on African Americans: 9n15.
  aristoi, artificial v. natural: 37, 180.
  on education: ix, xi, 44–45, 45n20, 56–58, 82, 111, 114, 125, 136, 149, 157, 160, 161, 162–64, 164n32, 171, 200, 202.
  and equality: 4, 37, 46, 47, 71, 74–86, 85n24, 109, 119, 129, 138, 140, 156, 165, 178, 179, 184, 187, 188, 199.
  and expansionism: 79–84, 187–88.
  on free presses: ix, 131, 154.
  on human agency: 86–96.
  on husbandry: 12.
  and Jesus: 176–79.
  and preserving laws of Virginia: 47.
  and liberty as disease: vii, ix, 185, 187.
  and liberty as empire: 179–84.
  and liberty, four senses of: 109–14.
  and liberty as thing: x–xii, 115.
  and liberty and reason: ix.
  as Lockean liberal or Classical republican: 174–75.
  as materialist: 71–74.
  on moral duties: 52.
  on moral sense: ix, 14, 16, 35, 46, 84–86, 89, 93, 97, 112, 159, 160–61, 173–75, 179, 180, 200.
  on Native Americans: 12.
  on nature of humans: 71–97.
  Opinion of French Treaties: 173–74.
  as patron of sciences/scientist: 65–68.
  and political relativism: 123–26.
  as president of American Philosophical Society: 69.
  as progressivist: 8, 11, 13, 36, 52, 53, 59, 61, 65, 92–93, 97, 99, 100, 123, 125–26, 193.
  on race: 4–9.
  on rationality: 4.
  on religious freedom: ix, xi, 129, 138, 154, 161, 162, 175, 179.
  on republicanism: ix, xi, 14, 36, 42, 44, 46, 47, 68, 71, 119, 126, 129–33, 140, 146, 148, 150 151, 152, 156–58, 161, 162, 164, 170, 172, 173–76, 178–80, 182, 183, 184, 185, 187–88, 194, 197, 200.
  on republicanism as experiment: 129–33.
  on republicanism as global: x, 187–88.
  on republicanism, principles of: 153–54.
  on revolution: 126–29.
  on Saxon myth: 43.
  systematicity of daily life: 3n2.
Johnson, William: 27–28.
Jordan, Dan: 21.

K

Kames, Lord: 11, 13, 88, 89–92, 93, 95, 97, 160.
Kant, Immanuel: 8, 9, 53, 59, 60, 88, 91–93, 96, 97.
Kentucky Resolutions: 147, 148.
Kepler, Johannes: 68–69.
Kercheval, Samuel: 125, 172–73.
Kidd, Thomas: 83.
King George III: 44, 76, 80–81, 138, 140, 165, 167, 168, 170.
Knox, Henry: 31, 146.
Kosciusko, Thaddeus: 194.
Kravchenko, Victor: xii.

L

Lafayette, Marquis de: vii, 122, 185.
Lavoisier, Antoine: 64.
Lee, Thomas Ludow: 161.
Lewis, George: 29, 40.
Linnaeus, Carl: 6–7.
Livy: 23, 25, 35, 36, 51n1.
Locke, John: 38–39, 42, 72, 75, 77, 87, 96, 97, 104, 151, 173, 175, 180.
Louisiana Purchase: 182.
Ludlow, William: 11, 12, 174, 185, 193.
Lyon, Matthew: 147.

M

McDonald, Forest: 110, 130, 201.
McLaughlin, Jack: 19.
McPherson, Isaac: 67–68.
Madison, James: 14, 27, 31, 142, 146, 147, 150, 162, 182, 185, 186, 189, 201.
Malone, Dumas: 55, 123, 126.

Marshall, John: 29.
Mason, George: 77, 131, 134, 161.
Matthews, Richard: 123, 126.
May, Henry: 59, 87, 127.
Mazzei, Philip: 28.
Melish, John: 146.
Mercier, Louis–Sébastien: 15, 53, 193.
Mill, John Stuart: x, 99–100.
Millar, John: 10, 11.
Miller, Sir Thomas: 134.
Mirkin, Harris G.: 127n22.
Monroe, James: 114, 183, 199.
Montesquieu: 53, 124, 125, 197.
Monticello: 54, 66, 72n2, 159, 199.
More, Thomas: 15.

N

Native Americans: 136, 183.
Nemours, Pierre Samuel Dupont: 170–71, 180.
Newton, Isaac: viii, 6, 38, 63, 64, 72–74, 87, 90, 91, 92.
Nietzsche, Friedrich: 25.
Notes on Virginia: 9n15, 14, 44, 55, 56, 66, 72, 134, 137, 163, 163, 175, 179, 193, 194, 196.

O

O'Brien, Conor Cruise: 21, 191, 192.
Onuf, Peter: 19, 21, 23n9, 54, 55.

P

Patterson, Caleb Perry: 124.
Peden, William: 137.
Peterson, Merrill: xiii, 16, 109, 110.

Plato: viii, viiin2, xin4, 10, 25, 77n14, 92, 114, 157–58, 160, 195, 197, 202, 203.
Plutarch: 25, 35.
political relativism, subjective and objective: 126.
Postmodernism: 19–23, 23n9, 25, 55, 58.
Priestley, Joseph: 131, 155.

R

Randolph (Bankhead), Anne: 36.
Randolph, Edmund: 31, 146.
Randolph, Isham: 136.
Randolph, Jane: 137.
Randolph, Martha (Jefferson): 174.
Randolph, Sarah: 159.
Ranke, Leopold von: 20, 21, 25, 29.
Revolution of 1800: vii, 10, 145–164.
Revolution, American: vii, x, 27, 30, 44, 51, 110, 119–43, 146, 150, 164, 165–70, 179.
Revolution, French: 43, 44, 122, 129, 148, 149, 185–88, 191, 192.
Revolutionary War: 133.
Rittenhouse, David: 71.
Roane, Spenser: vii, 145.
Robertson, William: 10.
Rousseau, Jean Jacques: 106–8.
Royal Proclamation of 1763: 167–68.
Rush, Benjamin: 9, 15, 59, 68, 122, 126, 140–41, 178–79.

S

Schelling, Friedrich: 25.
Schlegel, Friedrich: 25.
science today: 52.
Scientific societies: 64.

Shays' Rebellion: 127n22, 129, 142, 147, 188–93, 197.
Short, William: 30, 32, 43, 94, 129, 177, 178, 191.
Silverstein, Jake: 55–56.
1619 Thesis: 55–58.
Smith, Adam: 10, 11, 161–62.
Smith, Capt. John: 76.
Smith, John: 82.
Smith, T.V.: 128–29.
Smith, William Stephens: 126–27, 190.
stadial history: 9–13.
Stalin, Joseph: xii.
Stamp Act: 169.
Stewart, Dugald: 74.
Stoics: xin4, 88–89, 93.
Stuart, Archibald: 132.
Stuart, Josephus Bradner: 32, 169, 170, 173, 179.
Suffolk, Henry Howard: 134.
Summary View: 44, 65, 75, 76, 121, 134.

T

Tacitus: 5, 23, 35, 36, 37.
Taylor, Alan: 164n32.
Taylor, John: 171.
Tiffany, Isaac: 145.
Tracey, Destutt de: 73n4, 74, 94–95, 97.
Treaty of Paris: 168.
Trenchard, John: 101–2.
Trumbull, John: 51, 72, 72n2, 140.
Turgot, Anne-Robert-Jacques: 10.

U

University of Virginia: ix, 19, 41–42, 45n21, 112, 163, 164, 200.

University of Virginia, Rotunda of: ix.

V

Van der Kemp, Francis Adrienne: 74, 113.
Virgil: 16.
Virginia Resolutions: 147.
Volney, Constantin François de: 9.

W

Washington, George: 29, 29n21, 33n27, 51, 134, 139–40, 142, 146, 148, 149, 151, 159, 164, 173, 184, 194.
Wells, Charles E.: 68n37.
William and Mary College: 45, 52n4, 53, 137, 200.
Williams, David: 15.
Wirt, William: 29–30, 120–21, 149.
Wood, Gordon: 75, 110, 135.
Wythe, George: 161.

www.ingramcontent.com/pod-product-compliance
Lightning Source LLC
Chambersburg PA
CBHW072233290426
44111CB00012B/2080